国家一流本科专业（英语/翻译）建设配套参考书

思政经典中国特色语言英译指南

孙斐瑾　郑东升　夏桐枝　编著

南开大学出版社

天　津

图书在版编目(CIP)数据

思政经典中国特色语言英译指南 / 孙斐瑾，郑东升，夏桐枝编著． — 天津：南开大学出版社，2025.3.
ISBN 978-7-310-06704-6

Ⅰ．D64-62

中国国家版本馆 CIP 数据核字第 2025U62W52 号

版权所有　侵权必究

思政经典中国特色语言英译指南
SIZHENG JINGDIAN ZHONGGUO TESE YUYAN YINGYI ZHINAN

南开大学出版社出版发行
出版人：刘文华
地址：天津市南开区卫津路 94 号　　邮政编码：300071
营销部电话：(022)23508339　营销部传真：(022)23508542
https://nkup.nankai.edu.cn

天津泰宇印务有限公司印刷　全国各地新华书店经销
2025 年 3 月第 1 版　　2025 年 3 月第 1 次印刷
240×170 毫米　16 开本　15 印张　1 插页　261 千字
定价：75.00 元

如遇图书印装质量问题，请与本社营销部联系调换。电话：(022)23508339

本书系天津市教委科研计划项目（人文社科）一般项目"思政经典英译版中国特色语言研究"项目（项目编号：2022SK054）研究成果

序

党的十八大以来，习近平总书记高度重视我国的国际传播能力建设，强调要讲好中国故事，传播好中国声音，展示真实、立体、全面的中国。培养理论基础扎实、双语转换能力强、具有家国情怀和国际视野的翻译人才，是外语服务国家现实需要和战略需求的重要目标。思政经典汉英翻译文本乃是新时代翻译教学新鲜而有效的素材资源。《思政经典中国特色语言英译指南》的出版，既是编著者对新时代翻译教学使命的积极响应，也是外语服务国家形象对外传播的有益尝试。

翻译作为双语转换和面向传播的语义再生，从来不是简单的字面转换，而是涉及语言形式背后历史的、文化的、社会的等诸方面因素的复杂活动。本书以翻译理论为基础，聚焦于思政经典中的语汇、金句和典故三种转换类型，深入剖析中国特色语言英译特点。通过详细阐述相关的翻译理论，为读者搭建起一个理解翻译本质、原则和策略的框架，指导译者在从事思政经典翻译时依照恰当的理论来确保翻译准确性与恰当性的平衡。同时，本书极为注重实践层面的指导，通过丰富的、有代表性的实例，对照习作解析，对思政经典作品中的语汇、金句、典故翻译做出细致分析。无论是一词一句的斟酌，还是对典故背后深意的精准传达，都有清晰的讲解和呈现。通过理论与实践的结合，读者能够直观地感受到翻译实程中的难点与要点，从而做到在实际操作中有的放矢，不断提升翻译转换能力。此外，本书选取的素材均源于思政领域的经典之作，在国际上传播广泛、产生重要影响力的文本，因此具有权威性与代表性。以此为依托来讲解翻译，读者能够更好地把握不同语境下和差异化受众时思政经典语言的翻译策略和技巧。本书的最后板块精心整理出高频语汇、金句、典故，是学习者在实际翻译中会经常遇到的，集中呈现并加以详细解读，方便读者进行重点学习与记忆，能够极大地提高学习效率。这无疑是本书的一大亮点。

《思政经典中国特色语言英译指南》的出版，具有多维的意义。从教育教学的角度来看，它为广大师生提供了极为实用的参考工具。教师可以借助这本书，更加系统、专业地开展思政经典翻译教学，引导学生深入理解思政经典作品的内涵，提升教学效果。学生则可通过学习本书，树立翻译实践中的国家意识，不断夯实翻译基础，提高翻译技能，更好地完成相关课程的学习任务，为今后从事相关翻译工作奠定坚实基础。从文化传播的层面而言，它有助于构建中国特色话语体系。思政经典作品承载着中国共产党的理念、中国的发展理念以及中华民族的优秀文化传统等重要内容。准确地将这些内容翻译成英文，能够让国际社会更加全面、深入地了解真实、立体、全面的中国，打破文化隔阂与误解，增进相互理解与认同，从而有力推动中国特色话语体系在国际上的传播与确立。从时代使命的维度考量，它是新时代翻译界履行使命的有力支撑。新时代赋予了翻译界讲好中国故事、传播好中国声音、建设人类命运共同体的伟大使命，而这本指南通过提升翻译人才对思政经典作品的翻译能力，能够让更多优秀的翻译成果走向世界，让世界更好地听到中国的声音，看到中国的发展，进而助力人类命运共同体之愿景的实现。

翻译是人类交流的工具，具有中国特色的思政经典作品英译，是让其他国家理解中华文明和当代中国的窗口。相信这本指南在广大师生、翻译工作者和关心中国文化国际传播的人士手中，一定能发挥应有的作用，为翻译理论研究、翻译教学、人才培养做出独特的贡献。

2024 年 12 月 12 日

前言

一、编写目的

党的十八大以来,习近平总书记在多种场合就加强课程思政工作发表重要讲话,强调要培养具有家国情怀、国际视野的翻译人才。新时代翻译界担负着讲好中国故事,传播好中国声音,展示真实、立体、全面的中国,建设人类命运共同体的伟大使命。为落实课程思政育人效果,高等学校外国语言文学类专业指导委员会编写了"理解当代中国"系列教材。在开展教学的过程中,很多教师感到非常有必要出版一本针对思政经典作品翻译的指导手册,方便查阅和参考。本指南应广大师生要求编写,旨在切实提升课程思政育人实效,帮助学生提高思政经典作品的翻译能力,为构建中国特色话语体系和讲好中国故事提供指导和参考。

二、内容构成

本指南共六个单元。第一、二单元是关于思政经典中的词汇翻译,第三、四单元是关于思政经典中的句子翻译,第五单元是关于思政经典中的修辞翻译,第六单元是关于思政经典中的典故翻译。每个单元均包括三个部分,分别是相关知识及范例对照、知识与技能讲析、习作与范例对照解析。附录1是思政高频词汇,附录2是习近平金句,附录3是典故解析。

三、素材选取

本指南选取的素材,包括《习近平谈治国理政》中英文版、《中国共产党章程》中英文版、《共产党宣言》中英文版、"理解当代中国"系列教材、《习近平总书记教育重要论述讲义》中英文版、《中国日报》中有关习近平总书记重要讲话内容双语版,以及中国知网有关思政文献翻译的期刊论文等内容。

四、分工与致谢

本指南是全体编者通力合作的结晶。孙斐瑾构思和设计整体出版方案，郑东升、夏桐枝提出指南框架和单元结构，三位编者共同负责审校和定稿。具体章节的撰写分工如下：

第一单元：夏桐枝

第二单元：夏桐枝

第三单元：孙斐瑾

第四单元：孙斐瑾

第五单元：郑东升

第六单元：郑东升

附录1：孙斐瑾

附录2：孙斐瑾

附录3：孙斐瑾 郑东升

在本指南编写过程中，南开大学出版社张彤、宋立君两位老师提出了宝贵建议，任东升教授百忙中为本书作序，天津科技大学外国语学院各位领导给予了支持鼓励，天津科技大学外国语学院翻译系2020级、2021级本科生和2023级研究生贡献了正文习作译稿，郑东升指导的刘哲、张潇月、张楚帆三位研究生参与了部分中国特色术语、典故的查找工作，在此一并致谢。

因时间仓促，加之编者能力有限，书中难免有疏漏错误之处，恳请使用本书的教师和同学们给我们提出宝贵意见，以便再版时改进。

编者

2024年6月

第一单元　思政经典中的词汇翻译（一） ………………………… 1

第一部分：汉英词汇知识及范例对照 ……………………………… 1
1. 概念意义与内涵意义 …………………………………………… 1
2. 抽象意义与具体意义 …………………………………………… 2
3. 情感意义 ………………………………………………………… 3
4. 风格意义 ………………………………………………………… 3
5. 搭配意义 ………………………………………………………… 4

第二部分：知识与技能讲析 ………………………………………… 4
1. 词汇意义的多维层面 …………………………………………… 4
2. 词汇选择 ………………………………………………………… 7
3. 正式文体的词汇特点 …………………………………………… 8

第三部分：英译习作与文本词汇范例对照解析 ………………… 10
1. 概念意义与内涵意义 ………………………………………… 10
2. 抽象意义与具体意义 ………………………………………… 10
3. 情感意义 ……………………………………………………… 11
4. 风格意义 ……………………………………………………… 12
5. 搭配意义 ……………………………………………………… 12

第二单元　思政经典中的词汇翻译（二） ……………………… 14

第一部分：汉英文本词汇知识及范例对照 ……………………… 14
1. 词性转译 ……………………………………………………… 14
2. 词序调整 ……………………………………………………… 15
3. 增译与省译 …………………………………………………… 16
4. 文化词汇翻译 ………………………………………………… 17

第二部分：知识与技能讲析 ……………………………………… 18
1. 词性异同与词性转译 ………………………………………… 18
2. 词序与修饰语顺序 …………………………………………… 19
3. 词汇的增译与省译 …………………………………………… 20
4. 文化词汇翻译 ………………………………………………… 22

第三部分：英译习作与文本词汇范例对照解析 …… 27
　　　　1. 词性转译 …… 27
　　　　2. 词序调整 …… 27
　　　　3. 增译与省译 …… 28
　　　　4. 文化词汇翻译 …… 29

第三单元　思政经典中的句子翻译（一） …… 30
　　第一部分：思政经典汉英文本金句范例对照 …… 30
　　　　1. 句子结构及其类型 …… 30
　　　　2. 句子连贯 …… 31
　　　　3. 强调句 …… 31
　　　　4. 倒装句 …… 32
　　　　5. 平行句 …… 32
　　第二部分：知识与技能讲析 …… 33
　　　　1. 句子结构及其类型 …… 33
　　　　2. 句子连贯 …… 35
　　　　3. 确定主语、谓语 …… 35
　　　　4. 强调结构 …… 37
　　　　5. 排比句 …… 39
　　第三部分：英译习作与文本金句范例对照解析 …… 39
　　　　1. 句子结构及其类型 …… 39
　　　　2. 句子连贯 …… 40
　　　　3. 强调句 …… 40
　　　　4. 倒装句 …… 41
　　　　5. 平行句 …… 41

第四单元　思政经典中的句子翻译（二） …… 42
　　第一部分：思政经典汉英文本金句范例对照 …… 42
　　　　1. 区分主从 …… 42
　　　　2. 分译与合译 …… 43
　　　　3. 主动与被动翻译 …… 44
　　　　4. 无主句翻译 …… 45
　　　　5. 长句翻译 …… 45
　　第二部分：知识与技能讲析 …… 46

1. 区分主从 …… 46
2. 分译与合译 …… 47
3. 主动与被动翻译 …… 49
4. 无主句翻译 …… 50
5. 长句翻译 …… 52

第三部分：英译习作与文本范例金句对照解析 …… 53
1. 区分主从 …… 53
2. 分译与合译 …… 54
3. 主动与被动翻译 …… 55
4. 无主句翻译 …… 55
5. 长句翻译 …… 56

第五单元　思政经典中的修辞翻译 …… 57

第一部分：修辞的主要类型及范例对照 …… 57
1. 比喻 …… 57
2. 拟人 …… 58
3. 夸张 …… 59
4. 移就 …… 59
5. 类比 …… 60
6. 排比 …… 60
7. 反问 …… 61
8. 借代 …… 61
9. 通感 …… 61
10. 反复 …… 62

第二部分：知识与技能讲析 …… 63
1. 直译 …… 63
2. 意译 …… 63
3. 省译 …… 64
4. 增译 …… 65

第三部分：英译习作与修辞范例对照解析 …… 65
1. 比喻 …… 65
2. 拟人 …… 66
3. 夸张 …… 66

  4. 移就 ·· 66
  5. 类比 ·· 67
  6. 排比 ·· 67
  7. 反问 ·· 68
  8. 借代 ·· 68
  9. 通感 ·· 69
  10. 反复 ·· 69

第六单元　思政经典中的典故翻译 ······························ 71
 第一部分：典故的主要类型及范例对照 ···················· 71
  1. 成语 ·· 71
  2. 俗语 ·· 72
  3. 古诗文 ·· 73
 第二部分：知识与技能讲析 ·· 73
  1. 归化 ·· 73
  2. 异化 ·· 74
  3. 解释 ·· 74
  4. 注释 ·· 75
 第三部分：英译习作与典故范例对照解析 ················ 76
  1. 成语 ·· 76
  2. 俗语 ·· 76
  3. 古诗文 ·· 77

附录1　思政高频词汇 ·· 78
附录2　习近平金句 ·· 101
附录3　典故解析 ·· 151
主要参考书目 ·· 227

第一单元

思政经典中的词汇翻译（一）

第一部分：汉英词汇知识及范例对照

文章创作需要积字为句、积句为段、积段为篇，汉英翻译过程须遵循选词、造句、谋篇三个步骤。译者对词汇的理解和表达是篇章翻译的根本，所以在翻译过程中，如何选词达意是基础，也是难点之一。

1. 概念意义与内涵意义

词的概念意义是词典中的释义，即词的字面意思，构成词语意义的核心，相对固定，比较明确。词的内涵意义随着时代和社会的变迁而变化，因历史和文化的差异而不同。词汇翻译容易出错的根源在于两种语言中看似对等的词汇实际上并不对等，绝对对等的词汇极少，所以追求词汇意义的对等是错误的。例如：

原文：经过全党全国各族人民持续奋斗，我们实现了第一个百年奋斗目标，在中华大地上全面建成了小康社会，历史性地解决了绝对贫困问题，正在意气风发向着全面建成社会主义现代化强国的第二个百年奋斗目标迈进。这是中华民族的伟大光荣！这是中国人民的伟大光荣！这是中国共产党的伟大光荣！

译文：Through the continued efforts of the whole Party and the entire nation, we have realized the First Centenary Goal of building a moderately prosperous society in all respects. This means that we have brought about a historic resolution to the problem of absolute poverty in China, and we are now marching in confident strides towards the Second Centenary Goal of building China into a great modern socialist country in all respects. This is a great and glorious achievement for the Chinese nation, for the Chinese people, and for the Communist Party of China.

分析：如果按照字面意义翻译处理，则原文"伟大光荣"译为"glorious honor"最接近，看似对等。但是，习近平总书记《在庆祝中国共产党成立100周年大会上的讲话》中，这句话的背景是对中国所取得的伟大成就的总结，"honor"虽然意义是"荣耀、光荣"，但侧重指"荣誉、名誉"，而且是一个抽象概念；而"achievement"具体明确，更符合文本中社会主义现代化建设的历史性成就这一语义意图。

2. 抽象意义与具体意义

不同的历史和文化因素产生了不同的思维方式。从总体上看，中国文化思维有着较强的具体性，而西方文化思维则更具抽象性和笼统性。汉语具有具体、细致的特点，较多使用具有实指意义的具体词汇，以具体形象的表达代替抽象的内容，而英语中抽象的虚化词汇使用较多，现代英语的特点就是使用抽象名词。例如：

原文：让所有贫困人口脱贫，是中国政府对人民作出的承诺，也是我牵挂最多、花精力最多的一件事情。

译文：To lift all the remaining poor people out of poverty is a solemn commitment made by the Chinese government to the people. It is uppermost in my mind and I have spent more energy on poverty alleviation than anything else.

分析：汉语原文符合中国读者偏于具体明确概念的思维方式和表达习惯，英译则通过不定代词短语"anything else"把具有实指意义的具体明确概念抽象化、笼统化，符合英语母语者偏于抽象思维的行文表达习惯，措辞简练、语义明确。

3. 情感意义

由于历史和文化背景的差异，每一种语言中都有很大一部分词汇具有一定的褒贬情感意义，反映了其民族文化所特有的爱憎倾向，而其他文化却无法意会和理解。在汉英翻译时，词汇选择往往会涉及词汇褒义与贬义的辨析问题，译者应该考虑文化差异和译文的可理解性。例如：

原文：一百年来，中国共产党团结带领中国人民进行的一切奋斗、一切牺牲、一切创造，归结起来就是一个主题：实现中华民族伟大复兴。

译文：All the struggle, sacrifice and creation through which the Party has united and led the Chinese people over the past hundred years has been tied together by one ultimate goal – bringing about the rejuvenation of the Chinese nation.

分析："rejuvenation"表示"恢复青春""恢复活力"，体现出中华民族在世界历史长河中曾经创造出了灿烂的文明，如今将再创辉煌，而"rebirth"或者"renewal"只表示"再生"，属于中性词，缺少了赞美性情感色彩，无法反映原文讴歌赞美的主题意义。

4. 风格意义

词语的风格涉及不同的语体、文体和交际方式等因素，语体风格可简单分为正式、普通与非正式体。译者需要根据汉语材料的语体尺度来选择合适的词汇以满足相应语体的需要。了解和掌握运用英语不同语体在词汇选择上的一般规律，对于准确得体的翻译是非常重要的。英语存在着大量同义词，用法和含义不同，使用者需要根据语境选择适当的词汇。例如：

原文：马克思主义是我们立党立国的根本指导思想，是我们党的灵魂和旗帜。

译文：Marxism is the fundamental ideology upon which our Party and country are founded; it is the very soul of our Party and the banner under which it strives.

分析：词语的使用大都带有一定的语体色彩，语体的差异引起了词语使用在文本正式程度上的差异。"banner"源于拉丁语，非常正式，与汉语正式语体相对称和匹配，适合思政经典场合。我们在翻译时应该根据语体的需要选择合适的、能够反映汉语的语体尺度的词，关注词汇在语体上存在的分级性。

5. 搭配意义

任何一种语言在使用过程中都会形成一些固定的词组和搭配，大多数搭配不能直接翻译成另一种语言。同一个词与不同的词汇搭配会产生不同的意义。因此，将其译成英文时不可用同一个词汇套用，必须首先领会每个词语的内涵。同时，英语的介词非常活跃，而汉语的介词表现力很弱。据统计，英语介词大约有280个，和动词、名词构成难以计数的固定搭配，活跃在各种语境中。例如：

原文：全党要<u>关心和爱护</u>青年，为他们实现人生出彩<u>搭建舞台</u>。广大青年要坚定理想信念，<u>志存高远</u>、<u>脚踏实地</u>、<u>勇做时代的弄潮儿</u>，在实现中国梦的生动实践<u>中</u>放飞青春梦想，<u>在</u>为人民利益的<u>不懈奋斗中</u>书写人生华章！

译文：All of us in the Party should <u>care about</u> young people and <u>set the stage for</u> them to excel. To all our young people, you should have firm ideals and convictions, <u>aim high</u>, and <u>have your feet firmly on the ground</u>. You should <u>ride the waves</u> of your day; and <u>in the course of</u> realizing the Chinese Dream, fulfill your youthful dreams, and write a vivid chapter <u>in your tireless endeavors</u> to serve the interests of the people.

分析：汉英两种语言各有各的搭配，汉译英时应该按照英语的表达尤其是固定搭配习惯和规则来处理译文。译文使用了动词搭配"care about"（关爱）、"set the stage for"（为……做好准备）、"aim high"（志存高远）、"have one's feet on the ground"（脚踏实地）、"ride the waves"（顺势而为）和介词搭配"in the course of"（在……过程中）、"in one's/the endeavors"（在努力中）。

第二部分：知识与技能讲析

1. 词汇意义的多维层面

词是语言中最小的不可分割的可以运用的单位，可以由一个或几个词素组成，词在语言中的使用就是它的意义，词语的意义和语言使用者期望被理解的意图相关。杰弗里·利奇（Geoffrey Leech）把词汇意义分成七类：外延、内涵、风格、情感、联想、并列、主题，并认为除了主题意义，其他六种意义都和词义紧密相关。词汇意义大概可归纳为如下五个层面：

1.1 概念意义与内涵意义

词汇的意义不是单一的，需要置于情景和上下文关系中去分析和解读。概念意义是语言交际过程中词汇的基本意义，相对固定，比较明确，是词汇意义的核心。内涵意义附加在概念意义之上，随着时代和历史变迁而变化，翻译时很难找到对等词汇来进行简单替换。必须根据上下文判断和确定词汇的概念意义与内涵意义，按照翻译目标语的语言习惯灵活处理。最典型的就是东西方文化中表示颜色的词汇有时具有相似的内涵，但通常差异较大。例如：

原文 1：弘扬以伟大建党精神为源头的中国共产党人精神谱系，用好<u>红色资源</u>，深入开展社会主义核心价值观宣传教育，深化爱国主义、集体主义、社会主义教育，着力培养担当民族复兴大任的时代新人。

译文：We will carry forward the long line of inspiring principles for the Chinese Communists that originated with the great founding spirit of the Party; put <u>resources related to the Party's heritage</u> to great use; conduct extensive public awareness activities to promote the core socialist values; enhance commitment to patriotism, collectivism, and socialism; and foster a new generation of young people to shoulder the mission of realizing national rejuvenation.

原文 2：正是成千上万这样的中国女性，<u>白衣执甲</u>，逆行而上，以勇气和辛劳诠释了医者仁心，用担当和奉献换来了山河无恙。

译文：In fact, many women <u>medical</u> workers in China, like this girl, and in their tens of thousands, have taken on the virus bravely by putting themselves in harm's way. Their courage and hard work have shown the very best of the medical profession. Their devotion and sacrifice have kept the nation intact through difficult times.

众所周知，作为火焰和血液的颜色，红色在许多文化中象征着力量和活力，也代表着危险和警示。在中国文化中，红色象征着吉祥与喜庆、豪放与激情、革命与斗志。考虑到跨文化理解，"红色资源"没有按照颜色译出，而是根据语境把象征意义译出；同样，"白衣天使"是汉语词汇，虽然它融入了西方文化因素，把医护人员比喻为奉上帝的差遣到人间来救死扶伤的天使，但是，考虑到文化差异而放弃直译，采用"medical"表达更加具体确定，更适合英语语境。

1.2 抽象意义与具体意义

词语的抽象意义往往是笼统的、不具体的。笼统和具体不是绝对的，两个概念相互对立、相互依存，甚至可以互相转换。笼统意义的词汇一般只表明抽象的范畴，意义不明确，而具体意义的词语则表达更加明确的特定意义。有些汉语的抽象词无须译出，译出来反倒会破坏英语的行文习惯和规范。

1.3 情感意义——褒义、中性与贬义

由于历史和文化背景不同，每一种语言都有一部分词汇具有一定的社会意义和情感意义，汉译英时，应该考虑到中西文化差异和译文的可接受性。

1.4 风格意义

语体风格具体可表现为亲昵体、随便体、商谈体、正式体等，可简单分为正式、普通与非正式体。英语存在着大量同义词，用法和含义不同，使用者需要根据语境选择适当的词汇。汉译英时，需要把握同义词之间的语体差异，选择合适的词，准确地反映汉语的语体尺度、感情尺度、风格尺度。英语中具有语体色彩的同义词语有三类：英语本族语、外来词和习语同义词。通过这些词在言语和文本中所占的不同比例，就能确定出不同的语体风格，如源于拉丁语、希腊语、法语的词语往往比本族语更正式，多用于科技、学术文体中，具有书面特征；习语则生动活泼，具有口语特点。

1.5 搭配意义

英语中的名词、介词、形容词、副词表现能力很强，非常活跃。介词使用频率很高，具有超高的活跃性，并产生了大量的介词搭配，掌握并熟练运用介词搭配对英语学习者是不容小觑的挑战。一个词有着若干能够与之搭配的词，不同的词有着不同的搭配范围,同一个词与不同的词搭配就产生了不同的语境、不同的概念和不同的意义，在翻译时不能千篇一律地选用一个词。学习者需要在平时的学习中积累，尽量多记固定词组和常用搭配，才不会在翻译时断章取义、张冠李戴。例如：

原文 1：大会的主题是：高举中国特色社会主义伟大旗帜，全面贯彻新时代中国特色社会主义思想，<u>弘扬</u>伟大建党精神，自信自强、守正创新，踔厉奋发、勇毅前行，为全面建设社会主义现代化国家、全面推进中华民族伟大复兴而团结奋斗。

译文：The theme of this Congress is holding high the great banner of socialism with Chinese characteristics, fully implementing the Thought on Socialism with Chinese Characteristics for a New Era, <u>carrying forward</u> the great founding spirit of the Party, staying confident and building strength, upholding fundamental principles and breaking new ground, forging ahead with enterprise and fortitude, and striving in unity to build a modern socialist country in all respects and advance the great rejuvenation of the Chinese nation on all fronts.

原文 2：面对这些影响党长期执政、国家长治久安、人民幸福安康的突出矛盾和问题，党中央审时度势、果敢抉择，锐意进取、攻坚克难，团结带领全党全军全国各族人民撸起袖子加油干、风雨无阻向前行，义无反顾<u>进行</u>具有许多新的历史特点的伟大斗争。

译文：In the face of these acute problems and challenges, which undermined the Party's long-term governance, the security and stability of the country, and the wellbeing of the people, the Party Central Committee fully assessed the situation, made resolute decisions, and took firm steps. Under its leadership, the entire Party, the military, and the Chinese people were brought together. We rolled up our sleeves and got down to work, forging ahead with resolve to <u>carry out</u> a great struggle with many new features of our times.

"carry forward"和"carry out"是"carry"与不同的介词搭配构成的两个不同意义的词组，搭配不同，意义相异。

2. 词汇选择

词汇选择首先要根据词汇的意义，而词汇的意义又离不开语境。语境指语言使用的时间、地点以及使用者正在进行的活动，语境不同，选词用词不同。词典里的词语意义是词语在各种不同语境中的意义列举，词语的意义是由语境决定的，因此可以说，离开语境，大多数词汇是没有意义的。语境不同和上下文搭配不同导致一个词会有多种不同的翻译，所以，词语翻译必须参照语境。语境不仅仅指上下文的关系，还应包含时间、地点、场景以及交际方式。词汇选择首先要满足原语语体级别，翻译得体；其次要选择含义准确具体简练的词汇。

英语词汇的选择还要考虑词汇的形态。汉语没有形态的变化，主要依靠词语、词序及内在的逻辑关系来表达句子的含义；而英语词汇的形态非常丰富，名词有数的变化，动词有人称、时态、语态、语气以及非谓语动词（不定式、动名词、现在分词和过去分词）的变化，形容词和副词都有原级、比较级、最高级的变化，英语就是通过词汇的各种形态变化来表达句子丰富多彩的语言关系和多种逻辑关系。例如：

原文：我们要坚持绿色低碳，促进人与自然和谐共生。全球变暖不会因疫情停下脚步，应对气候变化一刻也不能松懈。我们要落实好应对气候变化《巴黎协定》，恪守共同但有区别的责任原则，为发展中国家特别是小岛屿国家提供更多帮助。中国愿承担与自身发展水平相称的国际责任，继续为应对气候变化付出艰苦努力。我不久前在联合国宣布，中国将提高国家自主贡献力度，采取更有力的政策和举措，二氧化碳排放力争于 2030 年前达到峰值，努力争取 2060 年前实现碳中和。我们将说到做到！

译文：We need to pursue green and low-carbon development, and promote harmony between humanity and nature. Global warming will not stop just because of Covid-19. To respond to climate change, we must never relax our efforts. We need to implement the Paris Agreement in good faith, stick to the principle of common but differentiated responsibilities, and provide more help to developing countries, particularly the small island developing states. China is ready to assume its international responsibilities as far as its current level of development permits, and will continue to make every effort to address climate change. I recently announced at the UN China's initiative to scale up our nationally determined contributions and adopt more forceful policies and measures to achieve peak carbon dioxide emissions by 2030 and carbon neutrality before 2060. China will keep its promise.

3. 正式文体的词汇特点

3.1 词源

英语正式文体词汇大都源于拉丁语、法语，个别源于古英语，而非正式文体词汇往往源于现代英语。思政经典文献具有极高的权威性和严肃性，以《决胜全面建成小康社会 夺取新时代中国特色社会主义伟大胜利——在中国共产党第十九次全国代表大会上的报告》（英文版）部分词汇为例，源于拉丁语的词汇最多，如：era, banner, rejuvenation, implement, etiquette, ethical, pursue；其次是源于法语的词汇，如：deliver, strive, mission, aspiration, formulate, launch, confront, issue, pioneer, session；源于古英语的词汇最少，如：seek。

3.2 首选单动词

英语存在着大量意义相近的词组，通常用于非正式的谈话体中；庄重的报告类文本单动词则是首选，而放弃具有口语特点的同义词组，因为动词尤其是实义动词最活跃、最有力量。与同义词组相比，单动词果断有力，字字千钧，更适合政论文体，如：seek (look for) happiness, uphold (stand for/stick to) the one-China principle, deter (prevent from) separatist, topple (pull down) the three mountains, withstand (hold out/strive against) major risks, highlight (put emphasis on) the importance, observe (abide by/adhere to) the Party's fundamental purpose, address (deal with/cope with) the concerns of the people, endeavor (make an effort) to develop an economy, ensure (make sure) China's food security。

3.3 避免非标准语

非标准语指不得体、不规范的表达，可适当用于谈话体中，正式文体中须谨慎使用。非标准语具体指如下三类：

3.3.1 俚语（Slang）

俚语是语言中极丰富多彩和富有活力的成分，多元、求新、趋俗的美国英语中俚语甚多，大部分源于社会的亚文化群体——黑社会、无业游民、吸毒者、赌徒等，大都粗俗不雅，英语学习者必须学会甄别，正式文体中切忌使用。

3.3.2 方言（Dialect）

方言即区域性语言，英语有多种方言。就英国本土来说，英国英语有苏格兰方言、威尔士方言、伦敦方言等。美国英语也因地域不同差别很大，不仅体现在语音方面，而且体现在拼写甚至语法规则方面。故方言也是正式文体之大忌，应坚决摒弃。

3.3.3 性歧视语（Sexist Language）

性歧视语指各种贬低或侮辱性尤其是针对女性的语言表现形式。语言反映了人类社会的历史文化、思维方式和价值观念。传统男权社会语言不可避免地存在着褒男贬女现象，女性因女性气质和特征被排斥在政治权利和某些职业之外，因此，重新审视狭义和有偏见的男性传统，还女性以真实，让她们真正成为"人"，并让女性价值得到理性的再现，符合她们身与心的必然状态。而今，一些带有偏见和误导性的语言仍很常见，英语学习者应努力避免，在正式文体中使用该类词汇时，建议译者采用中性的替代词汇（Hacker，1992）。以下是几个典型的例子：

chairman→ chairperson/moderator/chair/head

clergyman→ member of the clergy/minister/pastor

congressman→ member of Congress/representative/legislator

fireman→ firefighter

foreman→ supervisor

mailman→ mail carrier/postal worker/letter carrier

manpower→ personnel

policeman→ police officer

weatherman→ weather forecaster/meteorologist

salesman→ salesperson/sales representative/sales associate/sales clerk

workman→ worker/laborer

上述例子表明，在传统英语中，女性的角色就是妻子和母亲，体面的职业一般被认为只有男性才有资格从事，显然，这种词汇暗含针对女性的歧视性偏见。

第三部分：英译习作与文本词汇范例对照解析

1. 概念意义与内涵意义

原文：这一百年来开辟的伟大道路、创造的伟大事业、取得的伟大成就，必将<u>载</u>入中华民族发展<u>史册</u>、人类文明发展史册！

译文：The great path we have pioneered, the great cause we have undertaken, and the great achievements we have made over the past century will <u>go down in the annals</u> of the Chinese nation and of human civilization.

习作：The great road opened up in the past 100 years, the great cause created, the great achievement achieved, will surely be <u>recorded</u> in the history of the development of the Chinese nation and the history of human civilization.

范例对照解析：一个词语的内涵意义往往比其基本意义更加重要，所以对于遣词造句更加重要。"record"只是对人或物过去经历的记录和记载，属于中性词汇，习作者忽略了汉语的深刻含义；而"annals"源于拉丁语，它不是普通的记录，而是年鉴或者历史档案，"go down"意为"被载入""被铭记"，译文更接近汉语的内涵。出现问题的原因在于词汇的贫乏和单一，翻译时停留在就词论词的层面上。选择尺度把握不准，把握不住词的分寸和火候，要么用词过大和过重导致词义扩大，要么用词过小和过轻导致词义缩小，有时还会想当然地对号入座，这些都是学生翻译练习中的常见问题。

2. 抽象意义与具体意义

原文：勇于自我革命是中国共产党区别于其他政党的<u>显著标志</u>。

译文：A hallmark that distinguishes the Communist Party of China from other political parties is the courage to undertake self-reform.

习作：The courage of self-revolution is a remarkable sign of the CPC, which is different from other political parties.

范例对照解析：习作者没有准确把握词汇选择尺度，没有领会句子词汇的细微差别，"sign"表示所有迹象、符号及标志，意义笼统概括，选词过轻，过于抽象，不足以表现汉语的深刻意义；而"hallmark"原意是金银制品上表明纯度及制作时间、地点的印记，指具体的有特点和特征的标志和印记，所以与汉语文本的意义更接近。

3. 情感意义

原文：党中央号召你们，牢记初心使命，坚定理想信念，践行党的宗旨，永远保持同人民群众的血肉联系，始终同人民想在一起、干在一起，风雨同舟、同甘共苦，继续为实现人民对美好生活的向往不懈努力，努力为党和人民争取更大光荣！

译文：The Central Committee calls on every one of you to stay true to our Party's original aspiration and founding mission and stand firm in your ideals and convictions. Acting on the aims of the Party, you should always maintain close ties with the people, empathize and work with them, stand with them through good times and testing times, and continue working tirelessly to realize their aspirations for a better life and to bring still greater glory to the Party and the people.

习作：The Communist Party of China is calling all of you for keeping your original intention in mind and insisting your own ideal belief. Practicing the purposes of the Party, you should always maintain close ties with the people, always want to work together with the people, share weal and woe, continue to make unremitting efforts to realize the people's aspiration for a better life, and strive for greater glory for the Party and the people!

范例对照解析："intention"和"aspiration"都具有"目的""初衷"之意，但"intention"偏于中性和口语，指将要进行某种行为的思维活动，而"aspiration"更为书面，更多地表达"志向"与"抱负"，更符合中国共产党人为国为民的强烈愿望和追求的"使命"，因此是得体的译文；同样，"belief"和"convictions"都有"相信"的意思，但它们内含的情感不同，前者指单纯的主观上的"相信"，不需要什么根据，偏向于直观的感觉或者未经证实的想法，而后者则是基于事实和逻辑推理、经过深思熟虑后建立的坚定信念，所以，"convictions"更符合原文感情和场景。译者需要把握同义词之间的感情差异和风格差异，根据语体风格需要选择合适的词。

4. 风格意义

原文：我代表中共中央，向全国各族人民，向各民主党派、各人民团体和各界爱国人士，向香港特别行政区同胞、澳门特别行政区同胞和台湾同胞以及广大侨胞，向关心和支持中国现代化建设的各国朋友，表示衷心的感谢！

译文：On behalf of the Central Committee of the Communist Party of China, I express our heartfelt thanks to the people of all ethnic groups, to all other political parties, to the people's organizations, and to patriotic figures from all sectors of society, to our <u>fellow countrymen and women</u> in the Hong Kong and Macao special administrative regions and in Taiwan, to overseas Chinese, and to all our friends from around the world who have shown understanding and support for China's modernization.

习作：On behalf of the Central Committee of the Communist Party of China, I express our sincere thanks to the people of all races, to all political parties, to the people's organizations, and to patriotic people from all walks of society, to our <u>fellow countrymen</u> in the Hong Kong and Macao special administrative regions and in Taiwan, to overseas Chinese, and to all our friends from the world who have expressed their understanding and support for Chinese modernization.

范例对照解析：译文关注了对女性的尊重。"countrymen"意指"同胞"，但是，为规避对女性的疏忽之嫌而有意识地添加了"women"，此举看似微不足道，实则用心所致。显然，习作者缺少对英语词汇背后所折射的性别歧视偏见和态度的理解，缺乏对语言性别歧视的认知和研究。

5. 搭配意义

原文：<u>行百里者半九十</u>。中华民族伟大复兴，绝不是<u>轻轻松松</u>、<u>敲锣打鼓</u>就能实现的。

译文：As the Chinese saying goes, <u>the</u> last <u>leg of a journey</u> marks the halfway point. Achieving national rejuvenation will be no <u>walk in the park</u>; it will take more than <u>drum beating and gong clanging</u> to get there.

习作：A man who wants to walk 100 miles is only halfway there when he has gone 90 miles. The great rejuvenation of the Chinese nation will not be achieved by beating gongs and drums.

范例对照解析：译文中三个名词短语都是固定搭配："the leg of the/a journey"指长途旅行中的一段路程，如果像某网站一样把该搭配译为"行程中的（最后）一条腿"，那就闹笑话了；"walk in the park"意思是容易之事；"drum"和"gong"是中国文化中民间广泛使用的鼓和锣，"打"鼓必须用"beat"，"敲"锣必须用"clang"，而习作者对固定搭配掌握不够准确，只好按照汉语字面意思来译。

第二单元

思政经典中的词汇翻译（二）

第一部分：汉英文本词汇知识及范例对照

1. 词性转译

汉英两种语言使用和表达不尽相同，翻译时偶尔有个别句子可以逐词对应翻译，但大部分情况下不能机械地对译，需要在保持原文内容不变的前提下，改变原文中某些词的类别，以达到行文准确、流畅、自然，符合译语规范。例如：

原文：大会的主题是：<u>不忘初心</u>，<u>牢记使命</u>，高举中国特色社会主义伟大旗帜，决胜全面建成小康社会，夺取新时代中国特色社会主义伟大胜利，为实现中华民族伟大复兴的中国梦不懈奋斗。

译文：The theme of the Congress is: <u>Remain true to</u> our original aspiration and founding mission, hold high the banner of socialism with Chinese characteristics, secure a decisive victory in building a moderately prosperous society in all respects, strive for the great success of socialism with Chinese characteristics for a new era, and work tirelessly to realize the Chinese Dream of national rejuvenation.

分析：段落后面的几个句子谓语都是实义动词，为了避免动词堆积使用，译文通过词性转译，把原文中的动词"不忘"和"牢记"转化为系表结构搭配，降低了英语句子中动词的活跃度，使语言实现从静态到动态的过渡。

2. 词序调整

从词序角度来看，汉英两种语言有很多相似之处，句子的主要成分主语、谓语、宾语、表语顺序基本一致，但是两种语言的定语和状语位置差异很大。汉译英时译文采用什么样的语序要根据英语的表达习惯和规则，不能强调译文与原文句式和语序的绝对一致。例如：

原文：全面深化改革取得重大突破。蹄疾步稳推进全面深化改革，坚决破除各方面体制机制弊端。改革全面发力、多点突破、纵深推进，着力增强改革系统性、整体性、协同性，压茬拓展改革广度和深度，推出一千五百多项改革举措，重要领域和关键环节改革取得突破性进展，主要领域改革主体框架基本确立。中国特色社会主义制度更加完善，国家治理体系和治理能力现代化水平明显提高，全社会发展活力和创新活力明显增强。

译文：We have made major breakthroughs in deepening reform. We have taken comprehensive steps to deepen reform swiftly but steadily, and worked with resolve to remove institutional barriers in all areas. We have taken moves across the board, achieved breakthroughs in many areas, and made further progress in reform. We have pursued reform in a more systematic, holistic, and coordinated way, increasing its coverage and depth. Thanks to the launch of over 1,500 reform measures, breakthroughs have been made in key areas, and general frameworks for reform have been established in major fields. The system of socialism with Chinese characteristics has been further improved, with notable progress made in modernizing China's system and capacity for governance. Throughout society, development is full of vitality and is driven by greater creativity.

分析：从两种文本画线部分来看，主要区别在于定语和状语的位置。汉语中副词通常置于所修饰的动词之前，英语中副词通常放在动词之后；汉语中定语通常放在所修饰名词前，英语中定语若为单词或复合词则通常置于名词前，若为短语则后置。

15

3. 增译与省译

基于译文的可接受性，汉译英时对汉语进行结构调整、增加词汇或减少词汇是必要的。增译涉及英语语法规则所必需的因素，如必须增补汉语所没有的冠词、增补英语习惯用法的做主语和宾语的代词及物主代词、增补句法结构不可或缺的连词、增补涉及文化的解释词语等。省译也是翻译中的常见手段，目的在于使译文通顺、意义清楚，避免重复累赘，更加符合目的语的表达习惯。省译涉及汉语中一些笼统的范畴语，原文中的重复性词汇或近义词汇，实际意义不大、可有可无的词汇，含义在译文中不言而喻的词汇，某些从文化角度无法照字直译被理解和接受的词汇。

3.1 增译

原文 1：推进伟大工程，要结合伟大斗争、伟大事业、伟大梦想的实践来进行，确保党在世界形势深刻变化的历史进程中始终走在时代前列，在应对国内外各种风险和考验的历史进程中始终成为全国人民的主心骨，在坚持和发展中国特色社会主义的历史进程中始终成为坚强领导核心。

译文：All work to advance this project must go hand in hand with the struggle, the cause, and the dream. We must see that as history progresses and the world undergoes profound changes, the Party remains always ahead of the times; that as history progresses and we respond to risks and tests at home and abroad, the Party remains always the backbone of the nation; and that as history progresses and we continue to uphold and develop socialism with Chinese characteristics, the Party remains always a powerful leadership core.

分析："We must see"后面由"that"引导的三个平行的宾语从句，强调中国共产党在中国和国际历史进程中在三个方面一直发挥突出作用——走在世界前列，既是人民的主心骨又是坚强领导核心："ahead of the times""the backbone of the nation"和"a powerful leadership core"一气呵成，关联词"that"不省略，三次重复来强化主题。

原文 2：一百年来，中国共产党团结带领中国人民，以"为有牺牲多壮志，敢教日月换新天"的大无畏气概，书写了中华民族几千年历史上最恢宏的史诗。

译文：Over the past hundred years, the Party has united the Chinese people and led them in writing the most magnificent chapter in the millennia-long history of the Chinese nation, embodying the dauntless spirit that Mao Zedong expressed when he wrote, "Our minds grow stronger for the martyrs' sacrifice, daring to make the sun and the moon shine in the new sky."

分析：原文中引用了毛泽东1959年6月25日所创作的古诗作品《七律·到韶山》。回到阔别32年的家乡，毛泽东感慨万千，无数烈士的牺牲才换来了革命的胜利，尽管中华人民共和国成立仅十年，还是一穷二白，但是中国人民有信心让天地翻覆换新颜。为便于英文读者更充分地理解原诗作背景，译文采用了增译法，对汉语中具有文化色彩的成分进行补充性释译。

3.2 省译

原文：党中央决定对宪法进行适当修改是经过反复考虑、综合方方面面情况作出的……

译文：The Central Committee's proposed revisions are based on thorough consideration and comprehensive analysis…

分析：汉语中常用范畴词表示行为、现象所属的范畴，这些范畴词一般放在动词、形容词、名词之后，常用的有"领域""材料""问题""情况""状态""工作"等。汉译英时往往省译，只把它前面的修饰词译成名词即可。如果范畴词前面是名词，直接将该名词译出即可，这样处理使译文表达简洁精练。

4. 文化词汇翻译

文化离不开语言，文化因素体现在语言文字中，人类语言活动中处处都有文化印迹。翻译作为一种跨文化行为，不仅仅是语言之间的转换，更重要的是文化之间的转换。词汇是语言中最活跃、最敏感的要素，最为直接地反映着社会文化的特殊性和发展变化，翻译中的文化转换主要是通过词汇的文化信息体现出来的。例如：

扶贫工程 Anti-Poverty Project

菜篮子工程 Vegetable Basket Project

温饱工程 Decent-Life Project

西部大开发 Go-West Campaign

红色中国 socialist China

分析：翻译旨在促进思想文化交流，使人们对彼此间的民族文化有所了解。因此，翻译应以文化平等和文化传承为基本原则。考虑和照顾到英语读者文化接受的能力，上述文化词汇英译时再现了汉语的民族文化信息，达到了传播交流的目的。

第二部分：知识与技能讲析

1. 词性异同与词性转译

实践证明，了解汉英两种语言的差异在翻译过程中至关重要。凡是两种语言相同或者相似之处，翻译就容易处理，而两种语言差异很大之处，翻译起来难度就比较大。

汉英两种语言词类大部分重合，汉语中的名词、动词、形容词都可以做主语、谓语、宾语、表语，但是英语中只有名词、代词和相当于名词的动名词、不定式、名词从句做主语，充当谓语的只有动词。因此，翻译时不能拘泥于原文，要灵活地根据译文需要适当进行词性转译。汉英两种语言的词汇不是完全对等的，汉语的遣词造句在于动词，而英语则会通过名词、动词和介词词组形成互补。从理论上来讲，翻译中词类的转换是不受限制的。常见的词类转译有如下几种：

1.1 汉语动词的转译

汉语句子结构一个最典型特点就是可以有连动式和兼语式：一个句子中可以有好几个动词，一个动宾结构和一个主谓结构套在一起，前面动宾结构的宾语兼做后面主谓结构的主语，如："老师让我们背诵课文。"对比来看，英语要求只有一个谓语，英译时需要把汉语的动词译为名词、形容词、介词、副词或者非谓语动词，使译文更地道、自然，符合英语的规范要求。必须提到的是，汉语动词转译为介词短语是非常重要的技巧,因为英语介词的词汇意义极其丰富，不同的词组搭配意义不同，可以用来有效地表达汉语常见动词的意义。例如：

原文：现在，我代表第十九届中央委员会向大会作报告。

译文：<u>On behalf of</u> the 19th Central Committee of the Communist Party of China (CPC), I will now <u>deliver a report</u> to the 20th National Congress.

汉语是连动结构，英语译文把第一个动词转译成介词短语"on behalf of"，自然、流畅，符合英语行文的表达习惯。

1.2 汉语名词的转译

汉语名词做主语、宾语时可以译为对应的英文，但是不一定符合英语的表达习惯。因此，可转译为英语的动词、形容词、副词。首先，英语有词性变化，很多动词是从名词派生而来并保留着词根的基本意义；其次，部分英语名词同时也兼做动词，所以，汉语名词转译成动词并不显得生硬；最后，形容词加上英语中独特的定冠词，可以自然地成为名词。例如：

原文：自<u>成立</u>以来，我们党<u>团结带领</u>人民进行革命、建设、改革，<u>根本目的</u>就是为了让人民过上好日子，无论面临多大挑战和压力，无论付出多大牺牲和代价，这一点都始终不渝、毫不动摇。

译文：The fundamental goal for the Party since its <u>founding</u>, in <u>uniting</u> the people and <u>leading</u> them in revolution, construction and reform, is to give them a better life. The Party has never wavered in <u>pursuing</u> this goal no matter what challenges and pressure it faces, no matter the sacrifice and the cost.

不难发现，在英译句子中，汉语的动词"成立""团结""带领"以及主系表结构都是通过动名词和介词加动名词来表现，符合英语的表达习惯。

1.3 汉语形容词或副词的转译

英语词汇的派生特点使得同根词汇具有相同或相似的意义，由于句法和结构的需要，汉语形容词或副词可以比较自然地转译为英语名词，也可以转译为英语介词短语，汉语形容词可以转译为英语副词，汉语副词可以转译为英语形容词。例如：

原文：为了实现中华民族伟大复兴，中国共产党团结带领中国人民，浴血奋战、百折不挠，创造了<u>新民主主义革命</u>的伟大成就。

译文：To realize national rejuvenation, the Party united the Chinese people and led them in fighting bloody battles. With unyielding determination, we achieved great success <u>in the New Democratic Revolution</u> (1919-1949).

汉语中，"新民主主义革命"做定语修饰中心词"伟大成就"，在英译中被转换成后置介词短语，修饰前面的名词。

2. 词序与修饰语顺序

词序是指句子成分的排列顺序，它体现了词语之间的关系，汉英两种语言语系不同，母语使用者思维不同，语言表达顺序不同。就基本语序来讲，汉语和英语的主语、谓语和宾语位置相同，而定语和状语位置相异。汉英翻译必须考虑英语读者的习惯表达方式，适当对修饰语的语序进行调整。

2.1 定语位置

汉语定语总是放在中心词前面，而英语定语位置比较灵活，单词做定语时往往放在中心词之前，非单一词或者介词短语则置于中心词之后。汉语中不同类型词语并列做定语修饰一个名词时，往往把表示事物本质特点的词放在最前面，把描写性词语排列在后，而英语则恰恰相反，本质属性的定语一定要靠近中心词。如："社会主义核心价值观"译为"the core socialist values"，而不是"the socialist core values"。

当英语中心词前面有多个形容词修饰时，译者一定要考虑词汇顺序并按照一定的规则排列：限定词→评价性形容词→大小、形状、新旧形容词→颜色形容词→国籍、来源、材料形容词→目的、用途形容词。对照下面例子，可以看出汉英两种语言定语位置差异。

原文：全面建设社会主义现代化强国

译文：to make China <u>a great modern socialist country</u> in every dimension

2.2 状语位置

汉语状语通常放在主语和谓语之间，英语状语位置往往比较灵活，多放在句末，但也可以放在句首和句中。如果句子中有多个状语，汉语通常按照时间、地点、方式排列，英语则通常按照方式、地点、时间排列。对照下面例子，可以看出汉英两种语言状语位置差异。

原文：今天，<u>在中国共产党历史上</u>，<u>在中华民族历史上</u>，都是一个十分重大而庄严的日子。

译文：Today, the first of July, is a great and solemn day <u>in the history of both the Communist Party of China and the Chinese nation</u>.

3. 词汇的增译与省译

3.1 增译

汉译英时，经常需要在译文中增补一些没有对应表达的词，原文无其词却有其义。增补词汇主要出于三种考虑：

第一，语法需要：语法需要的增补涉及内容较多，如汉语中没有冠词，英译时必须增加；汉语原文省略较多，代词使用较少，通常采用省略或者重复，而英语中代词是常见的衔接手段；另外，介词甚至动词都可能需要增补。因此，汉译英时需要补全信息，如果照搬原文衔接手段，译文就会明显表现出中文式特点。汉语句子结构更多依靠语言内部逻辑关系，而英语依赖连词连接句子和指代关系，所以，汉译英时必须考虑增加并列连词和从属连词，增补连词是汉译英的重要任务之一。例如：

原文1：这一百年来开辟的伟大道路、创造的伟大事业、取得的伟大成就，必将载入中华民族发展史册、人类文明发展史册！

译文：The great path we have pioneered, the great cause we have undertaken, <u>and</u> the great achievements we have made over the past century will go down in the annals of the Chinese nation and of human civilization.

原文2：人民是历史的创造者，是真正的英雄。

译文：The people are the true heroes, <u>for</u> it is they who write history.

不难看出，汉语是两个分句，没有任何连贯，而英译范例增加了并列连词"and"和"for"，从而满足了英语句法的连贯衔接要求。

第二，语义需要：如果原文省略内容较多，一些具体信息没有交代，译者需要根据原文内容进行适当增补，从而使译文读者更清晰地了解原文希望传达的信息。例如：

原文：十月革命一声炮响，给中国送来了马克思列宁主义。

译文：With <u>the salvoes of Russia's October Revolution in 1917</u>, Marxism-Leninism was brought to China.

第三，文化需要：由于文化背景的差异，历史或文化典故往往带有较强的文化个性，英译时经常会增加一些原文中隐含的信息，以激发读者的兴趣，帮助读者更好地理解，所以需要进行小幅度的解释性增词，但切忌过多延展和演绎。例如：

原文：新的征程上，我们必须坚持党的全面领导，不断完善党的领导，增强"<u>四个意识</u>"、坚定"<u>四个自信</u>"、做到"<u>两个维护</u>"……

译文：On the journey ahead, we must continue to uphold and strengthen the Party's overall leadership. We must <u>be deeply conscious of the need to maintain political commitment, think in terms of the general picture, follow the core leadership of the CPC Central Committee, and act in accordance with its requirements. We must remain confident in the path, theory, system and culture of socialism with Chinese characteristics. We must uphold the core position of the general secretary on the Party Central Committee and in the Party as a whole, and uphold the authority of the Central Committee and its centralized, unified leadership</u>…

原文出现了"四个意识""四个自信"和"两个维护"重要政治概念，考虑到英语读者的认知，英译时增加了具体内容，表达更清晰全面，能更好地帮助读者理解当代中国。

3.2 省译

汉英两种语言构词方式和语法结构各异，因此，英译时对原语结构进行词语增译或省译的调整是必要的。汉语遣词造句，注重意合，而英语组织丰富，注重结构。英译省略的成分往往是被认为累赘的附属成分，省译后并没有减少所表达的思想内容，实现了译文简洁、凝练。汉语注重文采和修辞，词组中习惯含有修饰语，而英语词组里修饰成分不那么多，因此，汉译英时不一定把汉语全部译出。英文中修饰语过多或者辞藻过于华丽会产生烦冗累赘之感，所以，汉译英时需要考虑省译重复性词语、意义偏大而显得空洞的词语、实际意义不大的修饰词。也可以根据语法需要省译：汉语动词没有形态变化，时间概念靠副词表示，而英语的时间概念主要通过动词形态变化来表示，汉译英时通过动词的不同时态基本能表达出汉语的时间意义，可以省译。非正式语体中平行结构的关联词、介词等都可省略，而正式文体中却不能省略。例如：

原文：中国人民从来没有欺负、压迫、奴役过其他国家人民，过去没有，现在没有，将来也不会有。

译文：We have never abused, oppressed or subjugated the people of any other country, and we never will.

可以看出，汉语表达注重文采，语言略显华丽；而英语则重视简洁，现在完成时和一般将来时包含了原文的意义，从而避免了重复和累赘。

汉英两种语言存在着较多的差异，范畴词就是典型的例子之一。"方面""领域""方式""问题""情况""水平"之类的范畴词，在汉语中本身没有多少实际意义，但是可以使句子更加流畅，因此使用频率很高。汉译英时，往往省译，只须把其前面的词译成名词即可，如果范畴词前面是名词，直接将该名词译出即可，这样可避免译文的冗赘或中式英语的表达。例如：

原文：要继续推进法治领域改革，解决好立法、执法、司法、守法等领域的突出矛盾和问题。

译文：We must continue to carry forward reform in the domain of rule of law in order to solve prominent conflicts and problems in devising, enforcing, applying and observing the law.

4. 文化词汇翻译

文化词汇是指蕴含社会文化含义的词汇，与一国的政治、经济、文化、历史和民情民俗密切相关，是指某一特定文化所具有的事物和概念，从而在进行双语转换时形成一种词汇空缺。即某一个社会文化中具有某些独一无二的事物，其他社会文化中并没有，负载这一事物的词语在跨文化交际中就成为文化词汇。文化词汇差异主要表现在生态文化、物质文化、社会文化、宗教文化、肢体语言、习惯差异等方面。

另外一类文化词汇是文化含义词，其所指的事物和概念是对方有的，只是词义的维度和宽泛度不完全重合，即存在着某种程度的对等，不对等、不重合的部分有大有小，造成对方的词汇空缺。原因之一是词汇体系划分不同——由于社会文化不同，对客观事物和概念的不同划分和归类造成意义不重合，只有部分对等。原因之二是联想不同——尽管所指的事物相同，但由于社会文化不同，所产生的联想不同，造成文化含义不同。

翻译旨在促进思想文化交流，通过这种文化交流使人们对相互间的民族文化有所了解，因此译者应对其他民族文化平等对待，在考虑目的语读者文化接受能力的前提下，在译语中尽量再现原语的民族文化信息，从而真正达到传播交流的目的。文化词汇翻译策略主要有以下六种。

4.1 直译加补充信息（释译）

直译是在译文中保留原语民族文化色彩的最佳方法，但在一些情况下，特别是对于目的语初级和中级读者，其对原语文化接触时间不长，无法真正理解和接受外来文化，先直译再增补信息说明更有利于其理解和接受。例如：

原文 1：马来西亚有句谚语，"遇山一起爬，遇沟一起跨"。这正是亚太大家庭精神的精髓。

译文：There is a Malay proverb that goes, "bukit sama didaki, lurah sama dituruni", which means to climb the hill together and go down the ravine together. It aptly captures the spirit of our Asia-Pacific family.

原文 2：新中国成立后，党领导人民战胜政治、经济、军事等方面一系列严峻挑战，肃清国民党反动派残余武装力量和土匪，和平解放西藏，实现祖国大陆完全统一；稳定物价，统一财经工作，完成土地改革，进行社会各方面民主改革，实行男女权利平等，镇压反革命，开展"三反"、"五反"运动，荡涤旧社会留下的污泥浊水，社会面貌焕然一新。

译文：After the founding of the People's Republic, the Party led the people in surmounting a multitude of political, economic, and military challenges. It cleared out bandits and remnant KMT reactionary forces, peacefully liberated Xizang, and unified the entire mainland. It stabilized prices, unified standards for finances and the economy, completed the agrarian reform, and launched democratic reforms in all sectors of society. It introduced the policy of equal rights for men and women, suppressed counter-revolutionaries, and launched movements against the "three evils" of corruption, waste, and bureaucracy and against the "five evils" of bribery, tax evasion, theft of state property, cheating on government contracts, and stealing of economic information. As the stains of the old society were wiped out, China took on a completely new look.

原文 3：我们开展了史无前例的反腐败斗争，以"得罪千百人、不负十四亿"的使命担当祛疴治乱，不敢腐、不能腐、不想腐一体推进，"打虎"、"拍蝇"、"猎狐"多管齐下，反腐败斗争取得压倒性胜利并全面巩固，消除了党、国家、军队内部存在的严重隐患，确保党和人民赋予的权力始终用来为人民谋幸福。

译文：We have waged a battle against corruption on a scale unprecedented in our history. Driven by a strong sense of mission, we have resolved to "offend a few thousand rather than fail 1.4 billion" and to clear our Party of all its ills. We have taken coordinated steps to see that officials do not have the audacity, opportunity, or desire to be corrupt, and we have used a combination of measures to "take out tigers," "swat flies," and "hunt down foxes," punishing corrupt officials of all types. We have achieved an overwhelming victory and fully consolidated the gains in our fight against corruption. All this has helped remove serious hidden dangers in the Party, the country, and the military and ensured that the power granted to us by the Party and the people is always exercised in the interests of the people.

4.2 音意兼译

在翻译实践中比较常见的是音译加意译，又称为音意兼译。例如：

原文：面对"台独"势力分裂活动和外部势力干涉台湾事务的严重挑衅，我们坚决开展反分裂、反干涉重大斗争，展示了我们维护国家主权和领土完整、反对"台独"的坚强决心和强大能力，进一步掌握了实现祖国完全统一的战略主动，进一步巩固了国际社会坚持一个中国的格局。

译文：In response to separatist activities aimed at "Taiwan independence" and gross provocations of external interference in Taiwan affairs, we have resolutely fought against separatism and countered interference, demonstrating our resolve and ability to safeguard China's sovereignty and territorial integrity and to oppose "Taiwan independence." We have strengthened our strategic initiative for China's complete reunification and consolidated commitment to the one-China principle within the international community.

4.3 音译

反映中国特有事物的名称，汉译英时通常采用音译方法，把音和义都借过去，然后逐渐深入英语本土语言中，最后成为英语新词汇。例如：

原文 1：1938 年，毛泽东同志指出："如果我们党有一百个至二百个系统地而不是零碎地、实际地而不是空洞地学会了<u>马克思列宁主义</u>的同志，就会大大地提高我们党的战斗力量。"

译文：In 1938, Mao Zedong noted that "Our Party's fighting capacity will be much greater, if we have one or two hundred comrades with a grasp of <u>Marxism-Leninism</u> which is systematic and not fragmentary, genuine and not hollow."

原文 2：<u>孟子</u>认为这种人"同乎流俗，合乎污世"。

译文：<u>Mencius</u> denounced such people for "just following the herd and being in concord with the filthy world".

4.4 直译

直译法是指在不违背英语文化传统的前提下，在英文中完全保留汉语词语的指称意义，使汉语和英语在内容和形式上保持一致。通过直译，许多表达中国特有事物的词汇已经进入英语中，并成为标准英语的一部分，如："Project Hope"（希望工程）。这种方法既能传达原语的概念意义，又能再现原语的民族文化信息，是丰富语言、促进文化交流的理想途径。例如：

原文 1：共建<u>"一带一路"</u>是各国共同发展的大舞台，我们要推动共建"一带一路"倡议同各国发展战略及欧亚经济联盟等区域合作倡议深入对接，维护产业链供应链稳定畅通，促进各国经济融合、发展联动、成果共享。

译文：<u>Belt and Road</u> cooperation is a major platform for promoting development for us all. We need to strengthen complementarity between the Belt and Road Initiative and the development strategies of SCO countries, and with regional cooperation initiatives such as the Eurasian Economic Union. We should keep industrial and supply chains functioning smoothly, promote economic integration and interconnected development of all countries, and deliver shared benefits to all.

原文 2：中国共产党立志于中华民族千秋伟业，百年恰是风华正茂！回首过去，展望未来，有中国共产党的坚强领导，有全国各族人民的紧密团结，全面建成社会主义现代化强国的目标一定能够实现，中华民族伟大复兴的<u>中国梦</u>

一定能够实现！

译文：Today, a hundred years on from its founding, the Communist Party of China is still in its prime, and remains as determined as ever to achieve lasting greatness for the Chinese nation. Looking back on the path we have traveled and forward to the journey that lies ahead, it is certain that with the firm leadership of the Party and the great unity of all the Chinese people, we will achieve the goal of building a great modern socialist country in all respects and fulfill the Chinese Dream of national rejuvenation.

4.5 意译

意译法是指译者在受到译语社会文化差异的局限时，不得不舍弃原文的字面意义，以求得译文与原文内容的一致和主要语言功能的相似，即求"神似"，放弃"形似"。例如：

原文1：绿水青山就是金山银山。

译文：Lucid waters and lush mountains are invaluable assets.

原文2：要严防"三股势力"借疫生乱，遏制毒品泛滥趋势，打击极端主义思想通过互联网传播，提升成员国执法安全合作水平。

译文：It is important that we forestall terrorist, separatist and extremist attempts to exploit the pandemic for disruption, curb the proliferation of drugs, crack down on Internet-based propagation of extremist ideology, and deepen SCO members' law-enforcement cooperation.

4.6 借用

由于汉英两种语言的差异和民族文化背景的不同，相同的事物可能有不同的联想；相反，不同的事物也可能有相同的联想。而且文化具有共通性，汉英两种语言中有一些相同或相似的表达方式，这就为借用创造了条件。例如：

原文：三个臭皮匠，顶个诸葛亮。

译文：Two heads are better than one.

文化词汇是与我国的政治、经济、文化、历史和民情有关的词汇。文化词汇的翻译旨在让英语读者欣赏和领略中国文化的魅力，促进中西文化交流。翻译文化词汇时，译者绝不能拘泥于一种译法，必须根据具体情况，选择最适当的翻译技巧来传达原文信息，这对译者提出了更高的要求。

文化词汇反映了文化，承载着丰富的文化内涵，所以翻译起来有一定难度，译者不仅需要汉英语言能力，而且需要对双语文化知识，特别是两种民族的心理意识、文化形成、历史传统、宗教文化习俗等一系列因素有所了解。

第三部分：英译习作与文本词汇范例对照解析

1. 词性转译

原文：我们党团结带领人民找到了一条以农村包围城市、武装夺取政权的正确革命道路。

译文：Our Party united the people and led them in embarking on the right revolutionary path, using rural areas to encircle the cities and seizing state power with military force.

习作：Our Party united and led the people in finding a correct revolutionary road to seize power by encircling the cities with armed forces from the countryside.

范例对照解析：原文汉语一个句子中包含"团结""带领""找到"三个动词，是典型的连动结构。中国学生过分依赖动词，在选择谓语时往往习惯性地找动词对应，而英语中的谓语动词只能有一个，这就需要考虑三个动词的关系并且按照英语的习惯和规则处理。译文把"united"和"led"处理成并列关系，把动词"找到"用动名词做介词宾语处理："in embarking on"（开始一段旅程），符合英语语法，表达更地道。对照发现，习作者对汉语连动的英译处理技能有待提升。

2. 词序调整

原文：一百年前，中国共产党的先驱们创建了中国共产党，形成了坚持真理、坚守理想，践行初心、担当使命，不怕牺牲、英勇斗争，对党忠诚、不负人民的伟大建党精神，这是中国共产党的精神之源。

译文：A hundred years ago, the pioneers of communism in China established the Communist Party of China and developed the great founding spirit of the Party, which is comprised of the following principles: upholding truth and ideals, staying true to our original aspiration and founding mission, fighting bravely without fear of death, and remaining loyal to the Party and faithful to the people. This spirit is the Party's source of strength.

习作：100 years ago, the pioneers of the Communist Party of China founded the Communist Party of China, formed the ideal of adhering to the truth, practicing the original heart, undertaking the mission, not afraid of sacrifice, heroic struggle, loyalty to the Party, and living up to the people. This is the spirit of the Communist Party of China.

范例对照解析：翻译中语序处理的关键在于如何体现原文的主题意义和表现效果，了解汉英两种语言的差异在翻译过程中至关重要。凡是两种语言相同或者相似之处，翻译就容易；而两种语言差异很大之处，翻译起来难度就大。译文调整了词序，用非限定性定语从句来解释多个并列项，符合英语的表达习惯；而习作者无条件照搬原文语序，形成了中文式的机械译文，表达效果较差。

3. 增译与省译

3.1 增译

原文：中国特色社会主义进入新时代，我们党一定要有新气象新作为。<u>打铁必须自身硬</u>。

译文：As socialism with Chinese characteristics has entered a new era, our Party must get a new look and make new accomplishments. <u>As the saying goes, it takes a good blacksmith to forge good tools.</u>

习作：As socialism with Chinese characteristics enters a new era, our Party must take on a new outlook and make new achievements. The iron must be hard by itself.

范例对照解析：汉译英时不能照搬原文模式，而应对具有中国文化特点的词语进行适当解释。译文对汉语的谚语进行了补充解释，而习作者对应式翻译，忽略了英语读者的理解需求。

3.2 省译

原文：凡是在我国境内注册的企业，都要<u>一视同仁</u>、<u>平等对待</u>。

译文：All businesses registered in China will <u>be treated equally</u>.

习作：All businesses registered in China should be regarded as the same and treated equally.

范例对照解析：为了追求行文气势或者增强音韵效果，汉语往往采用重复法，对于汉语来说，这并不会影响文字的简洁性。但译成英语时，可能会造成累赘。因此，汉译英时应省略中文里重复出现的词语。汉语偏爱用字对仗工整，常常使用意义相近的对称结构，最常见的就是"一视同仁""平等对待"之类的四字词组，读起来朗朗上口，而英语则不同。所以，在翻译意义相近的词汇时，只需翻译其中一个部分，或者进行概括性翻译。习作者省译知识不足，担心减少词语翻译会漏掉原文信息，因此把对称的四字词组照搬到英语中，从而导致烦冗。

4. 文化词汇翻译

原文：长城内外、大江南北，全国人民心往一处想、劲往一处使，把个人冷暖、集体荣辱、国家安危融为一体，"天使白"、"橄榄绿"、"守护蓝"、"志愿红"迅速集结，"我是党员我先上"、"疫情不退我不退"，誓言铿锵，丹心闪耀。

译文：Our people across the country united as one with a single purpose in mind. We knew what was at stake: the wellbeing of every one of us, the common interests of our communities, and the safety of our nation. Doctors and nurses in white coats, military personnel in green uniforms, police officers in blue gear, and volunteers in red vests all played their part. Party members rushed to the front line, and their pledge to keep fighting until the virus was defeated has shown their loyalty to the Party and the people.

习作：Inside and outside the Great Wall, the north and south of the Great River, the people of the whole country are thinking in one place and making efforts in one place, integrating personal warmth and coldness, collective honor and disgrace, and national security. "Angel White", "Olive Green", "Guardian Blue", "Volunteer Red" quickly assembled. "I am a Party member. I will go first." and "If the epidemic does not retreat I do not retreat." The pledge is iron, and the heart shines.

范例对照解析：汉语包含了多个中国文化词汇，尤其是和颜色相关的词汇。由于颜色对于不同民族有着不同的文化寓意，如果直接按照原文来译，则影响英语读者的理解甚至产生误解。因此，解释性翻译是必要的。习作机械地按照原文去处理，原文的主题意义表现不够清晰。

第三单元

思政经典中的句子翻译（一）

第一部分：思政经典汉英文本金句范例对照

1. 句子结构及其类型

就句子成分和基本句型来讲，英语和汉语有一定的相似性，但是在句子结构方面存在着很大差异，具体表现在：汉语重意合，外形松散，分句短小，没有词形变化，语法关系和逻辑关系隐含在上下文中；英语重形合，呈现语块衔接，通过外部形态变化来表现各种语法和逻辑关系。因此，汉译英时，首先要处理好汉语句内的逻辑关系并运用适当连词表现出来。例如：

原文： 新时代的中国青年要以实现中华民族伟大复兴<u>为己任</u>，增强做中国人的志气、骨气、底气，<u>不负时代</u>，<u>不负韶华</u>，<u>不负党和人民的殷切期望</u>！

译文： In the new era, our young people should make it their mission to contribute to national rejuvenation and aspire to greater pride, confidence and assurance in their identity as Chinese, <u>so that</u> they can live up to the promise of their youth and the expectations of our times, our Party, and our people.

分析：汉语由多个分句组成，句型呈现连动结构，并无主从之分。译成英语时，按照英语中只能有一个谓语的规则，把汉语的"以……为己任"作为句子主干，将后面句子理解为其目的，用"so that"引导目的状语从句，从而明确表现了汉语句子的隐含逻辑关系，同时符合英语语言注重层次的表达习惯。

2. 句子连贯

汉语句子之间的逻辑关系通常蕴含在上下文中，多以短句、简约句子为主，连接词如连词、介词使用频率较低；英语句子与句子之间、句子内成分之间以及段落之间，通过词汇或者语法手段来实现连接和相互照应，是语篇连贯的最基本前提。了解汉英两种语言的这一显著特征，汉译英时，译者应当具有连贯意识，适当增补连接词，使译文更加连贯、逻辑清晰明了，也可以通过词语实现衔接。为了使语篇连贯，语言表层的调整是必要的。例如：

原文：……<u>坚持用马克思主义之"矢"去射新时代中国之"的"</u>，<u>继续推进马克思主义基本原理同中国具体实际相结合、同中华优秀传统文化相结合</u>，<u>续写马克思主义中国化时代化新篇章</u>。

译文：… should develop Marxism <u>while</u> upholding its basic tenets, combine them with the best of our traditional culture, <u>and</u> apply them in China's context, <u>so that</u> Marxism can continue to work in solving problems in China in the new era.

分析：汉语是含连动结构的三个分句，逻辑关系隐含在句中，译文选取了"继续推进"作为谓语动词，把"坚持用"作为并列动词，把"续写"转化为目的状语，明确了层次和逻辑关系，用"while""and"和"so that"实现了英语的语法衔接。

3. 强调句

原文：在近代以后中国社会的剧烈运动中，在中国人民反抗封建统治和外来侵略的激烈斗争中，在马克思列宁主义同中国工人运动的结合过程中，一九二一年中国共产党应运而生。

译文：With the advent of modern times, Chinese society became embroiled in intense upheavals; this was a time of fierce struggle as the Chinese people resisted feudal rule and foreign aggression. <u>It was</u> in the midst of this, in 1921, as Marxism-

Leninism was integrated with the Chinese workers' movement, that the Communist Party of China was born.

分析："It is/was…that"是英语中最常用的强调结构之一，使用灵活，可强调除了谓语之外的任何成分。

4. 倒装句

原文 1：……实现了中华民族由近代不断衰落到根本扭转命运、持续走向繁荣富强的伟大飞跃。

译文：Thus was made a great transition: The Chinese nation reversed its fate from the continuous decline of modern times to steady progress towards prosperity and strength.

分析：英语中把谓语动词提到主语之前构成全部倒装，是很常见的强调手法，"here""there""now""then"等副词比较常见，而"thus"倒装结构因极其正式，较多地使用在政论文体中。

原文 2：只有把基层党组织建设强、把基层政权巩固好，中国特色社会主义的根基才能稳固。

译文：Only with strong Party organizations and governments at the grassroots level can the foundations of Chinese socialism be solid.

5. 平行句

系列同词性，尤其是系列动词、系列名词和系列形容词的平行使用，可以使表现更有力量，文体更加庄重。例如：

原文：这个新时代，是承前启后、继往开来、在新的历史条件下继续夺取中国特色社会主义伟大胜利的时代，是决胜全面建成小康社会、进而全面建设社会主义现代化强国的时代，是全国各族人民团结奋斗、不断创造美好生活、逐步实现全体人民共同富裕的时代，是全体中华儿女勠力同心、奋力实现中华民族伟大复兴中国梦的时代，是我国日益走近世界舞台中央、不断为人类作出更大贡献的时代。

译文：This new era will be an era of building on past successes to further advance our cause, and of continuing in a new historic context to strive for the success of socialism with Chinese characteristics. It will be an era of securing a decisive victory in building a moderately prosperous society in all respects, and of moving on to all-out efforts to build a great modern socialist country. It will be an era for the Chinese people of all ethnic groups to work together and work hard to create a better life for themselves and ultimately achieve common prosperity for everyone. It will be an era for all of us, the sons and daughters of the Chinese nation, to strive with one heart to realize the Chinese Dream of national rejuvenation. It will be an era that sees China moving closer to center stage and making greater contributions to humanity.

分析：除了通过运用分号连接手段构成排比，有意识地运用结构重复也是首选模式之一。译文调整了原文的排比句，把第一个排比译成过渡句，引出关键词"新时代"，然后通过四次重复"It will be an era"实现了大段排比，突出了中国特色社会主义进入新时代的主题，同时使段落联结成为连贯的有机整体。

第二部分：知识与技能讲析

1. 句子结构及其类型

汉英翻译的关键是译文的准确表达，汉译英时首先需要考虑汉语的句子结构及表达意义，然后再考虑选择合适的英语结构来表现汉语内容。句子结构不是简单被动的词汇组合，而是应能够积极地反映作者的语义意图。

1.1 句子成分角度

从句子成分构成来看，汉英两种语言最基本的简单句有五种句型，而且主要成分顺序基本一致。

1.1.1 主语+谓语（不及物动词）

原文：……我国国际影响力、感召力、塑造力显著提升。

译文：…China's international influence, appeal, and power to shape have risen markedly.

1.1.2 主语+谓语（及物动词）+宾语

原文：我们全面加强党的领导……

译文：We have strengthened Party leadership in all respects…

1.1.3 主语+系动词+表语

原文：中华民族是世界上伟大的民族。

译文：The Chinese nation is a great nation.

1.1.4 主语+谓语+宾语+宾语补足语

原文：……紧紧围绕这个社会主要矛盾推进各项工作……

译文：…have made it clear that closing this gap should be the focus of all our initiatives…

1.1.5 主语+谓语+间接宾语+直接宾语

原文：要在一体化发展战略实施的过程中发现人才、培育人才、使用人才。

译文：In the course of implementing the integrated development strategy, you need to identify and cultivate the best talent and give them opportunities to shine.

1.2 句子结构角度

从句子的整体结构来看，英语句子可分为简单句、并列句和复合句。

1.2.1 简单句

简单句只包含一个主谓结构。例如：

原文：人民是我们党执政的最大底气。

译文：The people are our greatest strength in governance.

1.2.2 并列句

并列句由两个或两个以上的简单句组成，简单句之间可由并列连词"and" "but" "so" "for" "nor" "or" "yet"、并列副词"however" "therefore" "moreover" "furthermore" "nevertheless"或分号连接。例如：

原文 1：民之所忧，我必念之；民之所盼，我必行之。

译文：The people's concerns are my concerns, <u>and</u> the people's expectations are my goals.

原文 2：马克思主义是我们立党立国的根本指导思想，是我们党的灵魂和旗帜。

译文：Marxism is the fundamental ideology upon which our Party and country are founded<u>;</u> it is the very soul of our Party and the banner under which it strives.

1.2.3 复合句

复合句是由从属连词连接的各种句子，包括状语从句、定语从句、同位语从句、主语从句、宾语从句、表语从句等。例如：

原文：……解决了许多长期想解决而没有解决的难题，办成了许多过去想办而没有办成的大事，推动党和国家事业发生历史性变革。

译文：…have solved many tough problems <u>that</u> were long on the agenda but never resolved, and accomplished many things <u>that</u> were wanted but never done. With this, we have prompted historic shifts in the cause of the Party and the country.

2. 句子连贯

作为非字母语言，汉语的特殊性在于没有词尾变化和性、数、格、时态、语态等多种变化，语句组合往往不受制约，联系手段也不靠语法成分，而是依赖于内在结构和词汇搭配，所以汉语有着很强的"意合性"。而英语则注重形合，句子间通过连词、关系代词、关系副词、介词等进行有形连接。因此，汉英两种语言的明显特征差异之一在于连贯意识。

英语连贯指的是词语在语法或词汇方面的衔接，可以存在于句子内不同的成分之间或者句子与句子之间，韩礼德和哈桑（Halliday & Hasan）把英语句子的衔接手段分为四种：指代（reference）、替代（substitution）和省略（ellipsis）、连接（conjunction）、词汇衔接（lexical cohesion）。英语以形合为主，长句、复杂句非常多，连词、介词、关系代词、关系副词等都是连接词，将短语与短语、短语与句子、句子与句子连接起来，使用非常普遍。同时，英文句内与句间使用的连词能够表现相互的逻辑关系：原因、条件、比较与对照、递进、让步、结果等。相比较而言，汉语以意合为主，句子之间的逻辑关系通常蕴含在上下文中，句子往往呈现平行状态，句子内的成分间不用连词，而是通过语言内在的逻辑关系和意义结合在一起。可以说，句子衔接是英语最显著的语言特征之一。因此，汉译英时，译者应根据逻辑关系增补连接词，使译文既能够准确传意，又符合英语的行文规范。

句子翻译应注意下面三点：

第一，分析和划分原文句子信息层次是汉译英的第一步，只有将原文句子的信息层次弄清楚了，才能够按照英语的行文方式再现原文信息。

第二，找出汉语原文各个分句的主干成分，选择英语中的固定搭配或者其他表现形式再现原文信息，不能强调译文与原文句法结构的绝对一致。

第三，确定英语译文的时态、语态和语气。汉语动词没有复杂的形式变化，也没有时态之分，汉英两种语言"不对等"，因此汉译英时最容易出现语法错误。

3. 确定主语、谓语

英译文最首要的任务是确定主语、谓语，因为主语和谓语是句子的支撑性框架和主干。汉英两种语言的主语一般都在句首，但并非所有原文句子的主语都能直接切换成英语的主语，确定英语句子的主语是首要任务。汉语中几乎所有词都能直接做主语，而英语中只有名词性成分和代词能做主语，这种差异增加了确定英语主语的难度。最简单的方法就是通过对应把原文主语作为译文主语，但是译文必须进行词形变化以符合英语的语法要求。大多数情况下，译者需要重新选择和确定主语以实现译文的流畅和规范。如果汉语是无主句，译者则需要理解上下文，反复推敲来增补主语，可以使用泛指人称主语，也可以用代词"it"，或者选择使用"There be"结构。例如：

原文：世界上既不存在定于一尊的现代化模式，也不存在放之四海而皆准的现代化标准。

译文：There is no such a thing as a single authorized model of modernization, nor a universally applicable standard of modernization.

谓语的确定也同样重要，只有恰当地确定了主语和谓语，整个句子的结构关系才能脉络分明。汉英谓语差异较大，汉语中动词是遣词造句的主要成分，谓语范围非常宽泛，可以用来充当谓语的成分较多。相比之下，英语的谓语只有动词来充当。汉语的谓语没有人称和数的变化，谓语动词本身没有时间形态，时间概念依靠动词的排列顺序或者表示时间的状语来体现。英语中的动词是一个非常复杂的现象，它可用不同的形式来表示主语的人称、数量、时态和语态变化。动词选择错误常发生在表示动作和表示状态的同一类动词中。英译时谓语选择需要注意以下几点：

第一，谓语必须在人称和数上与主语保持一致。例如：

原文：我国现代化是全体人民共同富裕的现代化。

译文：Our modernization aims at common prosperity for everyone.

第二，谓语的时态与原文要保持一致。例如：

原文：历史已经并将继续证明，没有中国共产党的领导，民族复兴必然是空想。

译文：As history has shown and will continue to testify, without the leadership of the Communist Party of China, national rejuvenation would be just wishful thinking.

第三，原文谓语如果是形容词短语、名词性短语或介词短语，译文经常采用系表结构做谓语，翻译时应尽量仔细推敲表示动作还是状态，试用"名词化"动词，在形式上可为"v.+n."或"v.+to+n.+of"构成的短语，这样处理效果会缓和、委婉和耐人寻味，也更加书面化。例如：

原文：党的团结统一是党的生命，善于在总结历史中统一思想、统一行动，是我们党的成功经验。

译文：Unity <u>is</u> the lifeline of our Party. Our Party <u>is experienced in</u> unifying thinking and taking concerted action through reviewing history.

第四，原文如果有几个动词同时出现（前面提到的连动式或者兼语式），译文可选择一个主要动词做谓语，其他几个动词转换成其他形式。例如：

原文：必须构筑中华民族共有精神家园，使各民族人心归聚、精神相依，形成人心凝聚、团结奋进的强大精神纽带。

译文：We must <u>build</u> a cultural home shared by the Chinese nation, <u>creating</u> a strong bond among all ethnic groups and <u>inspiring</u> them to move forward in unity and interdependence.

4. 强调结构

英语中有几种强调结构。倒装是常用的强调手段，将助动词或情态动词移至主语前而谓语动词不变构成部分倒装；将句子主谓完全颠倒构成全部倒装。"here""there""now""then"等副词放在句首时，句子要全部倒装；否定副词如"no""never""seldom""little""hardly""rarely""scarcely"及含有"no"或"not"的短语放在句首时，句子要部分倒装。倒装多用于正式文体中，非正式文体中颇为少见。

英语表达强调功能的常见句子结构如下：

4.1 圆周句（periodical sentence）

圆周句就是把重要意思放在最后，直到最后句子结构才完整，读者必须读完整个句子才能获得完满的理解，因此圆周句在一定程度上制造了悬念，从而使文本信息环环相扣，对读者产生吸引力，激发读者的阅读兴趣，更具有强调功能，因而更多地用于正式文体中。例如：

原文：中国特色社会主义进入新时代，我国社会主要矛盾已经转化为人民日益增长的美好生活需要和不平衡不充分的发展之间的矛盾。

译文：As socialism with Chinese characteristics has entered a new era, the principal challenge facing Chinese society has evolved. What we now face is the gap between unbalanced and inadequate development and the ever-growing expectation of the people for a better life.

"as"引导的时间状语或方式状语放在句首构成圆周句。从句不是重点信息，后面的主句才是重点。

4.2 由 only 前置引起

原文：只有社会主义才能救中国，只有改革开放才能发展中国、发展社会主义、发展马克思主义。

译文：Only with socialism can we save China; only with reform and opening can we develop China, develop socialism, and develop Marxism.

4.3 由 thus 前置引起

"thus"源于拉丁语，副词，多用于严肃文体，表示结果，可引起倒装。按照英语语法解释，当方式状语、频率状语等移至句首时，有时引起局部倒装，如果主语较长，也可全部倒装。值得注意的是，因其极其正式，"thus"引起的倒装不太常见。例如：

原文：我们党团结带领人民进行改革开放新的伟大革命，破除阻碍国家和民族发展的一切思想和体制障碍，开辟了中国特色社会主义道路，<u>使中国大踏步赶上时代</u>。

译文：Our Party united the people and led them in launching the great new revolution of reform and opening up, in removing all ideological and institutional barriers to our country and nation's development, and in embarking on the path of socialism with Chinese characteristics. <u>Thus was China able to stride ahead to catch up with the times.</u>

译文强调结果：改革开放的伟大创举让中国大踏步赶上时代。

4.4 由 not only 前置引起

原文：我国稳定解决了十几亿人的温饱问题，总体上实现小康，不久将全面建成小康社会，人民美好生活需要日益广泛，不仅对物质文化生活提出了更高要求，而且在民主、法治、公平、正义、安全、环境等方面的要求日益增长。

译文：China has seen the basic needs of over a billion people met, has basically made it possible for people to live decent lives, and will soon bring the building of a moderately prosperous society to a successful completion. The requirements of the people to live better lives are increasingly broad. <u>Not only have their material and cultural needs grown; their demands for democracy, rule of law, fairness and justice, security, and a better environment are increasing</u>.

"not only"引起的"不仅……而且……"部分倒装结构强调的是后面的信息：新时代我国人民在精神文化方面的要求正在日益增长。

5. 排比句

排比（parallelism）即平行结构（parallel construction），指把结构相同或相似且意义密切相关、语气一致的三个或以上的词语或句子成串地排列，从而达到句式工整、节奏匀称的效果，给人留下深刻印象。排比可通过纯粹的语法结构如分号完成，也可借助结构重复或者相近词汇并列实现。通过相近词汇并列实现排比，有的排列词语意义不分主次轻重，是一种平等的列举关系，故词语位置并不重要；而有的排列在语法层面上属于并列关系，但在语义层面层层递进。例如：

原文：（中国）引导应对气候变化国际合作，成为全球生态文明建设的重要<u>参与者</u>、<u>贡献者</u>、<u>引领者</u>。

译文： Taking a driving seat in international cooperation to respond to climate change, China has become an important <u>participant</u>, <u>contributor</u>, and <u>torchbearer</u> in the global endeavor for eco-civilization.

这三个词按语义排列呈递进趋势，最后达到高潮，这也是一种常见强调手法——高潮序列（climactic sequence）。

第三部分：英译习作与文本金句范例对照解析

1. 句子结构及其类型

原文： <u>以上十四条</u>，构成新时代坚持和发展中国特色社会主义的基本方略。全党同志必须全面贯彻党的基本理论、基本路线、基本方略，更好引领党和人民事业发展。

译文： <u>The above 14 points form</u> the basic policy that underpins our endeavors to uphold and develop socialism with Chinese characteristics in the new era. All our members must fully implement the Party's underlying theories, basic guidelines, and fundamental policies <u>so as to</u> better steer the development of the Party and people's cause.

习作： <u>These 14 points</u> constitute the basic strategy for upholding and developing socialism with Chinese characteristics in the new era. All Party members must fully implement the Party's basic theory, line, and strategy to better guide the cause of the Party and the people.

范例对照解析：汉语句子比较松散、简短，几乎任何成分都可以做主语。原文"以上十四条"作为主语，和其他成分分开。译文首先规避语法错误，确定好主语和主干，同时，把最后分句降格处理为目的状语，更清晰地表现了句子之间的关系，符合英语句子外形严谨的要求。习作者虽然正确地确定了主谓关系，但是没有处理好句子之间的关系和衔接。

2. 句子连贯

原文：……制定实施香港特别行政区维护国家安全法，落实"爱国者治港"原则……

译文：… The Law on Safeguarding National Security in the Hong Kong Special Administrative Region was formulated and put into effect, ensuring that Hong Kong is administered by patriots…

习作：We will formulate and implement the Law on Safeguarding National Security in the Hong Kong Special Administrative Region and the principle of patriots governing Hong Kong.

范例对照解析：按照汉语两个分句的逻辑关系，译文把比较重要的信息"制定实施"处理成主干，用现在分词来处理次要信息。汉译英时，若汉语两个分句主语相同，可以将主要意义的分句译成主句，而次要意义的分句降格为非谓语动词或者定语从句，这样，两个分句通过语法或者关系代词连接起来，符合英语具有连贯特征的习惯用法。而习作者对于谓语的选择则是习惯性地找动词对应，忽略了句子之间的逻辑关系。

3. 强调句

原文：世界是丰富多彩的，多样性是人类文明的魅力所在，更是世界发展的活力和动力之源。

译文：Our world is characterized above all by diversity. It is diversity that makes human civilization what it is. It provides us a constant source of vitality and a driving force for world development.

习作：The world is rich and colorful. Diversity is the charm of human civilization. It is also the source of vitality and motivation for world development.

范例对照解析：通过使用强调句，译文凸显了重要信息"多样化"；习作者没有意识到汉语"所在"隐含的强调，使用一般结构，没有变通，照搬原文语序，译文略显生硬，表现力较差。

4. 倒装句

原文：基础不牢，地动山摇。只有把基层党组织建设强、把基层政权巩固好，中国特色社会主义的根基才能稳固。

译文：If the foundation is not solid, the building trembles. <u>Only with strong Party organizations and governments at the grassroots level can the foundations of Chinese socialism be solid.</u>

习作：The foundation is not solid, and the earth is shaking. The foundation of socialism with Chinese characteristics can be consolidated only by building primary-level Party organizations and consolidating primary-level political power.

范例对照解析：通过使用倒装结构，译文强调了重要信息"基层党组织"；习作者使用一般结构，没有表现出原文作者的语义意图，语言的表现力不够。

5. 平行句

原文：生态文明制度体系加快形成，主体功能区制度逐步健全，国家公园体制试点积极推进。

译文：Efforts to develop a system of institutions for building an eco-civilization have been accelerated; the system of functional zoning has been steadily improved; and progress has been made in piloting the national park system.

习作：The establishment of an ecological civilization system was accelerated, and the system of themed functional zones was gradually improved. Trials of a national park system were actively carried out.

范例对照解析：汉语是三个并列的分句，用逗号隔开。译文首先考虑避免标点符号使用错误，使用两个分号把译文直接变成平行结构。显然，习作者将译文处理成两个独立句，破坏了原文的平行关系，损坏了原文三个意义并列的逻辑关系。

第四单元

思政经典中的句子翻译（二）

第一部分：思政经典汉英文本金句范例对照

1. 区分主从

汉语行文层层展开，多用并列结构，有时一个长句可以包含几个并列短句（即主谓结构），有时一个主语可带几个并列谓语，各成分之间可能存在着各种不同的联系，但往往不用文字表示出来，表面上只是一个并列结构。英语行文讲究突出重点，重要的意思放在突出的位置，次要的意思则通过从句、分词、介词短语等手段放在次要的位置，各成分之间的关系呈现得一清二楚。例如：

原文：中国历来<u>重信守诺</u>，将以<u>新发展理念</u>为<u>引领</u>，在推动高质量发展中<u>促进</u>经济社会发展全面绿色转型……

译文：China always <u>honors its commitments</u>. <u>Guided by</u> our new development philosophy, we will <u>promote</u> greener economic and social development in all respects while pursuing high-quality development...

分析：原文中动词较多，谓语动词不明显。汉译英时，无论是处理成一个还是两个英语句子，都需要找到信息重点，并把它处理成句子的谓语动词。"重信守诺"是主要信息，所以单独成句；"促进"是第二主要信息，所以也译成谓语动词；其他次要信息译成非谓语动词结构。为使语篇连贯，语言层面进行了较大的调整。

2. 分译与合译

汉语有些长句习惯性地先做概括总结，然后进行分论和细节描述，或者先进行详尽阐述，再做概括总结。汉译英时，总结概括部分可单独译成一个句子，汉语的顺序关系用时间表示，译文则可用并列连词"and"表示顺序，省略了重复内容，句子结构更加紧凑。

2.1 分译

原文：我们要全面准确贯彻"一国两制"、"港人治港"、"澳人治澳"、高度自治的方针，落实中央对香港、澳门特别行政区全面管治权，落实特别行政区维护国家安全的法律制度和执行机制，维护国家主权、安全、发展利益，维护特别行政区社会大局稳定，保持香港、澳门长期繁荣稳定。

译文：We will stay true to the letter and spirit of the One Country, Two Systems policy, under which the people of Hong Kong administer Hong Kong, and the people of Macao administer Macao, both with a high degree of autonomy. We will ensure that the central government exercises overall jurisdiction over Hong Kong and Macao, and implement legal systems and enforcement mechanisms for the two special administrative regions to safeguard national security. While protecting China's sovereignty, security, and development interests, we will ensure social stability in Hong Kong and Macao, and maintain lasting prosperity and stability in the two special administrative regions.

分析：汉语含有多个层次的流水句，意义复杂，汉译英时，如果生搬原文句子和语序，将导致译文层次不清，甚至晦涩难懂。因此，首先考虑按照汉语层次和意义进行切分，按照英语表达习惯调整语序，把汉语的多个分句划分成三个大的层次，然后再对每个层次进行二次切分，从而规避了中式英语。

2.2 合译

原文：建设生态文明是中华民族永续发展的千年大计。必须树立和践行绿水青山就是金山银山的理念，坚持节约资源和保护环境的基本国策，像对待生命一样对待生态环境，统筹山水林田湖草系统治理，实行最严格的生态环境保护制度，形成绿色发展方式和生活方式，坚定走生产发展、生活富裕、生态良好的文明发展道路，建设美丽中国，为人民创造良好生产生活环境，为全球生态安全作出贡献。

译文：Building an eco-civilization is vital to sustain the Chinese nation's development. We must realize that lucid waters and lush mountains are invaluable assets and act on this understanding, implement our fundamental national policy of conserving resources and protecting the environment, and cherish the environment as we cherish our own lives. We will adopt a holistic approach to conserving our mountains, rivers, forests, farmlands, lakes, and grasslands, implement the strictest possible systems for environmental protection, and develop eco-friendly growth models and ways of life. We must pursue a model of sustainable development featuring increased production, higher living standards, and healthy ecosystems. We must continue the Beautiful China initiative to create good working and living environments for our people and play our part in ensuring global ecological security.

分析：原文第一句是总结性陈述，后面细节阐述使用了十个陈述分句。译文把系列分句整理成四个大的复合句，每个复合句中含有简单句、并列句和从句，符合英语层次性表达的习惯。

3. 主动与被动翻译

英语的另一个显著特点就是被动语态要比汉语使用频率高得多。选择使用被动结构会基于下几种情况：为了突出宾语，把宾语置于主语的位置，强调动作的承受者；不明确或者不需要指出动作的执行者；便于上下文连贯衔接；为了突出客观性，避免使用人称主语；为了措辞得当，语气委婉；固定用法的被动语态结构不能使用主动语态，翻译时随意添加动作的执行者并用作主语是不恰当的。例如：

原文：历史川流不息，精神代代<u>相传</u>。我们要继续弘扬光荣传统、赓续红色血脉，永远把伟大建党精神<u>继承</u>下去、发扬光大！

译文：As time moves steadily forward, the spirit of the Party <u>has been passed on</u> from generation to generation. We will continue to promote our glorious traditions and sustain our revolutionary legacy, so that the great founding spirit of the Party <u>will</u>

be passed down from generation to generation and carried forward.

分析：原文涉及"精神"和"建党精神"，动作的执行者已不重要，因此，选择使用被动语态更佳。

4. 无主句翻译

汉语是主题鲜明的语言，突出主题但不突出主语，因此，无主句非常常见。相反，英语是主语显著的语言，主语突出。汉译英时，汉语无主句可译成英语被动句，使句子保持完整，还可以套用"It is+过去分词+that""It is+形容词+to do sth."或者"There be"结构。例如：

原文1：不论谁在党纪国法上出问题，党纪国法决不饶恕。

译文：There will be zero tolerance for anyone who violates Party discipline and the law.

分析：英语"There be"句式的典型结构是地点/时间+存在动词+存在主体，表示人或事物的存在、出现或消失，该句型多表示静态存在状态，所以汉译英时使用这个结构来处理汉语的无主句是有效方法之一。

原文2：讲好中国故事，传播好中国声音，展示真实、立体、全面的中国，是加强我国国际传播能力建设的重要任务。

译文：To strengthen our international communication capacity, it is important to tell genuine and engaging stories, make our voice heard, and present an accurate, multidimensional and panoramic image of China.

分析：汉语是典型的无主句，英译采用"It is +形容词+to do sth."结构，处理比较恰当。

5. 长句翻译

汉语强调意合，结构较松散，因此简单句较多；英语强调形合，结构较严谨，因此长句较多。汉译英时要根据需要利用连词、分词、介词、不定式、定语从句、独立结构等把汉语短句连成长句。常用的方法有合并法、正译法和反译法、倒置法和插入法。例如：

原文：全党同志务必不忘初心、牢记使命，务必谦虚谨慎、艰苦奋斗，务必敢于斗争、善于斗争，坚定历史自信，增强历史主动，谱写新时代中国特色社会主义更加绚丽的华章。

译文：It is imperative that all of us in the Party never forget our original aspiration and founding mission, that we always stay modest, prudent, and hard-working, and that we have the courage and ability to carry on our fight. We must remain confident in our history, exhibit greater historical initiative, and write an even more magnificent chapter for socialism with Chinese characteristics in the new era.

分析：汉语是语义复杂的流水句，包含多个层次，汉译英时译者首先需要进行语义分析和层次逻辑分析。遵照汉语的语义和层次，译者再安排英语的行文层次和内容主次。第一步，把原长句拆分成两部分并建立两个独立句；第二步，选择合适的主从复合句结构来表现语义层次关系。

第二部分：知识与技能讲析

1. 区分主从

如前面所述，汉语的信息基本都体现在内在的逻辑关系上而不是语言表层的形式上。相比之下，英语句子注重信息的主次之分，主要信息放在突出位置，次要信息作为辅助性修饰手段。因此，汉译英时一定要把汉语的隐性主次关系发掘出来，译成英语的主次表达方式。通常，汉语中表示结果、行为动作、推论结论、本质、目的的部分会译成英语的主句或谓语部分；汉语中表示时间、地点、原因、条件、方式、方法、状态、说明、解释、非本质、修饰、否定的部分，在英语中则以从句或非谓语动词的形式体现。

1.1 行为与方式的主从

表示状态的信息应该从属于表示行为和动作的谓语部分或表语部分。例如：

原文：面对香港局势动荡变化，我们依照宪法和基本法有效实施对特别行政区的全面管治权……

译文：In the face of turbulent developments in Hong Kong, the central government exercised its overall jurisdiction over the special administrative region as prescribed by China's Constitution and the Basic Law of the Hong Kong Special Administrative Region.

1.2 手段与目的的主从

表示方法和手段的信息一般从属于表示目的的部分。例如：

原文：要健全制度体系，及时将实践中好的经验做法转化为制度规范。

译文：You can improve your institutions by turning successful experiences and practices into rules and norms.

"要健全制度体系"是目的，是主要信息，译为句子的主干；"转化为"表示手段，是次要信息，用非谓语动词或者从句处理。

1.3 原因与结果的主从

表示原因或条件的信息一般应从属于表示结果的部分。例如：

原文：在重大风险、强大对手面前，总想过太平日子、不想斗争是不切实际的，得"软骨病"、患"恐惧症"是无济于事的。

译文：Confronted by major risks, and powerful opponents, it is unrealistic to think confrontation can be avoided, nor will it help to fear it or evade it.

原句中"在重大风险、强大对手面前"表示条件，应该处理成非谓语动词，其他信息都是所产生的结果，应该成为主干部分。另外，译文采用"It is+形容词+ to do"来处理原文的无主问题。同时，由"nor"引出倒装结构进行强调。

2. 分译与合译

2.1 分译

分译是长句翻译常用技巧之一，就是把原文的一句话拆分成两个或者多个句子来译，因此也叫拆句。汉语有时候一句话很长，包含多个分句，含义较多，句子有时候呈现多个连动结构，界限不清。而英语句子结构比较严谨，句内的逻辑关系要通过各种连接词反映出来。而且，汉语长句内的一个分句往往就是一个意义完整的句子，因此，汉译英时往往需要把句子断开。这就需要译者首先按照英语的表达习惯拆分然后再译。下面情况的汉语适合分译：

第一，汉语的长句含有疑问句、感叹句、祈使句、反义问句。例如：

原文：疫情终将过去，胜利必将到来。让我们携起手来，风雨同舟、守望相助，坚持开放合作，畅通内外循环，共创共享亚太和世界更加美好的未来！

译文：The day will come when we finally beat Covid-19 and win victory in this fight. Let us work in solidarity and weather the storm together. Let us stay true to openness and cooperation and make development and circulations at home and overseas reinforce each other. Together, we can surely deliver a brighter future for all of us, both here in the Asia-Pacific and across the world!

汉语是包含几个分句和多个并列成分的长句，而且含有较长的祈使句和感叹句。英译微调了汉语语句内容顺序，采用了分译方法，把汉语的断句处理成含有一个中心谓语的独立句，使译文逻辑关系更加清晰。

第二，汉语长句内有"例如""以……为例"，通常将其单译。例如：

原文：<u>比如说</u>，生态环境保护就是为民造福的百年大计。

译文：<u>For example</u>, eco-environmental protection is of vital importance to the people.

第三，长句内含有概括句或阐述句，分述部分单独成句。例如：

原文：实践证明，<u>马克思主义是</u>我们认识世界、把握规律、追求真理、改造世界的强大思想武器，<u>是</u>我们党和国家必须始终遵循的指导思想。

译文：Our experience has shown that Marxism offers an inexhaustible theoretical wellspring for us to seek truth, understand the world and its laws, and transform it. <u>Therefore</u>, Marxism must always be the guiding philosophy of the Party and the state.

第四，含有对立句子的长句须分译，从中间断开，译文的逻辑关系会更加清晰明确。例如：

原文：人类面临的所有全球性问题，任何一国想单打独斗都无法解决，必须开展全球行动、全球应对、全球合作。

译文：No global problem can be solved by any one country alone. There must be global action, global response and global cooperation.

2.2 合译

合译也是汉英翻译中常见的技巧之一。英语长句在正式文体中极为常见，通过连词或语法手段把汉语的几个分句或者短句译成英语的简单句、并列句或复合句。合译能够避免语言拖沓和重复，使译文更加严谨、简洁、凝练，符合英文的表达习惯。合译通常有以下几种方式：

第一，通过补充关联词把汉语的两个分句合并成英语的并列句或复合句。例如：

原文：我们走出一条睦邻友好、合作共赢的光明大道，迈向日益紧密的命运共同体，为推动人类进步事业作出了重要贡献。

译文：We have embarked on a path of good-neighborliness and win-win cooperation, taken strides towards a closer community of shared future, <u>and</u> made an important contribution to human progress.

第二，通过增补关系代词或关系副词合译汉语的意合句。汉语的意合句包含多个分句，分句之间的联系不用关联词，而是通过其内在的逻辑纽带或语序表现出来。这类句子的英译必须首先分清汉语原文各分句的关系，然后根据英语的特点，选择恰当的关联词组织起来，使译文结构更加紧凑。例如：

原文：要在推动高质量发展中强化就业优先导向。就业是民生之本。

译文：In promoting high-quality development we should prioritize employment, which is pivotal to people's wellbeing.

第三，利用词、词组、名词性从句将汉语的分句表达出来，从而把原文的几句话合并成一个长句。例如：

原文：百年奋斗历史告诉我们，团结就是力量，奋斗开创未来；能团结奋斗的民族才有前途，能团结奋斗的政党才能立于不败之地。

译文：The Party's century-long history has shown that unity means strength and that hard work leads to a bright future. Unity of effort is what a nation relies on to build its future and what a political party counts on to remain resolute.

汉译英时常采用词类转换的手法，把汉语中的动词转换成英语的其他词类，这样，汉语的一个分句可以变成英语的词、词组或者从句。并不是所有的汉语分句在翻译时都需要合并。合译的主要目的是使译文更加符合表达习惯，读起来更加地道，没有翻译腔，是否合译应酌情处理。

3. 主动与被动翻译

主动与被动是两种不同的语态，表示句子谓语动词与其主语之间的逻辑关系，主动句的主语是谓语动词动作的执行者，而被动句的主语是谓语动词动作的承受者。被动结构突出了行为承受对象，因此主观色彩较少。汉语被动句使用较少，很多被动的句子用无主句来表示。

第一，汉语中典型被动句译成英语被动句："被""受""给""遭受""叫""让""予以""加以""为""被……所"。例如：

原文：……让资源更多向减贫、教育、卫生、基础设施建设等领域倾斜。

译文：More resources must be channeled to poverty reduction, education, health and infrastructure development.

第二，如果不知道原文谓语动作的执行者，或者出于礼貌或习惯回避施动者，或者主语是"大家""人们"等，或者句中含有"据说""据悉"等，常采用被动式。例如：

原文：要秉持共商共建共享原则，倡导全球事务由各国一起商量着办，治

49

理体系由大家携手建设，发展成果由各国人民共同分享。

译文：We need to follow the principle of extensive consultation, joint contribution and shared benefits, and build a world where global affairs are discussed by all, the governance system built by all, and development fruits shared by all.

第三，汉语的主动句译成英语的被动句。例如：

原文：广泛参与战后重建。战乱国家或地区签署和平协议后，帮助其恢复社会秩序、改善民生，是防止冲突再起、实现持久和平与稳定的治本之策。

译文：To participate extensively in post-conflict reconstruction. In a post-war country or region, when a peace agreement is reached, it is essential to restore livelihoods and social order in order to prevent the recurrence of conflict and achieve lasting peace and stability.

第四，为了加强上下文连贯和衔接。例如：

原文：首先，感谢普京总统和俄罗斯政府为这次金砖国家领导人会晤所做精心安排。当前，世纪疫情和百年变局交织，国际格局深刻演变。在这样一个重要时刻，我们举行这次会晤，共商抗疫合作大计，共绘金砖发展蓝图，具有特殊重要意义。

译文：I wish to begin by thanking President Putin and the Russian government for their thoughtful organization of this BRICS Summit. Right now, the world is caught between a pandemic of the century and momentous changes never seen in the last one hundred years. The international landscape keeps evolving in profound ways. At such a critical moment, we are meeting to discuss our joint response to Covid-19 and draw a blueprint for the future of BRICS. The meeting has thus taken on a special significance.

4. 无主句翻译

汉语不关注句法结构形式的完整，只要上下文意思清楚，省去句中的主语或者其他成分是很常见的，因此汉语存在大量的无主句。而英语句子必须保持结构完整，句子往往不能没有主语，因此英语是主语突出的语言。译成英语时，汉语无主句或者主语省略句应根据上下文增加主语或者变换句式。

第一，增加主语：中文往往省略第一人称，英译时需要补上。例如：

原文：必须高举中华民族大团结旗帜，促进各民族在中华民族大家庭中像石榴籽一样紧紧抱在一起。

译文：We must uphold the unity of the Chinese nation and ensure all ethnic groups remain closely united like the seeds of a pomegranate.

第二，思政经典中有很多祈使句，对读者或者听众发出劝告或指示等，翻译时须补上泛指意义的人称代词或名词。例如：

原文：回首过去，展望未来，有中国共产党的坚强领导，有全国各族人民的紧密团结，全面建成社会主义现代化强国的目标一定能够实现，中华民族伟大复兴的中国梦一定能够实现！

译文：Looking back on the path we have traveled and forward to the journey that lies ahead, it is certain that with the firm leadership of the Party and the great unity of all the Chinese people, we will achieve the goal of building a great modern socialist country in all respects and fulfill the Chinese Dream of national rejuvenation.

第三，汉语无主句译成英语被动句也可以使句子保持完整，还可以套用"It is+过去分词+that"或者"It is+形容词+to do sth."或者"There be"结构。例如：

原文：让大家过上更好生活，我们不能满足于眼前的成绩，还有很长的路要走。

译文：To ensure that everyone leads a better life, we must never rest on what we have achieved, and there is still a long way to go.

第四，口号式的句子译成英语祈使句。例如：

原文：让我们携起手来，共同建设清洁美丽的世界！

译文：Let us work together for a clean and beautiful world.

第五，英语句子可用汉语的无生命词（抽象概念）做主语。例如：

原文：最后，我要强调的是，社会主义中国发展到今天，取得的成就不是天上掉下来的，更不是别人恩赐施舍的，而是广大人民群众在党的领导下用勤劳、智慧、勇气干出来的！

译文：Finally, I want to emphasize that the achievements of our socialist country have not fallen like manna from Heaven, nor have they been granted by others. They have been achieved by our people through hard work, wisdom and courage under the leadership of the Party.

第六，无主句译成非谓语动词结构。例如：

原文：……要坚定理想信念，注重学习提升，矢志艰苦奋斗，从一点一滴做起，把小事当大事干，踏踏实实把正在做的事情做好，靠勤劳双手成就属于自己的人生精彩，共同创造我们的幸福生活和美好未来。

译文：…should have firm ideals and convictions, and study hard to improve yourselves. You should work hard in a pragmatic manner, <u>taking</u> one step at a time and <u>handling</u> every piece of work, big or small, with the utmost care and attention. I believe you will experience greater fulfillment in life through hard work, and together we will create a happy life and bright future for all.

5. 长句翻译

汉语习惯使用以意合为特征的多个短句进行有层次的叙述，它们组在一起也可成为含多层意义的长句。汉语长句一般表现为修饰语多、并列成分多、语言结构层次多。相比之下，英语习惯使用长句来表达比较复杂的概念，长句基本上是由简单句和复合句组合而成，句子结构呈树枝形，字数多，结构复杂，语义呈现多层次多阶梯形态。

汉译英时，首先对汉语的流水句进行语法分析，搞清楚词语之间及句子之间的语法和逻辑关系，尤其是各种代词具体所指；其次明确句子的主语、谓语和宾语，弄清句子的骨干结构框架，同时关注是否存在着信息省略；最后根据句子之间的逻辑关系和语义层次，按照英语的句子结构原则组句。长句的翻译一般采用下列方法：

5.1 顺序法

这种方法多用于单一主语的长句，按照原文的顺序进行翻译。当汉语长句的叙述层次和英语基本一致时，可以按照汉语原文的顺序翻译，但要分清句中的信息重心，译者需要掌握区分主从的翻译技能。例如：

原文：好的方针政策和发展规划都应该顺应人民意愿、符合人民所思所盼，从群众中来、到群众中去。

译文：Sound guidelines, policies and development plans must accord with the will, aspirations and expectations of the people. They should come from the people and serve their interests.

5.2 变序法

译文采用什么样的语序，要根据译文语言的表达习惯而定。汉译英长句翻译大部分情况下不能只单纯采用顺序法，还需要采用变序法。在翻译过程中，译者应该按照译文读者的思维习惯，对原文的语序进行调整，使译文表达正确无误、通俗易懂。这种方法需要译者认真分析，或按照时间先后顺序，或按照某种逻辑关系，调整原文语序，对全句信息进行主次区分，综合处理，最后译成既忠实于原文又层次清晰的译文。例如：

原文：广大人民群众众志成城、守望相助，特别是武汉人民和湖北人民识大体顾大局、<u>自觉配合疫情防控工作，展现了坚忍不拔的顽强斗志</u>。

译文：Our people have stood together in solidarity. The people of Wuhan and other parts of Hubei, in particular, put the greater interests of the country in the first place and <u>have shown unmatched perseverance and tenacity in their support for epidemic control</u>.

5.3 分译法和合译法

这两种方法在本单元已经提到。翻译较长且内容复杂的句子时，需要对原文层次进行切割式划分，译成两个或多个句子。汉语还有一种总分句的复句，先将主语、谓语、宾语浓缩成一个独立的分句，放在句首作为总述，后面放几个单句，这种句子通常需要分译。把两个以上的句子合译成一个英文句子，句子结构紧凑，同时又不会遗漏信息。例如：

原文：在这场同严重疫情的殊死较量中，中国人民和中华民族以敢于斗争、敢于胜利的大无畏气概，铸就了生命至上、举国同心、舍生忘死、尊重科学、命运与共的伟大抗疫精神。

译文：In the fierce battle against Covid-19, the Chinese people and the Chinese nation have shown extraordinary mettle and fought courageously for victory. While fighting the virus, we have put life above all else, rallied the entire country, braved danger, respected science, and stood together through adversity.

第三部分：英译习作与文本范例金句对照解析

1. 区分主从

原文：广大人民群众识<u>大体</u>、<u>顾大局</u>，自觉配合疫情防控斗争大局，<u>形成</u>了疫情防控的基础性力量。

译文：<u>Considering</u> the national interest and the general situation, the people have consciously <u>subordinated</u> their own needs to the overall interests of epidemic control, <u>becoming</u> the fundamental force in the battle.

习作：The broad masses of the people consider the overall situation and consciously cooperate with the overall situation of the epidemic prevention and control struggle, forming the basic force for epidemic prevention and control.

范例对照解析：原汉语行文表面上是一个多层次并列结构，包含几个主谓结构，但各成分之间存在着不同的联系，没有通过文字表示出来。汉译英时首先发掘汉语的隐性主次关系，然后再译成英语的主次表达方式。英语行文把重要的意思"subordinated"放在突出的位置，次要的意思则通过分词短语手段放在次要的位置，各成分之间的关系表现得清楚。译文把汉语中表示结果的部分译成英语的主句或谓语部分，次要信息以非谓语动词的形式体现。显然，习作者对汉语分句意义的主次分析不够，英语的表达缺少层次感，译文不够自然。

2. 分译与合译

2.1 分译

原文：两岸同胞是命运与共的骨肉兄弟，是<u>血浓于水</u>的一家人。

译文：Blood is thicker than water. People on both sides of the Taiwan Straits are brothers and sisters; we share the bond of kinship.

习作：Our compatriots on both sides of the Strait are brothers of flesh and blood who share a common destiny and are a family whose blood is thicker than water.

范例对照解析：汉语包含两个分句，虽然不是长句，但由于后面分句内的"血浓于水"是一个主谓结构的比较级，如果按照汉语做定语来处理，英语的流畅度必然减弱，因此，拆分出来单独译成一句效果更好。

2.2 合译

原文：一百年来，党和人民取得的一切成就都是团结奋斗的结果，团结奋斗是中国共产党和中国人民最显著的精神标识。

译文：All that the Party and the people have achieved over the past century derives from unity of effort, <u>which</u> is the most distinctive tradition of the CPC and the Chinese people.

习作：All the achievements of the Party and the people over the past 100 years are the result of united struggle. Unity and struggle is the most prominent spiritual symbol of the Communist Party of China and the Chinese people.

范例对照解析：汉语看似独立的两个分句存在着密切的联系，因为第二个句子在重复第一个句子的"团结奋斗"。如果后面句中重复使用前面的信息，译成英语时，可考虑选取关系代词"which"，它既可以指重复部分，又可以将两句有机地结合起来，这正是英语关系代词和关系副词的优势，能够使译文结构更加紧凑。而习作恪守原文语序的规则，没有遵照英语习惯，译文不够地道，带有明显的翻译腔。

3. 主动与被动翻译

原文：你们这边是吕梁山，挨着就是黄河了，再过去就是陕西。我插队那个延川县，离这儿也不远，地形也都是这样的丘陵沟壑。黄土高原生活着我们的祖祖辈辈，孕育着我们的中华文明。

译文：Your village is in the Lüliang Mountains, near the Yellow River, and across the river is Shaanxi Province. In the late 1960s, I was sent to work as a farmer in Shaanxi's Yanchuan County, which is not far from here. Its hilly terrain and ravines are similar to the landscape here. The Loess Plateau is our home, and the home of our ancestors. It has nurtured our Chinese civilization.

习作：On your side is the Lüliang Mountain, next to it is the Yellow River, and then past it is Shaanxi. Yanchuan County, where I worked, is not far from here, and the terrain is also such a hilly gully. The Loess Plateau has been home to our ancestors for generations and nurtured our Chinese civilization.

范例对照解析：汉语的"插队"是一个具有特殊意义的词汇，指中国20世纪六七十年代城市知识青年被安插在农村生产队或者去农场劳动。显然，使用被动语态更准确，习作者对这个词汇缺乏充分的理解，使用简单的"work"，淡化了原文的背景意义。

4. 无主句翻译

原文：稳健的货币政策要更加注重灵活适度，把支持实体经济恢复发展放到更加突出的位置，用好已有金融支持政策，适时出台新的政策措施。

译文：A prudent monetary policy should be pursued with greater flexibility as called for, support for the resumption of the operation of the real economy should be strengthened, current financial support policies should be fully used, and new policy measures should be enacted at the right time.

习作：We will adopt a prudent monetary policy to be more flexible and appropriate, and we will give greater priority to supporting the recovery and development of the real economy, make good use of existing financial support policies, and introduce new policies and measures at an appropriate time.

范例对照解析：原文为无主句，动作的执行者不明确，在没有语言环境的情况下，汉译英时无须说明或者补充。习作反映了大多汉译英者的问题：在选择做主语的词汇时，无论原句有没有人称主语，都自然而然地去找人称代词，似乎这样才有安全感。

5. 长句翻译

原文：抗击新冠肺炎疫情斗争取得重大战略成果，充分展现了中国共产党领导和我国社会主义制度的显著优势，充分展现了中国人民和中华民族的伟大力量，充分展现了中华文明的深厚底蕴，充分展现了中国负责任大国的自觉担当，极大增强了全党全国各族人民的自信心和自豪感、凝聚力和向心力，必将激励我们在新时代新征程上披荆斩棘、奋勇前进。

译文：The great strategic success we have achieved in the fight against Covid-19 is a testament to the strengths of the leadership of the CPC, China's socialist system, the Chinese people and the Chinese nation, our profound cultural heritage, and our sense of mission as a responsible major country. This success has significantly boosted the confidence, pride, unity, and cohesion of the entire Party and all the Chinese people. It will inspire us to keep forging ahead over all obstacles on our journey in the new era.

习作：The major strategic results achieved in the fight against Covid-19 fully demonstrate the remarkable strengths of the leadership of the Communist Party of China (CPC) and China's socialist system, the great strength of the Chinese people and nation, the profound heritage of the Chinese civilization, and China's sense of responsibility as a major country, which has greatly enhanced the confidence, pride, cohesiveness and centripetal force of the whole Party and the people of all ethnic groups in China, and will surely inspire us to break through hardships and forge ahead on a new journey in the new era.

范例对照解析：汉语是一个由多层次分句组成的长句，含义很多，句子界限不太明晰。译文按照汉语的逻辑关系和分句的意义，拆分成三个独立句，通过代词"This"和"It"使这三个部分保持衔接和连贯。习作者则按照汉语的流水句对译，句子结构汉语化，整个句子过长，影响了阅读和理解。

第五单元

思政经典中的修辞翻译

第一部分：修辞的主要类型及范例对照

陈望道先生认为，修辞是"调整语辞，使达意传情能够适切的一种努力"。张弓认为："修辞方式是适应社会交际的需要，根据民族语言的内部发展规律创造的具体的、一定的手法。"整体上看，修辞是用来提升语言表达效果的一种手法。在思政类作品中运用修辞手法，可以将表达内容清晰化、逻辑推理形象化、表达效果最佳化。因此，在翻译过程中，需要正确理解各种修辞手法的内涵和用法，运用恰当的词语进行翻译。下面我们以《习近平谈治国理政》中英双语文本中运用的修辞手法为例，展示一下其使用及传达效果。

1. 比喻

所谓比喻，就是打比方，它是最常见的一种修辞手法，有明喻、暗喻之分。无论明喻、暗喻，都是用喻体来描写本体，达到生动形象、微妙传神的修辞效果。在翻译过程中，恰当理解本体与喻体之间的深刻联系，是做好翻译的重要步骤。例如：

原文：形象地说，理想信念就是共产党人精神上的"钙"，没有理想信念，理想信念不坚定，精神上就会"缺钙"，就会得"软骨病"。

译文：Put figuratively, the ideals and convictions of Communists are the <u>marrow</u> of their faith. Without, or with weak, ideals or convictions, they would be deprived of their <u>marrow</u> and suffer from "<u>lack of backbone</u>".

分析：原文使用比喻的修辞手法，生动形象地将本体与喻体间抽象的关系具体化。"钙"对人体的重要性，等同于"理想信念"对共产党人的重要性。"缺钙"就会引起"软骨病"，文学色彩鲜明，也用形象的描述给读者留下深刻印象。在译文方面，原文的"钙"并没有翻译为"calcium"，而是译为"marrow"，因为原文中的"钙"并不是指现实生活中的化学元素，而是指"精神食粮"。与之相对应，形象具体的人体结构概念"marrow"——"骨髓"一词，在中华文化中具有深厚的表达意义，贴切地传达出原文的意思。这里的"软骨病"，并不是医学疾病，而是指骨头比较软的症状，引申为缺少强大精神力量支撑。在译文中，"软骨病"译为"lack of backbone"，非常符合语境，表达精妙。这段译文，在内容方面，再现原文深刻内涵，文学色彩浓厚；在情感方面，充分体现"坚定""信念"，情感充沛。

2. 拟人

所谓拟人，就是赋予事物以人的特征，给予其活力与情感，使其变得鲜活且具动感，从而引起读者共鸣，收到更好的艺术效果。在翻译过程中，我们需要找到贴切的词汇表达，实现生动形象、惟妙惟肖的翻译效果。例如：

原文：经过多年努力，我国科技整体水平大幅提升，一些重要领域跻身世界先进行列，某些领域正由"<u>跟跑者</u>"向"<u>并行者</u>"、"<u>领跑者</u>"转变。

译文：Years of painstaking efforts have resulted in great progress for China in science and technology, and China has entered the advanced ranks in the world in some important fields. In certain fields, it has become a "forerunner" or "parallel runner" instead of a "follower".

分析：原文把世界上的竞争形容为赛场，各个领域的竞争者如同赛场中的选手，跑在最前面的选手是"领跑者"，成绩相同的选手是"并行者"，跑在后面的选手是"跟跑者"，将各领域的"先进""落后"描写得绘声绘色。译文采用了直译方式，分别使用了"forerunner""parallel runner""follower"三个词语，形象地传达了我国的"某些领域"在世界竞争中的位置。

3. 夸张

所谓夸张，就是将事物故意夸大或贬抑，也就是"言过其实"，从而引起读者的联想和共鸣，达到认识事物本质的目标。在翻译过程中，能否准确传达夸张所具有的修辞效果，是检验翻译质量的重要因素。例如：

原文："自信人生二百年，会当水击三千里。"

译文：As Mao Zedong said, "Should I have 200 years to spare, I will surely swim for 3,000 li (1,500 km)."

分析：这是习近平同志在纪念五四运动100周年大会上发表讲话时，引用毛泽东同志1917年所写的《七古·残句》。毛泽东同志在湖南第一师范学校读书时，常和蔡和森、张昆弟、罗学瓒等人去湘江中游泳。他们在中流击水间，抒情言志；在迎风劈浪间，畅快淋漓。原文鼓励未来青年既要有豪迈情感，又要对未来满怀信心。在译文方面，采用直译加解释的方法，明确了诗词来历，借用毛泽东青年时期所具有的崇高精神，鼓励青年立大志、成大事，既准确传达原文意义，也有助于国外读者朋友了解当代中国。

4. 移就

所谓移就，就是将一种事物所具有的特征移到另一种本不具有该特征的事物上，通常是将人或动物所具有的特征移到其他事物上面，反之亦然。在翻译过程中，是采用形象词汇传达所蕴含的意义，还是平铺直叙展示其真实意义，对译者是一大考验。例如：

原文：在几千年历史长河中，中国人民始终革故鼎新、自强不息……治理了桀骜不驯的千百条大江大河……

译文：Over thousands of years, they have been able to discard the outdated and bring in the new. Our pursuit of progress has never paused…We have…harnessed numerous turbulent rivers…

分析："桀骜不驯"通常是指人或动物性情暴烈、不服管教。在原文中，"桀骜不驯"用来修饰大江大河，是指这些大江大河曾经给中国人民造成很大危害和困难，但是中国人民具有强大能力治理这些大江大河，这凸显了中国人民自强不息的精神。在译文方面，"turbulent"放在"rivers"前面，是指"汹涌湍急"，这是用大江大河所具有的汹涌湍急的特征，转译汉语中的"桀骜不驯"，似乎"汹涌湍急"的大江大河和"桀骜不驯"的人或动物具有相同特征，从而传达出中国人民在面对困难时所具有的自强不息精神。

5. 类比

所谓类比，就是在两个不同事物之间找到共同特征，加以比较，找到其异同点。在思政经典作品中，经常采用类比方式来生动体现事物之间的异同点。在翻译过程中，应考虑汉英两种文化之间是否具有相同的类比意义，或者采用其他方式表达，这对于翻译质量的提升非常关键。例如：

原文：常言道，先禁己身而后人，打铁还需自身硬。

译文：As the saying goes, one must discipline oneself before disciplining others, and one must be a good blacksmith to forge good tools.

分析：原文的意思是，要做成事情，自身先要优秀才行，要求别人做到的，自身先要做到，更要做好。原文使用"打铁"类比，让读者感知具体事物，体会内涵意义，从而让读者感受到中国文化的博大精深。在译文方面，译者采用意译的方式，即传达"好铁能做出好产品""没有好铁炼不出好钢"，充分解释了"先禁己身而后人"的深刻内涵。

6. 排比

所谓排比，就是多项结构相同的短语或句子排列在一起，集中表达相似的内容和情感。排比修辞的广泛运用，可以增强节奏感，凸显出语言魅力。无论英语还是汉语，皆有使用排比结构的偏好，所以在翻译过程中，采用排比方式传递信息，可以更好地为英语读者所接受。例如：

原文：亚洲的事情归根结底要靠亚洲人民来办，亚洲的问题归根结底要靠亚洲人民来处理，亚洲的安全归根结底要靠亚洲人民来维护。

译文：In the final analysis, let the people of Asia run the affairs of Asia, solve the problems of Asia and uphold the security of Asia.

分析：原文使用结构工整的三个主谓句，强调亚洲人民有能力和智慧解决亚洲的问题，亚洲的问题不受其他外来势力干涉干扰。在译文方面，使用了以"let"为首的祈使句，强化了"the people of Asia"的主体作用，凸显了亚洲人民是亚洲的真正主人，并通过反复使用"Asia"一词，与原文反复使用的"亚洲"一词形成照应，实现了功能对等。

7. 反问

所谓反问，就是利用疑问形式来表达确定的意思，从而加强语气、表达情感。也就是说，作者不会直接给出答案，而是反问对方，从而表达自己的观点。例如：

原文：有的党的高级干部编了一套暗语，家里人、身边人相互说话都用暗语，搞得像《潜伏》一样。这正常吗？

译文：Some high-ranking Party officials have even compiled a coded language, which they use when speaking with their families and those close to them, just like spies. Is this normal?

分析：原文通过反问，促使党的高级干部对自身存在的问题进行深入反思，既指出了当前党内存在的不足，又旗帜鲜明地表达了反对脱离群众的工作方式。在译文方面，采用了简洁明了的直译方式，无论句型还是用词，都一一对应，与原文简洁明了的立场形成呼应。

8. 借代

所谓借代，就是借用一种事物所具有的典型特征，赋予另一种事物，既可以以事代人，也可以以人代事，既可以以事代事，也可以以人代人，使得语言鲜活传神，达到幽默形象的效果。在翻译过程中，我们需要深刻了解事物所具有的文化背景和内涵，找到译入语中相同或相似的表达，才能更好地实现翻译目标。例如：

原文：世界上热点问题不少，按下葫芦起了瓢。

译文：Just when you press the gourd into the water, there floats the gourd ladle.

分析：原文采用借代方式，使用"葫芦"和"瓢"，分别指代形形色色的热点问题，因为葫芦和瓢都是在水中漂浮着，即使按下水面，也会自动浮上来，这是汉语习语的形象表达。在译文方面，采用了直译加注释（A traditional Chinese saying that means "tackling one problem only to find another emerging"）方式，用来解释此借代所蕴含的意义，非常符合文化翻译的特点。

9. 通感

所谓通感，就是将一种感觉通道转移到另一种感觉通道上去，也就是说，用一种感觉去描写另一种感觉，这是感官相通的很好例证。通感不但可以使描写更加生动鲜活，而且可以给人以难忘的感受，因为许多感受都是每个人与生俱来的感官能力。在翻译过程中，能否准确传达感官相通的意义，对于译者是一种能力考验。例如：

原文：我讲过，环境就是民生，<u>青</u>山就是美丽，<u>蓝</u>天也是幸福，<u>绿</u>水<u>青</u>山就是金山银山……

译文：As I previously mentioned, environment is livelihood, <u>green</u> mountains are beauty, <u>blue</u> sky is happiness, and <u>clear</u> water is wealth…

分析：原文充分利用颜色词，通过调动读者的视觉效果，传达美好环境所具有的特征，形象地展现了新发展理念、绿色发展理念。在译文方面，由于汉英两种语言之间颜色词所具有的文化意义比较类似，译者使用了直译方式，将颜色词充分运用到生态学的环保概念之中，既清楚表达了原文含义，也给读者以良好自然生态美感。

10. 反复

所谓反复，就是通过重复使用字词或句子，实现强调意味。在汉语中，使用反复修辞，是为强调所反复强调的对象；在英语中，使用反复修辞的频率要比汉语低一些。在翻译过程中，能否传递汉语所强调的对象和意义，是考验翻译效果的重要因素。例如：

原文：要防止和克服地方和部门保护主义、本位主义，<u>决不允许</u>"上有政策，下有对策"，<u>决不允许</u>有令不行、有禁不止，<u>决不允许</u>在贯彻执行中央决策部署上打折扣、做选择、搞变通。

译文：We must prevent or, if necessary, rectify departmental and local protectionism and parochialism, and <u>never allow</u> local policies to trump central policies, <u>never countenance</u> the sidelining of central decrees or prohibitions, and <u>never engage in</u> perfunctory or selective or compromised enforcement of the central leadership's policy decisions and plans.

分析：原文使用三个"决不允许"，强调地方和部门要严格贯彻党中央决策部署，不能有偏差和出入。在译文方面，使用三个意义相似的平行谓语"never allow""never countenance""never engage in"，使译文简洁流畅，实现了原文强调意味。

第二部分：知识与技能讲析

1. 直译

所谓直译，就是直接译出原文的本义。这是一种内容和形式完全对等、统一的翻译方法，换句话说，就是保持原文内容在用词、句法、修辞及风格特征等方面的一致。直译法的优点是可以直接传达原文意义和文化内涵，追求的是忠实于原文表达。在《习近平谈治国理政》英译本中，直译法被广泛应用。例如：

原文 1：中国特色社会主义

译文：socialism with Chinese characteristics

原文 2："大鹏之动，非一羽之轻也；骐骥之速，非一足之力也。"

译文："The roc soars lithely not merely because of the lightness of one of its feathers; the steed runs fast not merely because of the strength of one of its legs."

分析：直译的最大好处，就是尽可能地保留原文语言风格和结构，使读者能够更好地感受到原文韵味和特色，也更准确地传递原文文化背景和情感，使读者能够更好地理解和体验原文所表达的意义。上述例子，很好地采用了直译方式，将原文意义原原本本表达出来，体现了直译所具有的优点。另外，直译也有其不足之处。例如，因为语言之间存在着语法、修辞和文化上的差异，它可能导致译文在目标语中不通顺或不自然。

2. 意译

所谓意译，就是忠实于原文内容而不拘泥于原文句型结构、语法形式和修辞手法的翻译方法。在翻译过程中，根据目标语的语言习惯和文化背景，对原文进行适当调整和转换，以实现原文所具有的丰富内涵。例如，为了更好地传达中国文化的独特性，一些典故被意译为英文中的类似表达。例如：

原文 1："大道之行，天下为公。"

译文："A just world should be pursued for the common good."

原文 2：如果党的理论和路线方针政策在这里<u>失之毫厘</u>，到了基层就可能<u>谬以千里</u>……

译文：The slightest deviation from the theories, guidelines, principles and policies of our Party will lead to huge mistakes at the grassroots level…

分析：意译的最大好处，是可以根据目标语的语法和表达方式，使译文更通顺和自然，更符合读者的阅读习惯。意译有利于传达原文的深层含义，通过对原文的解释和转换，更准确地传达原文的深层含义和隐喻，使读者能够更好地理解原文的意义。根据目标文化的需求，通过意译对原文进行调整和改动，使译文更符合目标文化的审美和习惯。例如，将"大道"译为"a just world"，将"公"译为"the common good"，照顾到了目标语的相应表述。意译的不足之处在于，它充分考虑读者的感受，却忽略了所译内容的特色，可能会造成原文具有的文化内涵丧失。例如，将"失之毫厘"译为"the slightest deviation"，将"谬以千里"译为"huge mistakes"，丢掉了汉语成语所具有的深刻文化内涵。

3. 省译

所谓省译，是指省译原文内容，防止冗余产生，同时不失原文应有意义。作为一种常见的翻译技巧，省译只省其形而不省其义。出于语法、语义和修辞考虑，我们常常省译累赘词语，达到省去冗余、传达真实意义的目标。例如：

原文：坚持人民性，就是要把实现好、维护好、发展好最广大人民根本利益作为出发点和落脚点，坚持以民为本、以人为本。

译文：Serving the people means putting the people first and making realizing, safeguarding and developing the fundamental interests of the overwhelming majority of the people our starting point and goal.

分析：省译的最大好处，是可以非常简洁地表达原文所传达的意义，实现"精练就是美"的翻译效果。原文使用近义词表述方式，提升了语言文彩度，强化了文章表现力。例如，"出发点"和"落脚点"的意思相近，都是指目标；"以民为本"和"以人为本"都是将人民看作执政基础。译文使用"starting point and goal"把"出发点"和"落脚点"的意思加以概括，使用"putting the people first"把"以民为本、以人为本"的意思加以概括，因为"people"既指"民"，也指"人"。省译的不足之处在于，有时会缺失原文本身需要通过所谓的冗余实现的意义。例如，上述例子中的原文采用平行结构的两组词语，表达了"有始有终""人民至上"的执政理念。

4. 增译

所谓增译，就是增译原文内容，丰富原文省略的信息，补充缺失的文化，让读者了解原文所具有的内涵意义。与省译相反，增译实现的是增其形而不冗其义。例如：

原文：这就是《少年中国说》中所说的：少年智则国智，少年富则国富，少年强则国强，少年进步则国进步。

译文：As Liang Qichao said in his "Young China": "If the youth are wise, the country will be wise. If the youth prosper, the country will prosper. If the youth are strong, the country will be strong. If the youth progress, the country will progress."

分析：增译的最大好处，是充分传达原文具有的丰富内涵，补充读者所需的相关信息和背景知识，实现译文对原文信息的充分传递。例如，梁启超先生的《少年中国说》对于中国读者来说耳熟能详，但对于外国读者来说可能不太熟悉，译文通过补全作者信息，让外国读者进一步了解原文的重要意义。

第三部分：英译习作与修辞范例对照解析

1. 比喻

原文：……坚定不移"打虎"、"拍蝇"、"猎狐"……

译文：… have taken firm action to "take out tigers", "swat flies", and "hunt down foxes"…

习作：We must stand firm against "tigers", "flies" and "foxes".

范例对照解析：原文属于无主句，其中的"打虎""拍蝇""猎狐"，是我国当前反腐行动的不同称呼，针对的分别是高级干部、基层干部、逃亡海外的三类腐败分子。译文在补充主语的基础上，采取了典型的直译方式，将"打虎""拍蝇""猎狐"中的"打""拍""猎"使用不同动词体现出来，既形象又具体。习作采取了直译加省译的翻译方式，在增加主语的基础上，将"打虎""拍蝇""猎狐"中的"打""拍""猎"省去，而用"stand against"代替。这种处理方式虽然使得译文简洁明了，但似乎缺少了原文所表述的三种反腐行动的针对性。

2. 拟人

原文：人类发展活动必须尊重自然、顺应自然、保护自然，否则就会遭到大自然的<u>报复</u>，这个规律谁也无法抗拒。

译文：Human development activities must respect, accommodate, and protect nature; otherwise nature will <u>retaliate against</u> us. This is a law no one can deny.

习作：The development activities of human beings must show great respect for nature, as well as follow its law and protect it; otherwise we will be <u>revenged for</u> our disregard of the inevitable nature law.

范例对照解析：原文中的"报复"一词，用来指代大自然如同人类一样具有情感，人类破坏大自然的行为，可能让人类遭受自然灾害。译文翻译为"retaliate against"，意思是"反击"，让我们感受到大自然虽然对人类造成各种困难和灾害，但是常常以一种适当的方式，对人类破坏大自然的行为加以提醒。习作将"报复"翻译为"revenged for"，意思是"复仇"，虽然凸显出破坏大自然会让人类遭受自然灾害，但强调的是较为消极的一面，即大自然对人类进行无情反击，缺乏大自然对人类温情的一面。

3. 夸张

原文："忠诚印寸心，浩然充两间。"

译文："My loyalty comes from the bottom of my heart, and it stretches all the way from the Earth to the Heavens."

习作：Loyalty imprints in the heart, vast righteousness fills the space.

范例对照解析：这句话出自蔡和森所写的一首词《少年行》，原文表达的意思是"忠诚之志永驻心间，浩然之气充盈天地"，充分体现了党员对党的忠诚，心怀浩然正气。译文基本采用了直译方式，用词简单明了，结构工整有序，符合诗词译法和手段。习作虽然也注意使用词汇和句法，与原文字数匹配，但是"imprints"一词为及物动词，用词错误，由此可见习作者更多注重词的字面意思。

4. 移就

原文："为有牺牲多<u>壮志</u>，敢教日月换<u>新天</u>。"

译文："Our <u>minds</u> grow <u>stronger</u> for the martyrs' sacrifice, daring to make the sun and the moon shine in the <u>new sky</u>."

习作：The committed devotion to achieve the grand course can beat off the forces that hold us back.

范例对照解析：此句诗出自毛泽东的古诗作品《七律·到韶山》，原文表达的意思是"为伟大理想而勇敢牺牲，敢于挑战旧秩序，创造新天地"，充分体现了党员应具有伟大牺牲精神和革命精神。"壮志""新天"两个词语的翻译质量好坏，很大程度上体现译文的整体质量好坏。译文将"壮志"做具体化处理，翻译为"stronger minds"，强调意志强大的重要性，将"新天"直译为"new sky"，强调日月闪耀星空所具有的耳目一新的感受。习作将"壮志"翻译为"grand course"，与原文本义有所出入；将"换新天"翻译为"beat off the forces that hold us back"，缺少原文具体形象的特点。

5. 类比

原文："登高使人心旷，临流使人意远。"

译文："From a mountain top you will enjoy a broader outlook; down by the riverside you will enjoy a pleasant prospect."

习作：Climbing high mountain broadens the people's hearts and facing the river makes the mind wander distant.

范例对照解析：这句话出自明朝作家洪应明所著《菜根谭》。原文的意思是"登上高处，会让人感到心旷神怡；面对流水，会让人感到意境深远"。译文使用了将介词短语"From a mountain top""down by the riverside"放在句首的方式，表现强调的意味，使用了"enjoy"一词，充分表达"心旷""意远"给人带来的愉悦感。习作使用直译方式，虽然尊重原文的字面意义，但缺少了原文具有的深刻内涵。比如，"登高"翻译为"climbing high mountain"，"临流"翻译为"facing the river"，是名词动词化处理。原文是做名词，且具有非常深刻的意义和内涵，也就是说，"登高"不仅仅指的是登上高山，"临流"也不仅仅指的是站在河边。

6. 排比

原文：这是中华民族的伟大光荣！这是中国人民的伟大光荣！这是中国共产党的伟大光荣！

译文：This is a great and glorious achievement for the Chinese nation, for the Chinese people and for the Communist Party of China.

习作：This great glory not only belongs to the Communist Party of China, but also belongs to the Chinese people, as well as all Chinese descendants!

范例对照解析：原文通过排比修辞，强调伟大光荣属于中华民族、中国人民和中国共产党。排比句不仅结构相同，而且用词重复，凸显了浓厚的强调意味。译文将"伟大光荣"翻译为"great and glorious achievement"，凸显了事业伟大光荣的一面，并重复使用介词"for"引导的短语。习作重复使用了"belongs to"，并通过"not only""but also""as well as"将三个感叹句组合为一个句子，不如原文紧凑。此外，使用"great glory"作为主语，与原文实际主语（伟大光荣的成就）不符。

7. 反问

原文：如果没有中华五千年文明，哪里有什么中国特色？如果不是中国特色，哪有我们今天这么成功的中国特色社会主义道路？

译文：If there were no 5,000-year Chinese civilization, how could we build anything with what we describe today as "Chinese characteristics"? And if it were not for these characteristics, how could we have successfully embarked on the path to "socialism with Chinese characteristics"?

习作：If there were no 5,000-year-long Chinese civilization, how could we build "Chinese characteristics"? And if it were not for Chinese characteristics, how could we have successfully built today's "socialism with Chinese characteristics"?

范例对照解析：翻译质量的好坏，需要看对于原文的翻译是否贴切。原文中的反问，意思是中国特色离不开中华五千年文明这一基础，今天这么成功的中国特色社会主义道路离不开中国特色这一关键。考虑到原文中的两个反问，译文增加了部分词汇，补充了反问所具有的内涵。与译文相比，习作采用形式对等译法，虽然显得简洁，但是没有将反问句加以明确化，缺少了反问句中的关键词所具有的丰富内涵。

8. 借代

原文："安得广厦千万间，大庇天下寒士俱欢颜！"

译文："If only I could build a house with thousands upon thousands of rooms, I would bring all the poor people on the earth under its roof and bring smiles to their faces."

习作：How can I get a spacious house with myriad rooms to shelter people from all walks of life, bringing happiness to them!

范例对照解析：此句话出自唐朝诗人杜甫所写的《茅屋为秋风所破歌》，意思是希望有充裕的房屋，为读书人提供庇护场所，体现了诗人的崇高人格和博爱精神。这里的"广厦"具有非常广泛的意义，既可指物理空间之广，也可指社会空间之广。译文采用直译和省译方式，既照顾到形式，又照顾到内容，也照顾到外国读者群体的文本可读性。习作将原文处理为一个感叹句形式，没有采用虚拟条件句配合主句，缺少一种中文体现的对称美。

9. 通感

原文："横眉冷对千夫指，俯首甘为孺子牛。"

译文："Holding my head high in defiance of the enemy's attacks, bowing my head low in obedience to the people."

习作：When facing enemies, you can stand bravely to people who are opposed to you, sometimes, you can also bend yourself to be coordinated with your own ideas in a perfect way.

范例对照解析：这句话出自鲁迅先生的《自嘲》，意思是我们绝不向敌人投降屈服，而甘愿俯下身子为人民服务。译文采用意译的翻译方式，将"冷对"和"甘为"分别译为"in defiance of"和"in obedience to"，结构对称，意义明确，分别表现蔑视敌人和忠诚人民的态度和立场。习作亦采用意译的翻译方式，在翻译中误用词组如"stand to"，其他固定搭配过多，语言冗余，不够精准简练。

10. 反复

原文：这一百年来开辟的伟大道路、创造的伟大事业、取得的伟大成就，必将载入中华民族发展史册、人类文明发展史册！

译文：The great path we have pioneered, the great cause we have undertaken, and the great achievements we have made over the past century will go down in the annals of the Chinese nation and of human civilization.

习作：The great road opened up in the past 100 years, the great cause created, and the great achievement achieved, will surely be recorded in the history of the development of Chinese nation and the history of human civilization.

范例对照解析：原文反复使用"伟大"和"发展史册"，强调党的一百年历史对于中华民族和人类文明所具有的深远影响和意义。译文采用意译翻译方式，依照原文句子结构，将"伟大道路"翻译为"great path"；习作的"great road"明显将原文意义简单化、表面化。另外，对于"发展史册"一词的翻译，译文非常精练，而习作非常烦琐。

第六单元

思政经典中的典故翻译

第一部分：典故的主要类型及范例对照

我国关于典故最早的记载可以追溯至《后汉书》，不同学者对其界定也各不相同，学界一般将"典故"界定为"用典，也称用事引证，即引用或活用前人说过的话，或文学作品中记载的故事、神话等，用以比喻现实，抒写情怀，从而体现出简洁含蓄、发人深思的艺术效果"。为规范起见，本书采用《辞海》中"典故"定义的第二义项，即"诗文中引用的古代故事和有来历出处的词语"，并将典故分为成语、俗语和古诗文三类。下面我们以《习近平谈治国理政》中英双语文本中运用的典故为例，展示一下其使用及传达效果。

1. 成语

所谓成语，就是经过长期使用、锤炼形成的固定短语，通常为四字结构，因其富有深刻内涵、简短精辟等特点，非常受到作者青睐。在翻译过程中，译

者需要在理解成语所蕴含的文化信息基础上,准确传达文化意象和作者的使用意图。例如:

原文:"桃李不言,下自成蹊。"

译文:"Peaches and plums do not speak, but they are so attractive that a path is formed below the trees."

分析:此典故出自《史记·李将军列传》,原文用来赞扬李广将军为人真诚,严于律己,从而受到人们敬仰。原文表达的是桃树和李树不主动招引人,但人们都会看它们开花结果,在树下形成一条小路,比喻品德高尚的人不用宣传,就自然能受到尊重和敬仰。译文运用直译翻译方式和异化翻译策略,保留了原文的意象"桃李",以及原文拟人的修辞手法,使得译文鲜活生动。典故翻译需要忠实传递典故的含义,再现作者使用典故的意图。译文使用"they are so attractive"表达"下自成蹊"的原因,显化了典故所隐含的因果关系。习近平同志使用这一典故,指代"一带一路"结出了丰硕成果,并受到"一带一路"沿线各国人民发自内心的欢迎。译文既传递了中国文化意象,又通过因果关系促使读者理解这一典故,从而准确描写出共建国家对通过"一带一路"倡议实现合作共赢的感受。

2. 俗语

所谓俗语,就是约定俗成的惯用语,多为口语体,因其来自人民群众,具有通俗易懂的特征。俗语既包括谚语、歇后语,也包括具有地区特点的语言表达。与成语不同之处在于,俗语具有大众化特征,所以在翻译过程中,也应该使用大众化语言表达来传递原文意义。例如:

原文:还要注意区分轻重缓急,把对本地区改革发展稳定具有决定性意义的工作抓起来、管起来,不要<u>眉毛胡子一把抓</u>。

译文:In addition, local authorities should identify priorities and address themselves to tasks with a decisive bearing on reform and development in their localities, and refrain from <u>trying to attend to major and minor issues at one and the same time</u>.

分析:"眉毛胡子一把抓"出自李英儒所著的《野火春风斗古城》,是指主次不分,比喻做事不分轻重缓急,一齐下手。习近平总书记使用这个俗语,旨在提醒各级干部在工作中应分清主次,有序进行。这一俗语是中国文化中特有的表达,英文中并没有对应的词句。如果根据字面意思直译为"stroking eyebrow and beard at one and the same time",容易造成误解。如果译为"do not go about several tasks",只能传达出"不要多个工作同时进行"的意图,但并不能体现根据重要程度分清轻重缓急的意图。因此,译者采用意译的翻译方式,将其译为"trying to attend to major and minor issues at one and the same time",传达了俗语强调"不分主次、轻重"的含义。

3. 古诗文

所谓古诗文,主要是指古代的诗歌和散文。作为中国文化的瑰宝,古诗文具有悠久历史、深厚文化内涵,且具有语言精练、意蕴深刻和韵律优美的特点,常被作者引用。例如:

原文:"迟日江山丽,春风花草香。"

译文:"The land bathes in the spring sunshine, and the wind sends the aromas of grass and flowers."

分析:古诗文作为中国传统文化的代表,善于用精简的语言体现出庞大的信息量,这是对译者能否适应原文翻译生态环境的考验。《绝句·迟日江山丽》是唐朝诗人杜甫诗集《杜工部集》中的一首,诗人杜甫经过两年的流离奔波回到成都草堂之后,面对浣花溪一带的春光而作此诗,凸显春天日光和煦、万物欣欣向荣的特点,构成一幅明丽和谐的春色图。"迟日""江山""春风""花草"配以"丽""香",很好地传递出春天之美。译文采用直译的翻译方式,句式结构工整,用词形象具体,同时使用了尾韵手法,照顾到古诗文形式美、意境美。

第二部分:知识与技能讲析

1. 归化

所谓归化,就是在翻译过程中尽量减少译文中体现的异国文化和风格,让目的语读者读起来感到自然流畅,强调的是译入语文化,看重的是译文读者,目的是尽量消除文化差异,增强可读性。例如:

原文:"百尺竿头,更进一步。"

译文:We need to build on past success and promote cooperation in Asia.

分析:此处用典出自唐朝诗人吴融所写的《商人》一诗:"百尺竿头五两斜,

此生何处不为家。"习近平主席在博鳌亚洲论坛 2013 年年会主旨演讲中使用了这一典故，原意指学问、成绩等达到很高水平后继续努力，争取更大进步，此处用来表达亚洲地区需要继续协调各方利益诉求，更好地增进彼此之间的理解、凝聚共识、深化合作。原文"百尺竿头"，意为百尺高的竿子，结合语境采用了归化的翻译方法，译为"build on past success"，将"百尺高的"这种抽象描述具体表达为"past success"，省去了"竿子"这一无关意象，"更进一步"的翻译也添加了"cooperation"一词，表明是要更进一步地深化合作，同时在末尾添加了"Asia"一词，紧扣演讲主题。整个译文自然流畅，切合主题，目的语读者也可以轻松领会该典故内涵。

2. 异化

所谓异化，就是要求译文不按照目的语的方式表达，而尽量保持原文的文化底蕴，要求译者采取原文使用的表达方式，传达原文信息，强调的是原语文化，看重的是原文作者，目的是更好地丰富本族语言，促进文化交流。例如：

原文："自古雄才多磨难，从来纨绔少伟男。"

译文："A hard life breeds great talents, whereas an easy life is not the way to cultivate great men."

分析：此句用典出自近代诗人王宝池的励志诗《七律·劝学》。2014 年 5 月 30 日，习近平在北京市海淀区民族小学主持召开座谈会时指出，要引导少年儿童从小就培育和践行社会主义核心价值观。英译采用了异化的翻译策略，不仅保留了原文的意象，比如将"雄才""纨绔""伟男"分别翻译为"great talents""easy life""great men"，而且巧妙地忠实于原文的文风和句式，比如使用"whereas"表达出明确的转折意味，从而将原文中生动的表达方法引入目的语中，丰富了目的语的语言文化。在讲好中国故事，传播中华文化的大背景之下，习近平用典英译要在读者可理解的基础上保留其独特的文化内涵，包括原文的文风、意象和句式等，要把富含中国文化的典故尽量原汁原味地传达出去，促进文化交流。

3. 解释

所谓解释，就是对所翻译的对象和概念进一步阐释，从而让读者清楚其所蕴含的意义和背景信息。在翻译过程中，一些对象和概念常常具有丰富的内涵和意义，采用进一步解释的翻译方式，对于使外国读者更好地理解这些对象和概念非常有帮助。例如：

原文：新发展理念

译文：the philosophy of innovative, coordinated, green, open and inclusive development

分析："新发展理念"是新时代使用的一个术语，是指需要更加科学地认识当前的发展理念，也就是说，随着时代的发展，我们的发展不再是那种牺牲生态环境的、不可持续的发展方式，而是创新、协调、绿色、开放、共享的发展方式。在翻译过程中，将"新发展理念"这一术语加以具体化解释，能更加明确地展示这一术语所具有的内涵和意义。

4. 注释

所谓注释，就是形式上独立于原文，采用给原文作注的方式，对原文加以进一步解释。王雪明、杨子认为，注释是"将文本置于丰富的文化和语言环境中，使原语文化的特征得以保留，目的在于促进目的语文化对他者文化给予更充分的理解和更深切的尊重"。王振平将翻译中的注释分为科学术语、社会知识、文学典故、历史掌故、风土人情、重要人物、地理知识。他认为，翻译中的注释"一为帮助读者理解，二为传播科学文化知识"。在《习近平谈治国理政》英译本中，充分运用了该翻译方式，完美展现了博大精深的中华文化，为外国朋友更好地理解当代中国提供了合适的材料。例如：

原文：我们要通过行动回答"窑洞之问"，练就中国共产党人自我净化的"绝世武功"。

译文：In seeking the solution to breaking the cycle of rise and fall, we must act with force and continue to improve and renew ourselves.

原文注释：1945年7月，民主人士黄炎培在访问延安同毛泽东谈话时说，希望将来中国共产党建立的政权能够跳出旧政权"其兴也勃焉""其亡也忽焉"的周期率。毛泽东说："我们已经找到新路，我们能跳出这周期率。这条新路，就是民主。只有让人民来监督政府，政府才不敢松懈。只有人人起来负责，才不会人亡政息。"

译文注释：In a conversation with Mao Zedong during a visit to Yan'an in July 1945, Huang Yanpei, a prominent non-Party individual, expressed the hope that the government to be established by the CPC would bring an end to the cycle of rise and fall characteristic of governments in Chinese history. Mao Zedong replied that the

CPC had found a new path to break this cycle, and that the new path was democracy. Only under public scrutiny, will a government be clean and efficient; only when everyone takes responsibility, will good governance prevail.

分析：注释的最大好处，就是能将原文蕴含的深刻文化内涵详细解释清楚，为外国朋友了解中国文化提供详细背景。"窑洞之问"如果直接翻译为"the cycle of rise and fall"，难以体现出此概念所具有的深刻时代背景，采用注释的翻译方式，能很好地弥补所翻译概念的不足。

第三部分：英译习作与典故范例对照解析

1. 成语

原文："生于忧患，死于安乐。"

译文："One prospers in worries and hardships, and perishes in ease and comfort."

习作：Awareness of unexpected development leads to success and indulge in pleasure leads to failure.

范例对照解析：这一成语最早出自战国时期孟子及其弟子所著的《孟子·告子下》。原文为四字格的结构，且"生"与"死"对仗，"忧患"与"安乐"对仗，翻译时应考虑到反义词的使用，以及对仗结构的体现。译文使用"worries and hardships""ease and comfort"，很好地凸显了"忧患""安乐"的意义，也充分考虑了对仗的使用，比习作的翻译效果好一些。同时，译文认为"生""死"是指兴衰，翻译成动词"prosper""perish"，习作认为是成败，翻译成"success""failure"，译文比习作的翻译更地道。习作虽然考虑到了对仗和反义词的使用，但将"indulge"当作名词使用，语法上有误。习作翻译"忧患""安乐"时，没有充分考虑词的对仗。

2. 俗语

原文：面对复杂形势、复杂矛盾、繁重任务，没有主次，不加区别，<u>眉毛胡子一把抓</u>，是做不好工作的。

译文：When dealing with complex situations and difficult problems, or tasked with a demanding workload, no one will do well by trying to <u>attend to major and minor issues at one and the same time</u>.

习作：We can't complete work well without <u>grasping the main point</u> and telling the difference when facing complex situation, complicated opposition and strenuous tasks.

范例对照解析：原文中的"眉毛胡子"是指性质和类型不同的两种事物，翻译时应该注意"眉毛""胡子"是两个不同的词语。"眉毛胡子一把抓"非常形象地指代处理事物时没有条理、不分轻重缓急。译文考虑到俗语的内涵意义，采用直译方式处理，并将"眉毛胡子"翻译为"major and minor issues"，点明了其指代意义；习作对俗语的理解稍有偏差，采用意译方式处理，将"眉毛胡子"翻译为"main point"，没有注意到"眉毛""胡子"具有相反的意义。

3. 古诗文

原文："治国之道，富民为始。"

译文："The key to running a country is to first enrich the people."

习作：The way of governing a country starts with enriching its people.

范例对照解析：此句古诗文出自西汉司马迁的《史记·平津侯主父列传》。原文的意思是指治理好一个国家，首要的事情是让人民过上好日子。整体上看，能否翻译出原文具有浓厚中国文化要素的"道"字，是体现翻译质量的重要衡量标准。译文将"道"翻译为"key"，"key to running"主要凸显顺利管理国家的关键，并将"为始"理解为首先应做的事情。习作采用直译方式，将"道"翻译为"way"，将"治国"翻译为"governing a country"，也能忠实体现原文的意义，但将"为始"翻译为"starts with"，与"first"相比，显得不够精练。

附录1　思政高频词汇

A

爱国统一战线 the patriotic united front

爱国卫生运动 the public health campaign

爱国主义教育 patriotic education

安全共同体 a community of indivisible security

按劳分配 distribution with "to each according to their work"

"澳人治澳" the people of Macao administer Macao

B

"八大行动" the eight major initiatives (industrial development, infrastructure connectivity, trade facilitation, green development, capacity building, health care, cultural and people-to-people exchanges, and peace and security)

《巴黎协定》the Paris Agreement

霸权主义 hegemonism

百花齐放、百家争鸣的方针 the principle of letting a hundred flowers blossom and a hundred schools of thought contend

百年未有之大变局 change on a scale unseen in a century

保护主义 protectionism

北伐战争 the Northern Expedition

北京冬奥会 Beijing Winter Olympics

北京冬奥精神 the Spirit of the Beijing Winter Olympics

北京冬残奥会 Beijing Winter Paralympics

辩证唯物主义 dialectical materialism

不忘初心，牢记使命 remain/stay true to the Party's original aspiration and founding mission

C

长江经济带 the Yangtze River Economic Belt

长三角地区合作机制 the Yangtze River Delta cooperation mechanism

长三角一体化发展 the integrated development of the Yangtze River Delta

长征 the Long March

长征精神 the revolutionary spirit of the Long March

城乡区域发展 the development between urban and rural areas and between regions

城乡融合发展 integrated urban-rural development

创新发展 innovation-driven development

创新驱动 innovation-driven

创新驱动发展战略 the strategy of innovation-driven development

创新、协调、绿色、开放、共享的发展理念 the vision of innovative, coordinated, green, open and shared development

创新型国家 a country of innovators

创造性转化、创新性发展 the creative evolution and development

D

大革命 the Great Revolution

大历史观 a broad historical perspective

单边主义 unilateralism

党的初心和使命 the Party's original aspiration and founding mission

党的第二次全国代表大会 the Second National Congress of the CPC

党的各级领导班子 the Party leadership groups at all levels

党的基本方略 the Party's fundamental principles

党的基本理论 the Party's underlying theories

党的基本路线 the Party's basic guideline

党的集中统一领导 the Party's centralized and unified leadership

党的历史经验 the historical experience of the Party

党的领导 the leadership of the Party

党的全部工作 the overall work of the Party

党的全面领导 the overall leadership of the Party

党的群众路线 the Party's mass line

党的群众路线教育实践活动 the education campaigns among all Party members to increase awareness of honoring the Party's mass line

党的主要成就 the Party's major achievements

党的主要任务 the major tasks of the Party

党的宗教工作基本方针 the Party's basic policies on religious affairs

党的宗教工作理论 the Party's theory on religious affairs

党的宗教信仰自由政策 the Party's basic policies on freedom of religious belief

党和国家的事业 the cause of the Party and the country

党和人民事业 the cause of the Party and the people

党纪处分条例 Party disciplinary regulations

党史学习教育 the education campaign on CPC history

党委 the Party committees

党校 the Party schools

党性 Party consciousness; Party spirit

党章 the Party Constitution

党中央 the Party Central Committee

党中央权威和集中统一领导 the authority of the Party Central Committee and its centralized, unified leadership

党组 the Party leadership groups

道路自信 the confidence in our path

邓小平理论 Deng Xiaoping Theory

底线思维 worst-case scenarios

第二个百年奋斗目标 the Second Centenary Goal

第二十六届联合国大会 the 26th Session of the General Assembly of the United Nations

第十四个五年计划 the 14th Five-year Plan

第一个百年奋斗目标 the First Centenary Goal

地方组织 the local level units

地球生命共同体 a community of all life on earth

地缘政治挑战 the geopolitical challenges

顶层设计 top-level design

钉钉子精神 the perseverance to hammer away until a task is done

东北地区全面振兴 comprehensive revitalization of the northeast

东部发达地区 developed eastern regions

《东盟共同体愿景2025》ASEAN Community Vision 2025

《东南亚无核武器区条约》Protocol to the Treaty on the Southeast Asia Nuclear

Weapon-Free-Zone

《东南亚友好合作条约》the Treaty of Amity and Cooperation in Southeast Asia

东欧剧变 the dramatic changes in Eastern Europe

斗争精神 the fighting spirit

独立自主的和平外交政策 independent foreign policy of peace

对党忠诚 the loyalty to the Party

对美好生活的向往 the desire for a better life; the expectation for a better life

多边贸易体制 the multilateral trading system

多边主义 multilateralism

多党合作和政治协商制度 the system of multiparty cooperation and political consultation

F

发展不平衡、不充分的问题 imbalanced and insufficient development

发展中国家 developing countries

法律援助 legal aid

法治 rule of law

法治国家 a law-based country; a country under the rule of law

法治精神 the spirit of rule of law

法治社会 a law-based society

法治政府 a law-based government

法治中国 rule of law in China

反腐 combat corruption; anti-corruption

反腐败斗争 the battle against corruption

《反极端主义公约》Convention on Countering Extremism

反恐合作 cooperation against terrorism

反垄断法 the Anti-Monopoly Law

方舱医院 Temporary Treatment Centers

防范化解重大风险 guard against and defuse major risks

非典 SARS

非公有制经济 the non-public sector of the economy

非盟 African Union

非洲大陆自由贸易区 the African Continental Free Trade Area

非洲疾控中心总部 the Africa CDC headquarters

"枫桥经验" the "Fengqiao model"

负面清单 the negative list

G

改革创新精神 the spirit of reform and innovation

改革开放 reform and opening up

港澳台 Hongkong, Macao, Taiwan

"港人治港" the people of Hong Kong administer Hong Kong

高度自治 a high degree of autonomy

高排放、技术落后项目 projects with high emissions and outdated technology

高水平对外开放 high-standard opening up

高质量发展 high-quality development

革命老区 old revolutionary base areas

革命文化 the revolutionary culture

根本利益 the fundamental interests

工匠精神 the spirit of craftsmanship

公共安全 public security

公共服务 public service

公共卫生体系 public health system

公平、平等和非歧视的环境 the fair, equitable and nondiscriminatory environment

公有制经济 the public sector of the economy

供给侧结构性改革 supply-side structural reform

共产党 Communist Party

共产主义 communism

共产主义青年团 Communist Youth League

共产主义者 communist

共存互利 coexistence and mutual benefit

共商、共建、共享原则 the principles of extensive consultation, joint contribution, and shared benefits

共同富裕 common prosperity; shared prosperity

共同、综合、合作、可持续的安全观 vision of common, comprehensive, cooperative and sustainable security

共享经济 sharing economy

共享未来的全球社区 a global community of shared future

关键领域的核心技术 core technologies in key fields

关键少数 critical minority

关心关爱 care and compassion

《关于建国以来党的若干历史问题的决议》Resolution on Certain Questions in the History of Our Party Since the Founding of the People's Republic of China

《关于若干历史问题的决议》Resolution on Certain Questions in the History of Our Party

官僚主义 bureaucratism

官员腐败 the corruption among officials

国防和军队现代化 the modernization of our national defense and armed forces

国防和军队现代化新"三步走" the new three-step strategy for the modernization of national defense and the army

国际法 international law

国际关系民主化 the democracy in international relations

国际货币基金组织 International Monetary Fund (IMF)

国际金融危机 international financial crisis

国际社会 international community

国际秩序 international order

国家安全意识 awareness of national security

国家大数据战略 national big data strategy

国家人权行动计划 national human rights action plans

国家医疗保障局 National Healthcare Security Administration

国家治理体系和治理能力现代化 the modernization of the national governance system and capacity

国家主权、安全、发展利益 national sovereignty, security, and development interests

国内需求 domestic demand

国务院 State Council

国有企业　state-owned enterprises

H

海南自由贸易港　Hainan Free Trade Port
（海峡）两岸关系　cross-Straits relations
海洋经济　marine economy
海洋强国　a strong maritime nation/country
合作共赢　win-win cooperation
和平发展道路　the path of peaceful development
和平共处五项原则　the Five Principles of Peaceful Coexistence
和平统一　peaceful reunification
《横琴粤澳深度合作区建设总体方案》the Overall Plan for Building a Guangdong-Macao in-depth Cooperation Zone in Hengqin
红船精神　the Red Boat spirit; the spirit of the Red Boat
红军　the Red Army
《红岩》*Red Crag*
红岩精神　the revolutionary spirit of Hongyan
宏观经济政策　macroeconomic policy
"互联网+"行动计划　"Internet Plus" action plan
互联网大数据　the Internet big data
淮海战役　the Huai-Hai Campaign
黄河流域发展　development in the Yellow River Basin

J

《基本法》the Basic Law
基本国策　basic state policy
基本经济制度　the basic economic system
基本养老保险　basic pension insurance
基本医疗保险　basic medical insurance
基本政治制度　basic political system
基层群众自治制度　the system of community-level self-governance
基层组织　the primary level units

集体领导 collective leadership

集体主义 collectivism

集中国家资源 concentrate national resources

集中力量办大事 pool all our resources to complete major missions; pool our efforts to accomplish big tasks

集中统一领导 centralized and unified leadership

计划经济 planned economy

纪检监察 discipline inspection and supervision

加强党的政治建设 reinforce the Party's political foundations

坚持"一国两制" uphold the One Country, Two Systems policy

监察委员会 supervision commission

监督部门 department for supervision

《建国方略》The Plan for National Reconstruction

建军一百年奋斗目标 the Centenary Goal of the People's Liberation Army

建设世界科技强国 build China into a world leader in science and technology

健康中国行动 the Healthy China Initiative

节能环保 energy conservation and environmental protection

解放战争 the War of Liberation

金砖国家（巴西、俄罗斯、印度、南非及中国）BRICS

禁渔 ban on fishing

经济安全 economic security

经济发展 economic development

经济和社会发展五年计划 the Five-year Plan for Economic and Social Development

经济全球化 economic globalization

经济特区 special economic zone

经济体制改革 economic structural reform

京津冀协同发展 coordinated development of the Beijing-Tianjin-Hebei Region

精神文明建设 cultural-ethical progress

精准扶贫 targeted poverty alleviation

井冈山精神 the spirit of Jinggangshan

"九二共识" the 1992 Consensus

"九项工程" Nine Programs (the medical and health program; the poverty reduction and agricultural development program; the trade promotion program; the investment promotion program; the digital innovation program; the green development program; the capacity building program; the cultural and people-to-people exchange program; and the peace and security program)

绝对贫困 absolute poverty

《觉醒年代》 The Age of Awakening

K

开放型世界经济 an open world economy

开展立法工作 conduct legislative work

抗洪精神 the spirit forged in battles against floods

抗击新冠肺炎疫情 the fight against Covid-19

抗美援朝精神 the spirit of the War to Resist US Aggression and Aid Korea

抗美援朝战争 the War to Resist US Aggression and Aid Korea

抗日民族统一战线 national united front against Japanese aggression

抗日战争 War of Resistance Against Japanese Aggression

抗疫精神 the spirit of the fight against Covid-19

抗震救灾精神 the spirit forged in battles against earthquakes

科技创新 scientific and technological innovation

科技革命 revolution in science and technology

科技自立自强 self-reliance in science and technology

科教兴国战略 the strategy of invigorating China through science and education

科学发展观 the Scientific Outlook on Development

可持续发展 sustainable development

可持续发展议程 the Agenda for Sustainable Development

可控工业生态系统 controllable industrial ecosystems

扩大内需战略 the strategy of expanding domestic demand

L

劳动模范 model workers

冷战思维 a Cold War mindset

理论自信 confidence in our theory

理想信念 ideals and convictions

历史唯物主义 historical materialism

历史虚无主义 historical nihilism

历史周期率 historical cycle of rise and fall

利益共同体 a community of shared interests

联合国安理会 UN Security Council

联合国2030年可持续发展议程 the UN 2030 Agenda for Sustainable Development

联合国千年发展目标 the UN Millennium Development Goals

《联合国宪章》 the UN Charter

《联合国宪章》的宗旨和原则 the purposes and principles of the UN Charter

粮食安全 food security

"两不愁三保障" Their basic food and clothing needs have been guaranteed, and their access to compulsory education, basic medical services, and safe housing and drinking water has been ensured.

两大奇迹 two miracles (rapid economic growth and lasting social stability)

"两弹一星"精神 the spirit of "Two Bombs, One Satellite"

"两高"项目 energy-intensive and high-emission project

"两个毫不动摇" consolidate and develop the public sector, and at the same time encourage, support and guide the development of the non-public sector

"两个维护" the Two Upholds

"两个一百年"奋斗目标 the Two Centenary Goals

临床救治 clinical treatment

"六保" "Six Priorities"

六届七中全会 the Seventh Plenary Session of the Sixth CPC Central Committee

六届四中全会 the Fourth Plenary Session of the Sixth CPC Central Committee

"六稳" stabilize employment, finance, foreign trade, inbound investment, domestic investment and market expectations

鲁班工坊 Luban Workshops

绿色低碳发展 green and low-carbon development

绿色低碳技术评估 green and low-carbon technology assessment

绿色发展体系 green development system

绿色发展、循环发展、低碳发展 green, circular, and low-carbon development

绿色金融 green finance

绿水青山就是金山银山。Lucid waters and lush mountains are invaluable assets.

M

马克思列宁主义 Marxism-Leninism

马克思主义基本原则 the basic tenets of Marxism

马克思主义路线 Marxist line

马克思主义人权观 Marxist perspective on human rights

马克思主义信念 convictions in Marxism

马克思主义政治经济学 Marxist political economics

马克思主义执政党 Marxist governing party

马克思主义中国化时代化 adapt Marxism to the Chinese context and the needs of our times

马克思主义宗教观 Marxist view on religion

毛泽东思想 Mao Zedong Thought

茂物目标 Bogor Goals

《民法典》the Civil Code

民间外交 people-to-people diplomacy

民生福祉 the wellbeing of the people

民事法律制度 civil legal instruments

民营企业 private enterprises/businesses

民主集中制 democratic centralism

民主监督 democratic oversight

民族地区 areas with large ethnic minority population

民族复兴的中国梦 the Chinese Dream of national rejuvenation

民族区域自治 regional ethnic autonomy

民族区域自治制度 the system of regional ethnic autonomy

民族认同感 the sense of national identity

N

南北差距 North-South gap

南北对话 North-South dialogue
南昌起义 the Nanchang Uprising
南南合作 South-South cooperation
逆全球化 deglobalization
农民工 rural migrant workers
农业、农村地区和农村人口 agriculture, rural areas and rural people
农业现代化 agricultural modernization
女排精神 the spirit of the Chinese national women's volleyball team

O

欧亚经济联盟 Eurasian Economic Union

P

批评和自我批评 criticism and self-criticism
贫困地区 impoverished areas
乒乓外交 ping-pong diplomacy
平安中国 Peaceful China Initiative

Q

"七个有之"（七大歪风邪气）Seven Malpractices
"七一勋章" July 1 Medal
企业家精神 the spirit of entrepreneurship
前所未见之大变局 change on a scale unseen
强军哲学 philosophy on strengthening the military
强权政治 power politics
侨胞 overseas Chinese
亲诚惠容理念 the principle of amity, sincerity, mutual benefit and inclusiveness
庆祝中国共产党成立100周年大会 the Ceremony Marking the Centenary of the Communists Party of China
区块链 blockchain
《区域全面经济伙伴关系协定》Regional Comprehensive Economic Partnership (RCEP)

区域协调发展 coordinated development among regions
区域协调发展战略 the strategy of coordinated regional development
去产能、去库存、去杠杆、降成本、补短板（三去一降一补）cutting overcapacity, reducing excess inventory, deleveraging, lowering costs, and strengthening areas of weakness
全国各族人民 the Chinese people of all ethnic groups
全国工商联 the All-China Federation of Industry and Commerce
全国教育大会 National Education Conference
全国人大常委会 the Standing Committee of the National People's Congress (NPC)
全国人民代表大会 National People's Congress (NPC)
全国人民代表大会及其常务委员会 NPC and its Standing Committee
全国生态环境保护大会 National Conference on Eco-environmental Protection
全过程人民民主 whole-process people's democracy
全面从严治党 exercise full and rigorous self-governance of the Party; strict Party self-governance
全面开放体系 a system for opening up on all fronts
全面建成小康社会 the building of a moderately prosperous society in all respects
全面建设社会主义现代化国家 build a modern socialist country in all respects
全面深化改革开放 deepen reform and opening up across the board
全面乡村振兴 comprehensive rural revitalization
全面小康 moderate prosperity in all respects
全面依法治国 advance law-based governance in the whole country/in all respects
全球安全治理体系 global security governance system
全球产业链供应链 global industrial and supply chains
全球发展倡议 Global Development Initiative
全球发展命运共同体 global community of shared development
全球公共卫生治理 global public health governance
全球环境治理 global environmental governance
全球伙伴关系 global partnership
全球健康峰会 Global Health Summit
全球经济治理 global economic governance
《全球数据安全倡议》Global Initiative on Data Security

全球治理 global governance
全人类共同价值 common values of humanity
全心全意为人民服务 serve the people wholeheartedly
群团组织 people's organization
群众路线 mass line

R

人才强国 a talent-strong country
人大常委会 Standing Committee of the People's Congress
人的全面发展 well-rounded human development
人类命运共同体 a global community of shared future; a community of shared future for mankind
人类卫生健康共同体 a global community of health for all
人类文明新形态 new model for human progress
人民代表大会 the People's Congress
人民代表大会制度 the people's congress system
人民当家作主 people's position/status as masters of the country
人民对美好生活的向往 people's aspirations for a better life
人民民主 people's democracy
人民民主专政 people's democratic dictatorship
人民团体 people's organization
人民至上、生命至上 put the people and their lives front and center
人权 human rights
人与自然和谐共处 harmonious coexistence between humanity and nature; harmony between humanity and nature
儒家文化 Confucian culture

S

"三步走"战略 a three-step strategic plan
"三大法宝" three principal magic weapons
三大攻坚战 three critical battles; three tough battles
"三个代表"重要思想 the Theory of Three Represents

"三股势力" terrorism, separatism, extremism

"三农"问题 problems related to agriculture, rural areas, and rural people

"三期叠加" a shift in the growth rate, a painful structural adjustment, and a need to absorb the fallout of previous stimulus policies

"三医联动" reforms in medical treatment, medical insurance, and medicine supply

扫黑除恶 the fight against criminal gangs and organized crime

上海合作组织 Shanghai Cooperation Organization (SCO)

上海合作组织命运共同体 SCO community of shared future

上海精神 Shanghai Spirit

少数民族地区 ethnic minority areas

社保体系 social security system

社会保障 social security

社会发展和远景目标 social development and long range objectives

社会公平正义 social fairness and justice; social equity and justice

社会文明 civilized social conduct

社会稳定 social stability

社会愿景 community vision

社会治理 social governance

社会主义初级阶段 the primary stage of socialism

社会主义法制 socialist legal system

社会主义法治 socialist rule of law

社会主义核心价值观 core socialist values

社会主义基本经济制度 the basic socialist economic system

社会主义民主政治 socialist democracy

社会主义先进文化 advanced socialist culture

社会主义现代化 socialist modernization

社会主义现代化强国 a great modern socialist country

社会主义市场经济 socialist market economy

生态保护 eco-environmental protection

生态保护红线 red lines for ecological conservation

生态工业 eco-industries

生态红线 ecological red lines

生态环境 eco-environment

生态文明建设 build an eco-civilization

生态文明理念 philosophy of ecological civilization

生物安全 biosafety and biosecurity

《生物多样性公约》The Convention on Biological Diversity

十二届全国人大二次会议 the Second Session of the 12th National People's Congress

"十四五"规划 the 14th Five-year Plan

十一届三中全会 the Third Plenary Session of the 11th CPC Central Committee

十月革命 October Revolution

实事求是 seek truth from facts

实体经济 real economy

实现合作共赢 deliver win-win outcomes

实现政治稳定 deliver political stability

实现中华民族的复兴 realize the rejuvenation of the Chinese nation

示范区 demonstration zone

世界反法西斯战争 Global War Against Fascism; the World Anti-Fascist War

世界贸易组织 World Trade Organization (WTO)

《世界人权宣言》Universal Declaration of Human Rights

世界卫生组织 World Health Organization (WHO)

世贸组织的多边贸易体系 multilateral trading system with the WTO

守正创新 uphold fundamental principles and break new ground

数据云计算 data cloud computing

数字产业 digital industry

数字经济 digital economy

数字经济的健康发展 the sound growth of the digital economy

《数字经济发展战略纲要》Outline for the Digital Economy Development Strategy

数字经济与实体经济的融合 integration of the digital economy and the real economy

数字中国 digital China

双控 dual control over the volume and intensity of carbon emissions

"双碳" peak carbon and carbon neutrality

"双一流" Double First-Class; institutions of higher learning that aim to become first-rate universities or develop first-class disciplines

司法公正 judicial justice

丝绸之路经济带 the Silk Road Economic Belt

丝路精神 the Silk Road spirit

"丝路一家亲"行动 Silk Road Community Building Initiative

"四风" Four Malfeasances

"四个全面"战略布局 the Four-pronged Comprehensive Strategy

四个现代化 Four Modernizations

"四个意识" the Four Consciousnesses

"四个自信" the Four-sphere Confidence

四中全会 the Fourth Plenary Session

T

坦赞铁路 Tazara Railway

碳达峰 the peak carbon dioxide emissions

碳达峰十大行动 10 actions for achieving peak carbon dioxide emissions

碳排放 the carbon dioxide emissions

碳中和目标 carbon neutrality goals

《唐律疏议》Tang Code with Commentaries

特别行政区 special administrative region

统筹发展和安全 balance development with security

统筹国内国际两个大局 take a holistic approach to imperatives at home and abroad

统筹疫情防控和经济社会发展 coordinate epidemic response and economic and social development

统一战线 united front

《突发公共卫生事件应急条例》The Regulations on Response to Public Health Emergencies

《突发事件应对法》Emergency Response Law

土地革命战争 Agrarian Revolutionary War

推进祖国统一 promote national reunification

脱贫 poverty alleviation; poverty elimination

脱贫攻坚精神 the spirit of the battle against poverty

脱贫攻坚战 the fight against poverty

W

万隆精神 the Bandung Spirit

网络空间事务委员会 Cyberspace Affairs Commission

《网络强国战略实施纲要》the Outline for Implementing the National Cyber Development Strategy

唯物史观 historical materialism

伟大建党精神 the great spirit of our forerunners in creating the CPC

文化传统 cultural traditions

文化繁荣 cultural prosperity

文化基础设施网络 cultural infrastructure network

文化价值 cultural value

文化认同 cultural identity

文化事业 cultural undertakings

文化遗产 cultural heritage

文化自信 cultural confidence

文明交流互鉴 exchanges and mutual learning among civilizations

稳中求进原则 the general principle of pursuing progress while securing stability

污染防治攻坚战 a tough battle against pollution

无党派人士 prominent individuals without party affiliation

无畏精神 dauntless spirit

五四精神 the May 4th spirit

五四青年节 China's Youth Day

五四运动 the May 4th Movement

"五位一体"总体布局 the Five-sphere Integrated Plan

戊戌变法 Reform Movement of 1898

X

西柏坡精神 the revolutionary spirit of Xibaipo

习近平新时代中国特色社会主义思想 Xi Jinping Thought on Socialism with

Chinese Characteristics for a New Era

现代化经济体系 modern economy/economic system

现代农业 modern agriculture

乡村振兴战略 rural revitalization strategy

香港回归 Hong Kong's return to China

小康社会 a moderately prosperous society

辛亥革命 Revolution of 1911

新发展格局 the new development dynamic

新发展阶段 the new development stage

新发展理念 the new development philosophy

新冠肺炎疫情 Covid-19 pandemic

新民主主义革命 the New Democratic Revolution

新时代党的强军思想 the Party's philosophy on strengthening the military for the new era

新时代党的组织路线 the Party's organizational guideline for the new era

新时代军事战略 military strategy for the new era

新时代中国特色社会主义 socialism with Chinese characteristics for the new era

新时代中国特色社会主义法治思想 the thought on rule of law of socialism with Chinese characteristics for the new era

新时代中国特色社会主义外交思想 the thought on foreign affairs of socialism with Chinese characteristics for the new era

新文化运动 the New Culture Movement

新型大国关系 a new model of major-country relationship

新型工业化 a new type of industrialization

新型国际关系 a new model/type of international relations

新一轮科技革命和产业变革 a new round of revolution in science technology and industry

新一轮农村改革 a new round of rural reform

形式主义 favoring form over substance

学习型社会 a learning society

Y

鸦片战争　the Opium War

亚太经合组织　Asia-Pacific Economic Cooperation (APEC)

亚太命运共同体　Asia-Pacific community of shared future

亚洲金融危机　the Asian financial crisis

延安精神　the revolutionary spirit of Yan'an

炎黄子孙　descendants of Yan and Huang

"一带一路"　"Belt and Road"

"一带一路"倡议　"Belt and Road" Initiative

一个中国原则　one-China principle

"一国两制"　"One Country, Two Systems"

医疗服务　care and treatment

以德治国　rule of virtue

以国际法为基础的国际秩序　international order underpinned by international law

以人类和谐共处为特征的现代化　modernization characterized by harmonious coexistence of humanity

以人民为中心的发展思想　the people-centered philosophy of development

义和团运动　Boxer Uprising

义务教育　compulsory education

疫情防控　epidemic response; epidemic prevention and control

意识形态领域　the ideological domain

粤港澳大湾区　the Guangdong-Hong Kong-Macao Greater Bay Area

云计算技术　cloud computing technologies

Z

杂交水稻　hybrid rice

战略伙伴关系　strategic partnership

战略机遇　strategic opportunity

正常情况和紧急情况　both normal circumstances and emergencies

正确党史观　a rational outlook on Party history

政治安全　political security

政治规矩　political discipline and rules

政治局成员 members of the Political Bureau

政治领悟力 political understanding

政治判断力 political acumen

政治文明 political civilization

政治执行力 political capacity to deliver

政治制度 political system

知识产权 intellectual property rights

制定五年计划（五年规划）formulate the Five-year Plan

制度自信 confidence in our system

治国理政 the governance of China

治理能力 capacity for governance

中阿合作论坛 China-Arab States Cooperation Forum

中阿命运共同体 China-Arab community of shared future

中等收入群体 the middle-income group

《中非合作2035年愿景》China-Africa Cooperation Vision 2035

中非合作论坛 Forum on China-Africa Cooperation (FOCAC)

中非命运共同体 China-Africa community of shared future

中共中央委员会 the CPC Central Committee

中共中央政治局 the Political Bureau of the CPC Central Committee

中共中央政治局常务委员会 the Standing Committee of the Political Bureau of the CPC Central Committee

中国-东盟命运共同体 China-ASEAN community of shared future

中国-东盟全面战略伙伴关系 China-ASEAN comprehensive strategic partnership

中国-东盟自由贸易区 China-ASEAN Free Trade Area

中国方案 Chinese approach

中国高铁 China Railway High-speed (CRH); China's high-speed railway

中国工人运动 Chinese workers' movement

中国共产党 the Communist Party of China (the CPC)

中国共产党第二十次全国代表大会 the 20th CPC National Congress

中国共产党全国代表大会 the CPC National Congress

中国共产党人 Chinese Communists

中国国际进口博览会 China International Import Expo

中国精神 Chinese spirit

中国力量 Chinese strength

中国梦 Chinese Dream

中国人民解放军 the People's Liberation Army (PLA)

中国人民解放军百年目标 centenary goal of the People's Liberation Army

中国人民志愿军 Chinese People's Volunteers (CPV)

中国人权发展道路 Chinese path of human rights protection

中国（上海）自由贸易试验区 China (Shanghai) Pilot Free Trade Zone

中国少年先锋队 the Chinese Young Pioneers

中国式现代化 the Chinese path to modernization

中国特色大国外交 major-country diplomacy with Chinese characteristics

中国特色减贫道路 Chinese path to poverty reduction

中国特色社会主义法治 socialist rule of law with Chinese characteristics

中国特色社会主义理论体系 the system of theories of socialism with Chinese characteristics

中国特色社会主义伟大事业 the great cause of socialism with Chinese characteristics

中国天眼 the "China Sky Eye"

中华人民共和国 the People's Republic of China

《中华人民共和国宪法》 Constitution of the People's Republic of China

中华文化价值 Chinese cultural values

中华文明 Chinese civilization

中小微企业 micro, small and medium-sized enterprises

中央八项规定 the Central Committee's eight-point decision

中央财经领导小组 Central Leading Group for Financial and Economic Affairs

中央纪委 the Central Commission for Discipline Inspection

中央经济工作会议 the Central Economic Work Conference

中央军委 the Central Military Commission

中央全面深化改革委员会 the Central Commission for Comprehensively Deepening Reform

中央全面依法治国委员会 the Central Commission for Law-based Governance

中央调剂制度 central regulatory system

中央外事工作委员会 the Central Commission for Foreign Affairs

中央网络安全和信息化委员会 the Central Cyberspace Affairs Commission

中央委员会和中央军事委员会 the Central Committee and the Central Military Commission

中央预算 central government budgets

中央政治局常务委员会 the Standing Committee of the Political Bureau

重要战略机遇期 important period of strategic opportunity

珠江三角洲 the Pearl River Delta

诸子百家 Hundred Schools of Thought

自我革命 self-reform

自我净化、自我完善、自我革新、自我提高 self-purification, self-perfection, self-renewal and self-progression

自由贸易区 free trade area/zone

自由贸易试验区 pilot free trade zones

总体观 a holistic approach

总体国家安全观 a holistic approach to national security

祖国内地/大陆 the Chinese mainland

最高人民法院 Supreme People's Court

最高人民检察院 Supreme People's Procuratorate

遵义会议精神 the revolutionary spirit of the Zunyi Meeting

附录2　习近平金句

B

百年奋斗历史告诉我们，团结就是力量，奋斗开创未来；能团结奋斗的民族才有前途，能团结奋斗的政党才能立于不败之地。The Party's century-long history has shown that unity means strength and that hard work leads to a bright future. Unity of effort is what a nation relies on to build its future and what a political party counts on to remain resolute.

百年奋斗历史还告诉我们，围绕明确奋斗目标形成的团结才是最牢固的团结，依靠紧密团结进行的奋斗才是最有力的奋斗。Our century-long history has also revealed that unity under a clear goal is the strongest and that endeavor based on complete unity is the most powerful.

办好中国的事情，关键在党。China's success hinges on the Party.

保护生物多样性有助于维护地球家园，促进人类可持续发展。Protecting biodiversity helps protect the earth, our common homeland, and contributes to humanity's sustainable development.

必须促进各民族广泛交往交流交融，促进各民族在理想、信念、情感、文化上的团结统一，守望相助、手足情深。We must promote interactions, exchanges and integration among all ethnic groups, and reinforce their affinity and unity in terms of ideals, convictions, mindset and culture, so that they will support each other like brothers and sisters.

必须高举中华民族大团结旗帜，促进各民族在中华民族大家庭中像石榴籽一样紧紧抱在一起。We must uphold the unity of the Chinese nation and ensure all ethnic groups remain closely united like the seeds of a pomegranate.

必须更好发挥法治固根本、稳预期、利长远的保障作用，在法治轨道上全面建设社会主义现代化国家。We must give better play to the role of the rule of law in consolidating foundations, ensuring stable expectations, and delivering long-term benefits, and we must strive to build a modern socialist country in all respects under the rule of law.

必须构筑中华民族共有精神家园，使各民族人心归聚、精神相依，形成人心凝聚、团结奋进的强大精神纽带。We must build a cultural home shared by the Chinese nation, creating a strong bond among all ethnic groups and inspiring them to move forward in unity and interdependence.

必须坚持党对民族工作的领导，提升解决民族问题、做好民族工作的能力和水平。We must uphold the Party's leadership over work related to ethnic affairs, and increase our ability and performance in handling ethnic affairs.

必须坚持各民族一律平等，保证各民族共同当家作主、参与国家事务管理，保障各族群众合法权益。We must uphold the equality of all ethnic groups, and see to it that they are the masters of the country and participate in the management of state affairs, and that their legitimate rights and interests are protected.

必须坚持依法治理民族事务，推进民族事务治理体系和治理能力现代化。We must manage ethnic affairs in accordance with the law and actively modernize our system and capacity for handling ethnic affairs.

必须坚决维护国家主权、安全、发展利益，教育引导各民族继承和发扬爱国主义传统，自觉维护祖国统一、国家安全、社会稳定。We must resolutely safeguard our national sovereignty, security, and development interests, and encourage, through education and guidance, all ethnic groups to carry forward the patriotic tradition and consciously safeguard the unity of the country, national security and social stability.

必须牢固树立和践行绿水青山就是金山银山的理念，站在人与自然和谐共生的高度谋划发展。We must uphold and act on the principle that lucid waters and lush mountains are invaluable assets, and we must remember to maintain harmony between humanity and nature when planning our development.

必须强调的是，新时代新阶段的发展必须贯彻新发展理念，必须是高质量发展。It should be emphasized that during the new era and at the new stage we must follow the new development philosophy and ensure high-quality growth.

不断造福人民。Constantly work for the benefit of the people.

不论谁在党纪国法上出问题，党纪国法决不饶恕。There will be zero tolerance for anyone who violates Party discipline and the law.

C

长江经济带经济发展总体平稳、结构优化，人民生活水平显著提高，实现了在发展中保护、在保护中发展。The YREB region has generally enjoyed steady economic growth under an optimized structure. Local living standards have significantly improved, and economic growth has been achieved together with improvements in environmental protection.

城乡经济循环是国内大循环的题中应有之义，也是确保国内国际双循环比例关系健康的关键因素。The economic flow between urban and rural areas is an inherent part of the domestic economy, and is also key to ensuring a healthy balance between the domestic economy and international engagement in the double development dynamic.

创新是推动经济社会发展、应对人类共同挑战的决定性因素。Innovation is a decisive factor in economic and social development and in addressing common challenges to humanity.

从历史依据来看，新发展阶段是我们党带领人民迎来从站起来、富起来到强起来历史性跨越的新阶段。From a historical standpoint, this new stage will see our Party lead the people in completing the historic transformation from standing up and becoming better off to growing in strength.

从现在起，中国共产党的中心任务就是团结带领全国各族人民全面建成社会主义现代化强国、实现第二个百年奋斗目标，以中国式现代化全面推进中华民族伟大复兴。From this day forward, the central task of the Communist Party of China will be to lead the Chinese people of all ethnic groups in a concerted effort to realize the Second Centenary Goal of building China into a great modern socialist country in all respects and to advance the rejuvenation of the Chinese nation on all fronts through a Chinese path to modernization.

D

大家来自基层和生产一线，代表各行各业，要坚定理想信念，注重学习提升，矢志艰苦奋斗，从一点一滴做起，把小事当大事干，踏踏实实把正在做的事情做好，靠勤劳双手成就属于自己的人生精彩，共同创造我们的幸福生活和美好未来。All of you are from the grassroots or the front line, and you represent various sectors and industries. You should have firm ideals and convictions, and study hard to improve yourselves. You should work hard in a pragmatic manner, taking one step at a time and handling every piece of work, big or small, with the utmost care and attention. I believe you will experience greater fulfillment in life through hard work, and together we will create a happy life and bright future for all.

当代中国正在经历人类历史上最为宏大而独特的实践创新，改革发展稳定任务之重、矛盾风险挑战之多、治国理政考验之大都前所未有，世界百年未有之大变局深刻变化前所未有，提出了大量亟待回答的理论和实践课题。What contemporary China is experiencing is an innovative social transformation unique in history. In this context, the magnitude of our tasks to advance reform and development and to maintain stability, the multitude of problems, risks, and challenges we face, and the difficulties involved in the governance of the country are all unprecedented. As the world experiences change on a scale unseen in a century, a plethora of questions need to be answered in theory and in practice.

当今世界正经历百年未有之大变局。The world today is undergoing change on a scale unseen in a century.

党的百年奋斗历程告诉我们，党和人民事业能不能沿着正确方向前进，取决于我们能否准确认识和把握社会主要矛盾、确定中心任务。什么时候社会主要矛盾和中心任务判断准确，党和人民事业就顺利发展，否则党和人民事业就会遭受挫折。The Party's history over the past century tells us that for the cause of the Party and the people to progress, we must have a thorough understanding of the principal challenge facing our society and properly identify our central task. Only when this is done can the cause of the Party and the people progress smoothly. Otherwise our cause will suffer setbacks.

党的百年奋斗史，贯穿着党团结带领人民为争取人权、尊重人权、保障人权、发展人权而进行的不懈努力。Throughout its century-old history, the CPC has led the people in a tireless effort to realize, respect, protect and develop human rights.

党的团结统一是党的生命，善于在总结历史中统一思想、统一行动，是我们党的成功经验。党的团结统一首先是政治上的团结统一。Unity is the lifeline of our Party. Our Party is experienced in unifying thinking and taking concerted action through reviewing history. This unity is, first and foremost, political unity.

党用伟大奋斗创造了百年伟业，也一定能用新的伟大奋斗创造新的伟业。The Party has made spectacular achievements through its great endeavors over the past century, and our new endeavors will surely lead to more spectacular achievements.

党中央权威是危难时刻全党全国各族人民迎难而上的根本依靠。The authority of the CPC Central Committee is the fundamental guarantee for the whole Party and all the people in overcoming difficulties at critical moments.

对困难和挑战、阻力和变数，我们既不能遮掩回避、视而不见，也不能惊慌失措、乱了阵脚。Whatever the difficulties, challenges, obstacles and changes, we shall never cover them up, avoid them, turn a blind eye to them, panic, or become confused.

E

二十国集团要共担数字时代的责任，加快新型数字基础设施建设，促进数字技术同实体经济深度融合，帮助发展中国家消除"数字鸿沟"。The G20 should shoulder its responsibilities in the digital era, accelerate the development of new types of digital infrastructure, promote deeper integration of digital technologies with the real economy, and help developing countries eliminate the digital divide.

二十国集团应该合力挖掘创新增长潜力，在充分参与、广泛共识基础上制定规则，为创新驱动发展营造良好生态。The G20 should join forces to unleash the potential for innovation-driven growth and draw up rules based on extensive participation and broad-based consensus to foster an enabling environment for innovation-driven development.

F

腐败是危害党的生命力和战斗力的最大毒瘤，反腐败是最彻底的自我革命。只要存在腐败问题产生的土壤和条件，反腐败斗争就一刻不能停，必须永远吹冲锋号。Corruption is a cancer to the vitality and ability of the Party, and fighting corruption is the most thorough kind of self-reform there is. As long as the breeding grounds and conditions for corruption still exist, we must keep sounding the bugle and never rest, not even for a minute, in our fight against corruption.

G

敢于斗争、敢于胜利，是中国共产党不可战胜的强大精神力量。Having the courage to fight and the fortitude to win is what has made our Party invincible.

敢于斗争是我们党的鲜明品格。我们党依靠斗争走到今天，也必然要依靠斗争赢得未来。Being ready for the fray is a distinctive quality of our Party. It is through struggle that our Party has developed to its present state, and that is what will create a bright future.

高质量发展是全面建设社会主义现代化国家的首要任务。To build a modern socialist country in all respects, we must, first and foremost, pursue high-quality development.

共产党就是给人民办事的，就是要让人民的生活一天天好起来，一年比一年过得好。Our Party's mission is to serve the people and to improve their lives.

共同富裕是社会主义的本质要求，是人民群众的共同期盼。我们推动经济社会发展，归根结底是要实现全体人民共同富裕。As an essential requirement of socialism and a shared aspiration of the people, common prosperity is our ultimate goal in social and economic development.

共同富裕是中国特色社会主义的本质要求。Common prosperity is an essential requirement of socialism with Chinese characteristics.

构建开放创新生态，参与全球科技治理。We should build an open innovation ecosystem and participate in global science and technology governance.

构建新发展格局的关键在于经济循环的畅通无阻，就像人们讲的要调理好统摄全身阴阳气血的任督二脉。The key to building a new development dynamic is to ensure unimpeded economic flow, as is the case in traditional Chinese medicine, one must remove blockages to stimulate the free flow of vital energy and maintain the body's balance.

构建新发展格局是把握发展主动权的先手棋，不是被迫之举和权宜之计。Creating the new development dynamic is neither a passive response to pressure nor a stopgap measure, but a proactive move aiming to seize the initiative in development.

构建新发展格局最本质的特征是实现高水平的自立自强。The essence of the new development dynamic is realizing a high level of self-reliance.

广大人民群众识大体、顾大局，自觉配合疫情防控斗争大局，形成了疫情防控的基础性力量。Considering the national interest and the general situation, the people have consciously subordinated their own needs to the overall interests of epidemic control, becoming the fundamental force in the battle.

广大人民群众众志成城、守望相助，特别是武汉人民和湖北人民识大体顾大局、自觉配合疫情防控工作，展现了坚忍不拔的顽强斗志。Our people have stood together in solidarity. The people of Wuhan and other parts of Hubei, in particular, put the greater interests of the country in the first place and have shown unmatched perseverance and tenacity in their support for epidemic control.

广大医务工作者义无反顾、日夜奋战，展现了救死扶伤、医者仁心的崇高精神。Our health workers have proved their dedication to their profession, shouldering this daunting mission and working around the clock to save lives.

国家统一、民族复兴的历史车轮滚滚向前，祖国完全统一一定要实现，也一定能够实现！The wheels of history are rolling on toward China's reunification and the rejuvenation of the Chinese nation. Complete reunification of our country must be realized, and it can, without doubt, be realized!

H

好的方针政策和发展规划都应该顺应人民意愿、符合人民所思所盼，从群众中来、到群众中去。Sound guidelines, policies and development plans must accord with the will, aspirations and expectations of the people. They should come from the people and serve their interests.

和平、发展、公平、正义、民主、自由是全人类的共同价值，是中非双方孜孜以求的共同目标。Peace, development, equity, justice, democracy and freedom are common values of humanity and represent the abiding aspirations of both China and Africa.

和平是我们最大的共同利益，也是各国人民最大的共同期盼。Maintaining peace is our greatest common interest and the most cherished aspiration of people of all countries.

和平与发展是我们的共同事业，公平正义是我们的共同理想，民主自由是我们的共同追求。Peace and development are our common cause, equity and justice our common aspiration, and democracy and freedom our common goal.

回顾党的百年奋斗历程，坚持党指挥枪、建设自己的人民军队，是党在血与火的斗争中得出的重大结论。Through a century of struggle, the Party has reached a key conclusion – that the Party must command the gun and build up the people's armed forces. This is a conclusion drawn from the war of blood and fire during the revolutionary years.

回顾党的百年历程，党的民族工作取得的最大成就，就是走出了一条中国特色解决民族问题的正确道路。The history of our Party shows that our greatest achievement in ethnic work is that we have adopted a Chinese approach to ethnic issues.

J

基础不牢，地动山摇。只有把基层党组织建设强、把基层政权巩固好，中国特色社会主义的根基才能稳固。If the foundation is not solid, the building trembles. Only with strong Party organizations and governments at the grassroots level can the foundations of Chinese socialism be solid.

激发各类人才创新活力，建设全球人才高地。We should foster innovation vitality in talented people from all fields, and build China into a global leader in terms of talent resources.

既不能对不同地区采取"一刀切"的做法、阻碍经济社会秩序恢复，又不能不当放松防控、导致前功尽弃。A one-size-fits-all approach for different places will impede the restoration of economic and social order. However, relaxing controls indiscriminately will only put all our gains at risk.

加强生物安全建设是一项长期而艰巨的任务，需要持续用力、扎实推进。Strengthening our biosecurity management will be a long and arduous task requiring constant and concrete efforts.

加强原创性、引领性科技攻关，坚决打赢关键核心技术攻坚战。We should devote more effort to original and pioneering research and make breakthroughs in core technologies in key fields.

坚持党对人民军队绝对领导，朝着党指引的方向奋勇前进，人民军队就能不断发展壮大，党和人民事业就有了坚强力量支撑。As long as the people's armed forces progress under the absolute leadership of the Party, they will continue to grow in strength and provide firm support for the undertakings of our Party and our people.

坚持和完善人民代表大会制度，是全党全社会的共同责任。Upholding and improving the people's congress system is the common responsibility of the whole of the Party and society.

坚持人民至上。Always put the people first.

坚持尊重各国主权、领土完整，不干涉别国内政，尊重各国人民自主选择的发展道路和社会制度。We should respect the sovereignty and territorial integrity of all countries, oppose interference in internal affairs, and recognize the independent choice of development paths and social systems made by peoples of different countries.

坚守中华文化立场，提炼展示中华文明的精神标识和文化精髓，加快构建中国话语和中国叙事体系，讲好中国故事、传播好中国声音，展现可信、可爱、可敬的中国形象。We will stay firmly rooted in Chinese culture. We will collect and refine the defining symbols and best elements of Chinese culture and showcase them to the world. We will accelerate the development of China's discourse and narrative systems, better tell China's stories, make China's voice heard, and present a China that is credible, appealing, and respectable.

江山就是人民、人民就是江山，打江山、守江山，守的是人民的心。The country is the people and the people are the country. As we have fought to establish and consolidate our leadership over the country, we have in fact been fighting to earn and keep the people's support.

教育、科技、人才是全面建设社会主义现代化国家的基础性、战略性支撑。Education, science and technology, and human resources are the foundational and strategic pillars for building a modern socialist country in all respects.

解决台湾问题是中国人自己的事，要由中国人来决定。Resolving the Taiwan question is a matter for the Chinese, a matter that must be resolved by the Chinese.

紧紧依靠人民。Rely on the people.

经过不懈努力,党找到了自我革命这一跳出治乱兴衰历史周期率的第二个答案,自我净化、自我完善、自我革新、自我提高能力显著增强,管党治党宽松软状况得到根本扭转,风清气正的党内政治生态不断形成和发展,确保党永远不变质、不变色、不变味。Through painstaking efforts, the Party has found a second answer to the question of how to escape the historical cycle of rise and fall. The answer is self-reform. We have significantly boosted the Party's ability to purify, improve, renew, and excel itself, addressed the problem of lax and weak self-governance in Party organizations at the root, and steadily fostered and developed a political atmosphere of integrity within the Party. By doing so, we have ensured that the Party will never change its nature, its conviction, or its character.

经济全球化背景下，各国经济彼此依存，利益交融前所未有，以诚相待、普惠共享是根本之计。In this age of economic globalization, countries share a new level of economic interdependency and interlinked interests. To treat each other with sincerity and pursue shared benefits holds the key to state-to-state relations in today's world.

K

科学社会主义在二十一世纪的中国焕发出新的蓬勃生机，中国式现代化为人类实现现代化提供了新的选择，中国共产党和中国人民为解决人类面临的共同问题提供更多更好的中国智慧、中国方案、中国力量，为人类和平与发展崇高事业作出新的更大的贡献！Scientific socialism is brimming with renewed vitality in 21st-century China. Chinese modernization offers humanity a new choice for achieving modernization. The Communist Party of China and the Chinese people have provided humanity with more Chinese insight, better Chinese input, and greater Chinese strength to help solve its common challenges and have made new and greater contributions to the noble cause of human peace and development.

苦难铸就辉煌。没有一个国家、民族的现代化是顺顺当当实现的。Glory comes from adversity. No country or nation can achieve modernization easily.

L

牢牢植根人民。Take root in the people.

理想信念是中国共产党人的精神支柱和政治灵魂，也是保持党的团结统一的思想基础。As the source of strength and political soul of China's Communists, the ideals and convictions are the ideological basis for maintaining the Party's solidarity and unity.

历史车轮滚滚向前，时代潮流浩浩荡荡。历史只会眷顾坚定者、奋进者、搏击者，而不会等待犹豫者、懈怠者、畏难者。The wheels of history roll on; the tides of the times are vast and mighty. History looks kindly on those with resolve, with drive and ambition, and with plenty of guts; it does not wait for the hesitant, the apathetic, or those shy of a challenge.

历史告诉我们，和平发展、公平正义、合作共赢才是人间正道。History tells us that peaceful development, fairness and justice, and win-win cooperation are the right way forward for humanity.

历史告诉我们，拥抱世界，才能拥抱明天；携手共进，才能行稳致远。As history has taught us, we can only embrace the future when we embrace the world, and we can only travel safe and far when we walk together.

历史和现实都告诉我们，农为邦本，本固邦宁。History and our experience show that only when agriculture is stable can a country enjoy peace.

历史和现实都证明，中国共产党是始终保持青春特质的党，是永远值得青年人信赖和追随的党。Both history and our experience show that the CPC is a political party that has always maintained its youthful energy, a party that is worthy of young people's trust, and a party that is worth following.

历史总在不断前进，世界回不到从前。我们今天所作的每一个抉择、采取的每一项行动，都将决定世界的未来。Time moves on, and the world will not go back to what it was. Every choice and move we make today will shape the world of the future.

绿水青山就是金山银山。Lucid waters and lush mountains are invaluable assets.

M

马克思主义是我们立党立国的根本指导思想，是我们党的灵魂和旗帜。Marxism is the fundamental ideology upon which our Party and country are founded; it is the very soul of our Party and the banner under which it strives.

面对复杂形势、复杂矛盾、繁重任务，没有主次，不加区别，眉毛胡子一把抓，是做不好工作的。When dealing with complex situations and difficult problems, or tasked with a demanding workload, no one will do well by trying to attend to major and minor issues at one and the same time.

面对快速变化的世界和中国，如果墨守成规、思想僵化，没有理论创新的勇气，不能科学回答中国之问、世界之问、人民之问、时代之问，不仅党和国家事业无法继续前进，马克思主义也会失去生命力、说服力。In a fast-changing world and a fast-growing country, we cannot be fettered to old conventions and rigid thinking, and we must be bold enough to update our theory. If we cannot answer questions concerning the present and future of China and its people and the wider world, we will lose momentum in advancing the cause of the Party and the country, Marxism will wither, and people will lose faith in it.

面对这些影响党长期执政、国家长治久安、人民幸福安康的突出矛盾和问题，党中央审时度势、果敢抉择，锐意进取、攻坚克难，团结带领全党全军全国各族人民撸起袖子加油干、风雨无阻向前行，义无反顾进行具有许多新的历史特点的伟大斗争。In the face of these acute problems and challenges, which undermined the Party's long-term governance, the security and stability of the country, and the wellbeing of the people, the Party Central Committee fully assessed the situation, made resolute decisions, and took firm steps. Under its leadership, the entire Party, the military, and the Chinese people were brought together. We rolled up our sleeves and got down to work, forging ahead with resolve to carry out a great struggle with many new features of our times.

民法典要实施好，就必须让民法典走到群众身边、走进群众心里。To implement the Civil Code properly, we must ensure it is widely understood and well received by the public.

民之所忧，我必念之；民之所盼，我必行之。The people's concerns are my concerns, and the people's expectations are my goals.

民主不是装饰品，不是用来做摆设的，而是要用来解决人民需要解决的问题的。Democracy is not an ornament to be put on display, but an instrument for addressing the issues that concern the people.

民主是各国人民的权利，而不是少数国家的专利。Democracy is the right of the people of all countries, not the prerogative of a few nations.

民主是全人类的共同价值，是中国共产党和中国人民始终不渝坚持的重要理念。Democracy is a shared human value and an ideal that has always been cherished by the CPC and the Chinese people.

Q

强国必须强军，军强才能国安。A strong country must have strong armed forces, and only strong armed forces can keep the country safe.

强化国家战略科技力量，提升国家创新体系整体效能。We should increase our country's strategic capacity in science and technology and improve the overall efficiency of the national innovation system.

青年兴则国家兴，青年强则国家强。青年一代有理想、有本领、有担当，国家就有前途，民族就有希望。A nation will prosper only when its young people thrive; a country will be full of hope and have a great tomorrow only when its younger generations have ideals, ability, and a strong sense of responsibility.

全党必须牢记，全面从严治党永远在路上，党的自我革命永远在路上，决不能有松劲歇脚、疲劳厌战的情绪，必须持之以恒推进全面从严治党，深入推进新时代党的建设新的伟大工程，以党的自我革命引领社会革命。All of us in the Party must bear in mind that full and rigorous self-governance is an unceasing endeavor and that self-reform is a journey to which there is no end. We must never slacken our efforts and never allow ourselves to become weary or beaten. We must persevere with full and rigorous self-governance, continue to advance the great new project of Party building in the new era, and use our own transformation to steer social transformation.

全党全国各族人民要紧密团结在党中央周围，高举中国特色社会主义伟大旗帜，锐意进取，埋头苦干，为实现推进现代化建设、完成祖国统一、维护世界和平与促进共同发展三大历史任务，为决胜全面建成小康社会、夺取新时代中国特色社会主义伟大胜利、实现中华民族伟大复兴的中国梦、实现人民对美好生活的向往继续奋斗！We, the entire Party and the Chinese people of all ethnic groups, should rally closely around the Party Central Committee, and uphold socialism with Chinese characteristics. We should keep on working with great determination to accomplish the three historic tasks of advancing modernization, realizing China's reunification, and preserving world peace and promoting common development; we should secure a decisive victory in finishing the building of a moderately prosperous society in all respects, strive for the great success of socialism with Chinese characteristics for a new era, realize the Chinese Dream of national rejuvenation, and see that our people realize their aspirations for a better life.

全党全军全国各族人民要紧密团结在党中央周围，牢记空谈误国、实干兴邦，坚定信心、同心同德、埋头苦干、奋勇前进，为全面建设社会主义现代化国家、全面推进中华民族伟大复兴而团结奋斗！Let the whole Party, the entire military, and the Chinese people of all ethnic groups stay closely rallied around the Party Central Committee. Let us keep in mind that empty talk will do nothing for our country; only solid work will make it flourish. Let us maintain firm confidence, unite as one, and forge ahead with resolve. And let us strive in unity to build a modern socialist country in all respects and advance national rejuvenation on all fronts.

全党同志务必不忘初心、牢记使命，务必谦虚谨慎、艰苦奋斗，务必敢于斗争、善于斗争，坚定历史自信，增强历史主动，谱写新时代中国特色社会主义更加绚丽的华章。It is imperative that all of us in the Party never forget our original aspiration and founding mission, that we always stay modest, prudent, and hard-working, and that we have the courage and ability to carry on our fight. We must remain confident in our history, exhibit greater historical initiative, and write an even more magnificent chapter for socialism with Chinese characteristics in the new era.

全党要关心和爱护青年，为他们实现人生出彩搭建舞台。广大青年要坚定理想信念，志存高远，脚踏实地，勇做时代的弄潮儿，在实现中国梦的生动实践中放飞青春梦想，在为人民利益的不懈奋斗中书写人生华章！All of us in the Party should care about young people and set the stage for them to excel. To all our young people, you should have firm ideals and convictions, aim high, and have your feet firmly on the ground. You should ride the waves of your day; and in the course of realizing the Chinese Dream, fulfill your youthful dreams, and write a vivid chapter in your tireless endeavors to serve the interests of the people.

全党一定要保持艰苦奋斗、戒骄戒躁的作风，以时不我待、只争朝夕的精神，奋力走好新时代的长征路。All of us in the Party must work hard and live simply, guard against arrogance and impetuosity; and lose no time in progressing along the long march of the new era.

全党一定要自觉维护党的团结统一，保持党同人民群众的血肉联系，巩固全国各族人民大团结,加强海内外中华儿女大团结,团结一切可以团结的力量,齐心协力走向中华民族伟大复兴的光明前景。We must consciously safeguard the solidarity and unity of the Party, maintain the Party's deep bond with the people, and strengthen the great unity of the Chinese people of all ethnic groups and the great unity of all the sons and daughters of the Chinese nation at home and abroad. We must unite all the forces that can be united and work as one to progress towards the brilliant future of national rejuvenation.

全过程人民民主是社会主义民主政治的本质属性,是最广泛、最真实、最管用的民主。Whole-process people's democracy is the defining feature of socialist democracy; it is democracy in its broadest, most genuine, and most effective form.

全面建成小康社会不是终点,而是新生活、新奋斗的起点。The achievement of moderate prosperity is not the end, but the starting point of a new life and a new round of hard work.

全面建设社会主义现代化国家、全面推进中华民族伟大复兴,关键在党。Our Party has a pivotal role in building China into a modern socialist country in all respects and in advancing the rejuvenation of the Chinese nation on all fronts.

全体中国共产党员!党中央号召你们,牢记初心使命,坚定理想信念,践行党的宗旨,永远保持同人民群众的血肉联系,始终同人民想在一起、干在一起,风雨同舟、同甘共苦,继续为实现人民对美好生活的向往不懈努力,努力为党和人民争取更大光荣!The Central Committee calls on every one of you to stay true to our Party's original aspiration and founding mission and stand firm in your ideals and convictions. Acting on the aims of the Party, you should always maintain close ties with the people, empathize and work with them, stand with them through good times and testing times, and continue working tirelessly to realize their aspirations for a better life and to bring still greater glory to the Party and the people.

R

让大家过上更好生活,我们不能满足于眼前的成绩,还有很长的路要走。To

ensure that everyone leads a better life, we must never rest on what we have achieved, and there is still a long way to go.

让我特别感动的是，在各种急难险重任务和风险挑战面前，广大人民群众总是同心同德、齐心协力、顽强奋战，作出了重大贡献。党和国家事业取得胜利都是人民的胜利！人民是真正的英雄！What impresses me most is that, in the face of urgent and difficult tasks and dangerous and severe challenges, our people have always acted with one heart, united their efforts, and fought tenaciously. They have made a great contribution. These victories of our Party and our country are all victories won by our people, who are the true heroes.

人才是创新的第一资源，人才资源是我国在激烈的国际竞争中的重要力量和显著优势。Talent is the primary driver of innovation. Talented people are a key strength that will enable China to prevail in fierce international competition.

人类面临的所有全球性问题，任何一国想单打独斗都无法解决，必须开展全球行动、全球应对、全球合作。No global problem can be solved by any one country alone. There must be global action, global response and global cooperation.

人类是命运共同体，团结合作是战胜疫情最有力的武器。Humanity shares a common future. Solidarity and cooperation are our most powerful weapons to defeat the virus.

人民民主是社会主义的生命，没有民主就没有社会主义，就没有社会主义的现代化，就没有中华民族伟大复兴。People's democracy is the lifeblood of socialism; without democracy, there would be no socialism, socialist modernization, or national rejuvenation.

人民群众获得感、幸福感、安全感更加充实、更有保障、更可持续，共同富裕取得新成效。We have ensured a more complete and lasting sense of fulfillment, happiness, and security for our people, and we have made further progress in achieving common prosperity for all.

人民是历史的创造者,是真正的英雄。The people are the true heroes, for it is they who write history.

人民是我们党执政的最大底气。The people are our greatest strength in governance.

人民至上、生命至上,保护人民生命安全和身体健康可以不惜一切代价!We act on our belief that the people come first, and life matters most. We are willing to protect people's lives and health at any cost.

人权是历史的、具体的、现实的,不能脱离不同国家的社会政治条件和历史文化传统空谈人权。Human rights are concrete, rooted in history, and based on current realities. We cannot mouth empty words on human rights regardless of the social and political conditions and the historical and cultural traditions of a country.

任何人都不要低估中国人民捍卫国家主权和领土完整的坚强决心、坚定意志、强大能力!No one should underestimate the resolve, the will, and the ability of the Chinese people to defend their national sovereignty and territorial integrity.

任何人任何势力企图通过霸凌手段把他们的意志强加给中国、改变中国的前进方向、阻挠中国人民创造自己美好生活的努力,中国人民都绝不答应!We, the Chinese people, will never allow any force or any person to impose their will on China, change our course forward, or obstruct our efforts to create a better life.

任何想把中国共产党同中国人民分割开来、对立起来的企图,都是绝不会得逞的!9500多万中国共产党人不答应!14亿多中国人民也不答应!Any attempt to divide the Party from the Chinese people or to set the people against the Party is bound to fail. More than 95 million Party members and more than 1.4 billion Chinese people will never allow such a thing to come to pass.

如期实现建军一百年奋斗目标,加快把人民军队建成世界一流军队,是全面建设社会主义现代化国家的战略要求。Achieving the goals for the centenary of the People's Liberation Army in 2027 and more quickly elevating our people's armed forces to world-class standards are strategic tasks for building a modern socialist country in all respects.

S

什么时候都不能忘记一个道理，经济发展和社会保障是水涨船高的关系，水浅行小舟，水深走大船，违背规律就会搁浅或翻船。We must always remember that the economy and social security are like water and a boat – shallow water allows for a small boat, and deeper water allows for a larger boat. If this rule is not respected the boat may be swamped, or run aground.

十年来，我们经历了对党和人民事业具有重大现实意义和深远历史意义的三件大事：一是迎来中国共产党成立一百周年，二是中国特色社会主义进入新时代，三是完成脱贫攻坚、全面建成小康社会的历史任务，实现第一个百年奋斗目标。The past decade marked three major events of great immediate importance and profound historical significance for the cause of the Party and the people: We embraced the centenary of the Communist Party of China; we ushered in a new era of socialism with Chinese characteristics; and we eradicated absolute poverty and finished building a moderately prosperous society in all respects, thus completing the First Centenary Goal.

时代呼唤着我们，人民期待着我们，唯有矢志不渝、笃行不怠，方能不负时代、不负人民。The times are calling us, and the people expect us to deliver. Only by pressing ahead with unwavering commitment and perseverance will we be able to answer the call of our times and meet the expectations of our people.

时与势在我们一边，这是我们定力和底气所在，也是我们的决心和信心所在。The fact that time and momentum are on our side gives us reassurance, resolve and confidence.

实践证明，马克思主义是我们认识世界、把握规律、追求真理、改造世界的强大思想武器，是我们党和国家必须始终遵循的指导思想。Our experience has shown that Marxism offers an inexhaustible theoretical wellspring for us to seek truth, understand the world and its laws, and transform it. Therefore, Marxism must always be the guiding philosophy of the Party and the state.

实践再次证明，只要心里始终装着人民，始终把人民利益放在最高位置，我们就一定能够作出正确决策，并依靠人民战胜一切艰难险阻。Experience has proved once again that we can make correct decisions and overcome all difficulties as long as we put the people at the center of our concerns, regard their interests as the top priority, and always rely on their support.

实现建军一百年奋斗目标，是我军的责任，也是全党全国的责任。Achieving the centenary goal of the armed forces is the shared responsibility of all members of the military, the Party, and the country.

实现中国梦是一场历史接力赛，当代青年要在实现民族复兴的赛道上奋勇争先。Realizing the Chinese Dream of national rejuvenation is a relay race through time, in which you young people should give of your best in running your leg.

实现中华民族伟大复兴，是全体中国人共同的梦想。Realizing the rejuvenation of the Chinese nation is a dream shared by all of us as Chinese.

世界命运握在各国人民手中，人类前途系于各国人民的抉择。中国人民愿同各国人民一道，推动人类命运共同体建设，共同创造人类的美好未来！The future of the world rests in the hands of the people of all countries; the future of humanity hinges on the choices they make. We, the Chinese, are ready to work with the people of all other countries to build a global community of shared future and create a bright tomorrow for all of us.

世界上的问题错综复杂，解决问题的出路是维护和践行多边主义，推动构建人类命运共同体。The problems confronting the world are intricate and complex. Their solutions will come through upholding multilateralism and building a global community of shared future.

世界上既不存在定于一尊的现代化模式，也不存在放之四海而皆准的现代化标准。There is no such a thing as a single authorized model of modernization, nor a universally applicable standard of modernization.

世界上最大的幸福莫过于为人民幸福而奋斗。Working for the good of the public is the greatest joy in the world.

世界是丰富多彩的，多样性是人类文明的魅力所在，更是世界发展的活力和动力之源。Our world is characterized above all by diversity. It is diversity that makes human civilization what it is. It provides us a constant source of vitality and a driving force for world development.

世界正处于大发展大变革大调整时期，和平与发展仍然是时代主题。The world is undergoing major developments, transformation, and adjustment, but peace and development remain the call of our day.

适应人民群众需求变化，努力办好各项民生事业，让老百姓的日子越过越好，是社会主义生产的根本目的。Satisfying the people's changing demands, improving their wellbeing in all respects, and ensuring a better life for all are the ultimate goals of socialist production.

思想就是力量。一个民族要走在时代前列，就一刻不能没有理论思维，一刻不能没有思想指引。Theories and ideas give people power. Theoretical thinking and guidance are pivotal for a nation to be ahead of the times.

T

推动长江经济带发展是党中央作出的重大决策，是关系国家发展全局的重大战略。The YREB represents a major policy decision on the part of the CPC Central Committee. It is an important strategy with a bearing on China's overall development.

推进科技体制改革,形成支持全面创新的基础制度。We should advance the reform of scientific and technological systems and form basic institutions supporting all-round innovation.

脱贫攻坚伟大斗争，锻造形成了"上下同心、尽锐出战、精准务实、开拓创新、攻坚克难、不负人民"的脱贫攻坚精神。Our struggle against poverty has forged such a spirit, through which we have all come together, put our all into the fight, made precise and pragmatic efforts, launched pioneering initiatives, overcome difficulties, and worked hard to live up to the people's expectations.

脱贫摘帽不是终点，而是新生活、新奋斗的起点。Shaking off poverty is not the finish line, but rather the starting point of a new quest and a new endeavor.

W

完善全球环境治理，积极应对气候变化，构建人与自然生命共同体。We need to improve global environmental governance, actively respond to climate change, and create a community of life for humanity and nature.

网络文明是新形势下社会文明的重要内容，是建设网络强国的重要领域。As an important element of civilized social conduct in the new era, a sound cyber culture will contribute to China's growing strength in cyberspace.

唯有主动迎战、坚决斗争才有生路出路，才能赢得尊严、求得发展，逃避退缩、妥协退让只会招致失败和屈辱，只能是死路一条。 Meeting challenges ahead-on is the only way to survive, to develop, and to win dignity. Retreat, compromise or concession will only lead to defeat and humiliation.

伟大的事业必须有坚强的党来领导。只要我们党把自身建设好、建设强，确保党始终同人民想在一起、干在一起，就一定能够引领承载着中国人民伟大梦想的航船破浪前进，胜利驶向光辉的彼岸！A great cause calls for leadership of a strong party. As long as our Party keeps itself competent and strong, always remains true to the people's aspiration and works in concert with the people, we can and will navigate the great ship bearing the great dream of the Chinese people to conquer the waves and reach our destination.

伟大抗疫精神，同中华民族长期形成的特质禀赋和文化基因一脉相承，是爱国主义、集体主义、社会主义精神的传承和发展，是中国精神的生动诠释，丰富了民族精神和时代精神的内涵。The great spirit that we have forged in the battle against Covid-19 is deeply rooted in the character of the Chinese nation and our cultural genes. It carries and builds on patriotism, collectivism, and socialism, and illustrates and enriches the ethos of both our nation and our times.

伟大事业孕育伟大精神，伟大精神引领伟大事业。A great cause breeds a great spirit, and is in turn guided by it.

为了人民而发展，发展才有意义；依靠人民而发展，发展才有动力。Development is meaningful only when it advances the people's interests, and can be sustained only when it is driven by the people.

为了实现中华民族伟大复兴，中国共产党团结带领中国人民，解放思想、锐意进取，创造了改革开放和社会主义现代化建设的伟大成就。To realize national rejuvenation, the Party united the Chinese people and led them in freeing the mind and forging ahead, achieving great success in reform, opening up and socialist modernization.

为了实现中华民族伟大复兴，中国共产党团结带领中国人民，浴血奋战、百折不挠，创造了新民主主义革命的伟大成就。To realize national rejuvenation, the Party united the Chinese people and led them in fighting bloody battles. With unyielding determination, we achieved great success in the New Democratic Revolution (1919-1949).

为了实现中华民族伟大复兴，中国共产党团结带领中国人民，自力更生、发愤图强，创造了社会主义革命和建设的伟大成就。To realize national rejuvenation, the Party united the Chinese people and led them in endeavoring to build a stronger China with a spirit of self-reliance, achieving great success in socialist revolution and construction.

为了实现中华民族伟大复兴，中国共产党团结带领中国人民，自信自强、守正创新，统揽伟大斗争、伟大工程、伟大事业、伟大梦想，创造了新时代中国特色社会主义的伟大成就。To realize national rejuvenation, the Party has united the Chinese people and led them in pursuing a great struggle, a great project, a great cause, and a great dream through a spirit of self-confidence, self-reliance and innovation, achieving great success of socialism with Chinese characteristics in the new era.

稳健的货币政策要更加注重灵活适度，把支持实体经济恢复发展放到更加突出的位置，用好已有金融支持政策，适时出台新的政策措施。A prudent monetary policy should be pursued with greater flexibility as called for, support for the resumption of the operation of the real economy should be strengthened, current financial support policies should be fully used, and new policy measures should be enacted at the right time.

我多次强调，人与自然是生命共同体，人类必须尊重自然、顺应自然、保护自然。I have consistently emphasized that humanity and nature form a community of life. As human beings, we must respect nature, follow its ways, and protect it.

我反复讲，中国人的饭碗任何时候都要牢牢端在自己手中，我们的饭碗应该主要装中国粮。I have consistently emphasized that we in China must always have control over our own food supply and that we should mainly rely on domestic food supplies.

我国社会主义民主是维护人民根本利益的最广泛、最真实、最管用的民主。China's socialist democracy is the most broad-based, genuine and effective democracy that safeguards the fundamental interests of the people.

我国现代化是全体人民共同富裕的现代化。Our modernization aims at common prosperity for everyone.

我国现代化是人口规模巨大的现代化。Our modernization is for a huge population.

我国现代化是人与自然和谐共生的现代化。Our modernization features a harmonious coexistence between humanity and nature.

我国现代化是物质文明和精神文明相协调的现代化。Our modernization balances material and cultural-ethical progress.

我国现代化是走和平发展道路的现代化。Our modernization follows a path of peaceful development.

我呼吁，让我们携起手来，共同佑护各国人民生命和健康，共同佑护人类共同的地球家园，共同构建人类卫生健康共同体！To conclude, I call on all of us to come together and work as one. Let us make a concerted effort to protect the lives and health of all people in all countries. Let us work together to safeguard planet earth, our common home. Let us work together to build a global community of health for all.

我们必须复苏经济，推动实现更加强劲、绿色、健康的全球发展。发展是实现人民幸福的关键。We must revitalize the economy and pursue more robust, greener and more balanced global development. Development holds the key to human wellbeing.

我们必须以越是艰险越向前的精神奋勇搏击、迎难而上。We must maintain our commitment, step up to the fight, and confront these challenges, whatever difficulties may lie ahead.

我们不断发展全过程人民民主，推进人权法治保障，坚决维护社会公平正义，人民享有更加广泛、更加充分、更加全面的民主权利。To ensure that our people enjoy fuller and more extensive democratic rights, we have put in place whole-process people's democracy and legal protection for human rights, and defended social fairness and justice.

我们党来自人民、植根人民、服务人民。Our Party comes from the people, has its

roots among the people, and is dedicated to serving the people.

我们党立志于中华民族千秋伟业，致力于人类和平与发展崇高事业，责任无比重大，使命无上光荣。Our Party has dedicated itself to achieving lasting greatness for the Chinese nation and committed itself to the noble cause of peace and development for humanity. Our responsibility is unmatched in importance, and our mission is glorious beyond compare.

我们党没有自己特殊的利益，党在任何时候都把群众利益放在第一位。The Party has no special interests of its own and it shall, at all times, give top priority to the interests of the people.

我们党在内忧外患中诞生、在历经磨难中成长、在攻坚克难中壮大，锤炼了不畏强敌、不惧风险、敢于斗争、敢于胜利的风骨和品质。Founded amid domestic turmoil and foreign aggression, our Party has been tempered through numerous tribulations, and grown strong by surmounting difficulties. It does not fear powerful enemies or any risk or challenge; it has the courage to fight and the mettle to win.

我们的军队是人民军队，我们的国防是全民国防。我们要加强全民国防教育，巩固军政军民团结，为实现中国梦强军梦凝聚强大力量！ Our military is the people's military, and our national defense is the responsibility of every one of us. We must raise public awareness about the importance of national defense and strengthen unity between the government and the military and between the people and the military. Let us work together to create a mighty force for realizing the Chinese Dream and the dream of building a powerful military.

我们坚持精准扶贫、尽锐出战，打赢了人类历史上规模最大的脱贫攻坚战，全国八百三十二个贫困县全部摘帽，近一亿农村贫困人口实现脱贫，九百六十多万贫困人口实现易地搬迁，历史性地解决了绝对贫困问题，为全球减贫事业作出了重大贡献。By galvanizing the entire nation to carry out targeted poverty alleviation, we have won the largest battle against poverty in human history. A total of 832 impoverished counties and close to 100 million poor rural residents have been lifted out of poverty, and, among them, more than 9.6 million poverty-stricken people have been relocated from inhospitable areas. We have, once and for all, resolved the problem of absolute poverty in China, making significant contributions to the cause of global poverty reduction.

我们坚持绿水青山就是金山银山的理念。We have acted on the idea that lucid waters and lush mountains are invaluable assets.

我们坚信，只要包括港澳台同胞在内的全体中华儿女顺应历史大势、共担民族大义，把民族命运牢牢掌握在自己手中，就一定能够共创中华民族伟大复兴的美好未来！We remain firm in our conviction that, as long as all the sons and daughters of the Chinese nation, including our compatriots in Hong Kong, Macao, and Taiwan, follow the tide of history, work together for the greater national interests, and keep our nation's destiny firmly in our own hands, we will, without doubt, be able to achieve the great rejuvenation of the Chinese nation.

我们经过接续奋斗，实现了小康这个中华民族的千年梦想，我国发展站在了更高历史起点上。We have achieved moderate prosperity, the millennia-old dream of the Chinese nation, through persistent hard work. With this, we have elevated China to a higher historical starting point in development.

我们就是要不忘初心、牢记使命，一代接着一代干，到中华人民共和国成立100周年时，中国、中华民族就会更加坚强昂扬地屹立于世界东方，就会为全人类作出更大的贡献。We will stay true to the Party's original aspiration and founding mission and do solid work, generation after generation, so that by the centenary of the PRC in 2049, our nation will stand taller and stronger in the East and make a greater contribution to humanity.

我们要坚持多边主义，维护世界和平稳定。We need to stay true to multilateralism, and safeguard global peace and stability.

我们要坚持共同、综合、合作、可持续的安全观，共同维护世界和平和安全。

We should stay committed to the vision of common, comprehensive, cooperative and sustainable security, and work together to maintain world peace and security.

我们要坚持民生优先，推进全球可持续发展。发展是解决一切问题的总钥匙。We need to prioritize people's wellbeing in our efforts for sustainable global development. Development holds the key to resolving all problems.

我们要坚持人民至上、生命至上，调集一切资源、尽一切努力保护人民生命安全和身体健康。We should put people's lives and health first, pool all available resources, and do everything we can to protect people's safety and wellbeing.

我们要落实新时代党的建设总要求，健全全面从严治党体系，全面推进党的自我净化、自我完善、自我革新、自我提高，使我们党坚守初心使命，始终成为中国特色社会主义事业的坚强领导核心。We must meet the overall requirements for Party building in the new era, improve the systems for exercising full and rigorous self-governance, and comprehensively advance our efforts to purify, improve, renew, and excel ourselves. This will enable our Party to stay true to its original aspiration and founding mission and remain the strong leadership core in building socialism with Chinese characteristics.

我们要顺应数字化、网络化、智能化发展趋势，共同致力于消除"数字鸿沟"，助推服务贸易数字化进程。We need to adapt to the trend towards digital-driven, Internet-based and smart growth, jointly eliminate the "digital divide", and advance the digitalization of trade in services.

我们要推动以团结取代分歧，以理性消除偏见，扫除"政治病毒"，凝聚起各国携手抗疫的最大合力。We need to eliminate division through unity, replace bias with reasoning, and stamp out the "politicization of the virus". By doing so, we will build a powerful global synergy to beat the virus.

我们要为人民福祉着想，秉持人类命运共同体理念，用实际行动为建设美好世界作出应有贡献。We must keep people's wellbeing close to our hearts and strive to build a global community of shared future. With concrete actions, we can make the world a better place for everyone.

我们要在全社会大力弘扬伟大抗疫精神，使之转化为全面建设社会主义现代化国家、实现中华民族伟大复兴的强大力量。We should promote this great spirit that we have forged in the battle against Covid-19 in our society and turn it into a powerful force for building a modern socialist country and realizing the rejuvenation of the Chinese nation.

我们要准确把握时代大势，勇于站在人类发展前沿，聆听人民心声，回应现实需要，坚持解放思想、实事求是、守正创新，更好把坚持马克思主义和发展马克思主义统一起来，坚持用马克思主义之"矢"去射新时代中国之"的"，继续推进马克思主义基本原理同中国具体实际相结合、同中华优秀传统文化相结合，续写马克思主义中国化时代化新篇章。We need to gain a keen appreciation of the underlying trends of the times, and stand boldly at the forefront of human development. We should listen to the people, respond to their needs, continue to free our minds, seek truth from facts, and maintain the right political direction and break new ground. We should develop Marxism while upholding its basic tenets, combine them with the best of our traditional culture, and apply them in China's context, so that Marxism can continue to work in solving problems in China in the new era.

我们应该携手推动构建人类命运共同体，共同建设持久和平、普遍安全、共同繁荣、开放包容、清洁美丽的世界。We should join together to build a global community of shared future, and work together to build an open, inclusive, clean and beautiful world that enjoys lasting peace, universal security, and common prosperity.

我们走出一条睦邻友好、合作共赢的光明大道，迈向日益紧密的命运共同体，为推动人类进步事业作出了重要贡献。We have embarked on a path of good-neighborliness and win-win cooperation, taken strides towards a closer community of shared future, and made an important contribution to human progress.

我们走中国特色社会主义道路，一定要推进马克思主义中国化。As we have opted

for the path of socialism with Chinese characteristics, we must adapt Marxism to the Chinese context.

五年规划编制涉及经济社会发展方方面面，同人民群众生产生活息息相关，需要把加强顶层设计和坚持问计于民统一起来，鼓励广大人民群众和社会各界以各种方式建言献策。The formulation of the Five-year Plan involves all aspects of economic and social development, and is closely related to the work and life of the people. It is necessary to strengthen top-level design and at the same time collect ideas from the people, encouraging all sectors of society to submit opinions and suggestions in various ways.

五年来，我们党团结带领人民，攻克了许多长期没有解决的难题，办成了许多事关长远的大事要事，推动党和国家事业取得举世瞩目的重大成就。Over the past five years, our Party has rallied the people and led them in solving a great number of problems that had long gone unsolved, securing many accomplishments that hold major future significance, and achieving impressive advances in the cause of the Party and the country.

X

新发展格局决不是封闭的国内循环，而是开放的国内国际双循环。The new development dynamic is not a closed loop but a blend of domestic and international economic flows.

新时代的伟大成就是党和人民一道拼出来、干出来、奋斗出来的！The great achievements of the new era have come from the collective dedication and hard work of our Party and our people.

新时代的中国青年，生逢其时、重任在肩，施展才干的舞台无比广阔，实现梦想的前景无比光明。For China's youth in the new era, the timing is ideal to do great things since you have a vast stage to display your talents, and brighter prospects than ever before of realizing your dreams.

新时代的中国青年要以实现中华民族伟大复兴为己任，增强做中国人的志气、骨气、底气，不负时代，不负韶华，不负党和人民的殷切期望！In the new era, our young people should make it their mission to contribute to national rejuvenation and aspire to greater pride, confidence and assurance in their identity as Chinese, so that they can live up to the promise of their youth and the expectations of our times, our Party, and our people.

新时代十年的伟大变革，在党史、新中国史、改革开放史、社会主义发展史、中华民族发展史上具有里程碑意义。The great transformation over the past 10 years of the new era marks a milestone in the history of the Party, of the People's Republic of China, of reform and opening up, of the development of socialism, and of the development of the Chinese nation.

Y

亚太合作未来的路怎么走，关乎地区发展，关乎人民福祉，关乎世界未来。Which way should Asia-Pacific cooperation be heading? The answer will have a profound impact on the development of our region, the wellbeing of our people, and the future of the world.

亚太经济合作从来不是零和博弈、你输我赢的政治游戏，而是相互成就、互利共赢的发展平台。Economic cooperation in the Asia-Pacific region has never been a zero-sum political game in which one gains at the expense of others. Rather, our cooperation has provided us with a development platform that delivers gains to us all.

要把为民造福作为最重要的政绩。We must consider serving the people and working for their wellbeing to be our primary political goal.

要倡导和平、发展、公平、正义、民主、自由的全人类共同价值，深化文明交流互鉴，用好地区多元文化特色和优势。We should advocate peace, development, equity, justice, democracy and freedom, which are the common values of humanity, increase exchanges and mutual learning between civilizations, and fully leverage our region's unique strength of cultural diversity.

附录 2 习近平金句

要从党的百年奋斗史中汲取智慧和力量，加强中央政治局自身建设。The Political Bureau should draw wisdom and strength from our Party's century-long history of struggle to improve itself.

要更加聚焦人民群众普遍关心关注的民生问题，采取更有针对性的措施，一件一件抓落实，一年接着一年干，让人民群众获得感、幸福感、安全感更加充实、更有保障、更可持续。We must focus more on issues of public concern that affect people's lives, take more targeted measures, and ensure effective implementation to solve each and every one of them, so that the people will have a growing, guaranteed, and sustained sense of gain, fulfillment and security.

要坚持把政治标准作为第一标准，确保干部队伍政治上信得过、靠得住、能放心。Political commitment and integrity must be the primary criteria for selecting officials to ensure they are trustworthy and reliable.

要坚持发展和治理相统一、网上和网下相融合，广泛汇聚向上向善力量。We need to coordinate development and governance, and online and offline efforts, and bring together all positive forces for the common good.

要坚持用全面、辩证、长远的眼光分析当前经济形势，努力在危机中育新机、于变局中开新局…… We need to take a comprehensive, dialectical and long-term view of the current economic situation, develop new opportunities in the midst of crisis, and open up new prospects in the midst of change…

要坚定走绿色低碳发展道路，推动流域经济发展质量变革、效率变革、动力变革。We will be committed to green and low-carbon development, and work hard for better quality, higher efficiency, and more robust drivers in economic growth in the Yellow River Basin.

要健全法律面前人人平等保障机制，维护国家法制统一、尊严、权威，一切违反宪法法律的行为都必须予以追究。Efforts will be made to guarantee that everyone is equal before the law, to safeguard the consistency, dignity and authority of the legal system, and to call to account anyone who violates the Constitution or other laws.

要健全制度体系，及时将实践中好的经验做法转化为制度规范。You can improve your institutions by turning successful experiences and practices into rules and norms.

要讲清楚，实施好民法典是坚持以人民为中心、保障人民权益实现和发展的必然要求。It must be made clear that the implementation of the Civil Code is essential to protecting the people's rights and interests and achieving people-centered development.

要扩大金融等服务业对外开放。要继续优化营商环境，做好招商、安商、稳商工作，增强外商长期投资经营的信心。We should further open up finance and other services, continue to improve the business environment, and attract and retain foreign investment, so as to boost international confidence in long-term investment and business operations in China.

要培育文明健康、向上向善的诚信文化，教育引导资本主体践行社会主义核心价值观，讲信用信义、重社会责任、走人间正道。We should advocate a healthy culture of credibility and integrity, and encourage players in the capital market to practice the core socialist values, uphold business ethics, and fulfill their social responsibilities.

要深化对人与自然生命共同体的规律性认识，全面加快生态文明建设。生态文明这个旗帜必须高扬。We must understand fully how humanity and nature form a community of life and step up efforts on all fronts to build an eco-civilization. We must always prioritize eco-environmental progress.

要深化干部制度改革，推动形成能者上、优者奖、庸者下、劣者汰的正确导向。You should improve the management of officials to ensure the capable are promoted, the excellent rewarded, the mediocre demoted, and the incompetent dismissed.

要深化理论研究，认真总结参政党建设经验，把握参政党建设规律。You can conduct in-depth theoretical research, review your experience gained as political parties participating in state governance, and turn your insights into institutional practices.

要深入推动能源革命，促进能源消费、供给、技术、体制改革，加强国际合作，加快建设能源强国。We should promote the energy revolution, push forward reform in energy use, supply, technology, and institutions, strengthen international cooperation, and build up our strength in energy.

要始终坚持人民至上、生命至上，坚持科学精准、动态清零，尽快遏制疫情扩散蔓延势头。We should always put the people and their lives first, take a science-based and targeted approach to implement the dynamic zero-Covid policy, and act promptly to curb the spread of the virus.

要提高党把方向、谋大局、定政策、促改革的能力和定力，为长三角一体化发展提供坚强政治保障。Efforts should be made to reinforce the Party's ability and resolve to steer the course, make overall plans, devise policies, and promote reform, so as to provide a strong political guarantee for the integrated development of the Yangtze River Delta.

要提高科学精准防控水平，不断优化疫情防控举措，加强疫苗、快速检测试剂和药物研发等科技攻关，使防控工作更有针对性。We should continue our science-based and targeted Covid-19 response, and improve response measures. We should expedite the research and development of vaccines, medicines, and rapid test reagents, and make our response more targeted.

要用好"我为群众办实事"实践活动形成的良好机制，推动各级党组织和广大党员、干部满腔热情为群众办实事、解难事，走好新时代党的群众路线。Through the mechanisms established in the campaign "I do solid work for the people", Party organizations and members should continue to help solve problems that concern the people most, and carry our Party's mass line into the new era.

要用好用活各方面人才，坚持以用为本，精准高效配置军事人力资源，确保人才得到最佳配置、发挥最大效能。We will make effective and flexible use of talent in all fields, and ensure precise and efficient allocation of human resources, so that they can best play their role in the most suitable positions.

要在推动高质量发展中强化就业优先导向。就业是民生之本。In promoting high-quality development we should prioritize employment, which is pivotal to people's wellbeing.

要在一体化发展战略实施的过程中发现人才、培育人才、使用人才。In the course of implementing the integrated development strategy, you need to identify and cultivate the best talent and give them opportunities to shine.

要增强思想政治建设的时代性、针对性、实效性，不断巩固共同团结奋斗的思想政治基础。It is crucial to update your theoretical and political training and make it more targeted and effective, to consolidate the foundations of our concerted efforts.

要重点抓好防治力量的区域统筹，坚决把救治资源和防护资源集中到抗击疫情第一线，优先满足一线医护人员和救治病人需要。We must focus on coordinating prevention and treatment forces across regions, pool medical resources and protective equipment on the front line, and prioritize the needs of medical workers and patients.

一百年来，党和人民取得的一切成就都是团结奋斗的结果，团结奋斗是中国共产党和中国人民最显著的精神标识。All that the Party and the people have achieved over the past century derives from unity of effort, which is the most distinctive tradition of the CPC and the Chinese people.

一百年来，中国共产党弘扬伟大建党精神，在长期奋斗中构建起中国共产党人的精神谱系，锤炼出鲜明的政治品格。Over the past hundred years, the Party has carried forward this great founding spirit. Through its protracted struggles, it has developed a long line of inspiring principles for China's Communists and tempered a distinct political character.

一百年来，中国共产党团结带领中国人民进行的一切奋斗、一切牺牲、一切创造，归结起来就是一个主题：实现中华民族伟大复兴。All the struggle, sacrifice and creation through which the Party has united and led the Chinese people over the past hundred years has been tied together by one ultimate goal – bringing about the rejuvenation of the Chinese nation.

一百年前，中国共产党的先驱们创建了中国共产党，形成了坚持真理、坚守理想，践行初心、担当使命，不怕牺牲、英勇斗争，对党忠诚、不负人民的伟大建党精神，这是中国共产党的精神之源。A hundred years ago, the pioneers of communism in China established the Communist Party of China and developed the great founding spirit of the Party, which is comprised of the following principles: upholding truth and ideals, staying true to our original aspiration and founding mission, fighting bravely without fear of death, and remaining loyal to the Party and faithful to the people. This spirit is the Party's source of strength.

一个国家、一个民族要振兴，就必须在历史前进的逻辑中前进、在时代发展的潮流中发展。For any country or nation to thrive, it must follow the logic of history and develop in line with the trend of the times.

一个民族之所以伟大，根本就在于在任何困难和风险面前都从来不放弃、不退缩、不止步，百折不挠为自己的前途命运而奋斗。A nation is great because it never gives up, never retreats, and never stops moving forward. No matter what setbacks it faces, it will keep fighting for a better future.

一个现代化的社会，应该既充满活力又拥有良好秩序，呈现出活力和秩序有机统一。Modernity is built on a balance between order and dynamism.

"一国两制"是中国特色社会主义的伟大创举，是香港、澳门回归后保持长期繁荣稳定的最佳制度安排，必须长期坚持。The policy of One Country, Two Systems is a great innovation of socialism with Chinese characteristics. It has proven to be the best institutional arrangement for ensuring sustained prosperity and stability in Hong Kong and Macao after their return to the motherland. This policy must be adhered to over the long term.

……一件一件抓落实,一年接着一年干,努力让群众看到变化、得到实惠。We must make concrete efforts year after year to deliver tangible results and real benefits to the people.

依法治军是我们党建军治军的基本方式,是实现党在新时代的强军目标的必然要求。Running the military in accordance with the law is our Party's basic strategy in building and running the military, and a necessary requirement for achieving the Party's goal of building a stronger military for the new era.

以史为鉴、开创未来,必须继续推进马克思主义中国化。As we put conscious effort into learning from history to create a bright future, we must continue to adapt Marxism to the Chinese context.

以史为鉴、开创未来,必须坚持和发展中国特色社会主义。As we put conscious effort into learning from history to create a bright future, we must uphold and develop socialism with Chinese characteristics.

以史为鉴、开创未来,必须坚持中国共产党坚强领导。As we put conscious effort into learning from history to create a bright future, we must uphold the firm leadership of the Party.

以史为鉴、开创未来,必须团结带领中国人民不断为美好生活而奋斗。As we put conscious effort into learning from history to create a bright future, we must unite the Chinese people and lead them in working ceaselessly for a better life.

疫情对产业发展既是挑战也是机遇。Covid-19 poses both a challenge and an opportunity for industrial development.

疫情防控不只是医药卫生问题,而是全方位的工作,是总体战,各项工作都要为打赢疫情防控阻击战提供支持。Virus prevention and control is not only a medical and health issue. It is a battle across various fields, and all sectors should engage in the battle and strive for victory.

勇于自我革命是中国共产党区别于其他政党的显著标志。A hallmark that distinguishes the Communist Party of China from other political parties is the courage to undertake self-reform.

Z

在平等相待基础上开展合作，在相互尊重基础上化解分歧，是亚太经济发展繁荣的根本。We should pursue cooperation on the basis of equality and dissolve differences with mutual respect because this is essential to delivering economic development and prosperity in the Asia-Pacific region.

在脱贫攻坚斗争中，1800多名同志将生命定格在了脱贫攻坚征程上，生动诠释了共产党人的初心使命。In the fight against poverty, more than 1,800 Party members laid down their lives for the ideals that we as Communists have always cherished.

在我们这么一个有着14亿人口的国家，每个人出一份力就能汇聚成排山倒海的磅礴力量，每个人做成一件事、干好一件工作，党和国家事业就能向前推进一步。For a country with a population of 1.4 billion, individual contributions gather into an earth-shaking force. If everyone can do one thing or one job well, the cause of the Party and the state will advance one step further.

在新的历史条件下，要永葆党的马克思主义政党本色，关键还得靠我们党自己。在为谁执政、为谁用权、为谁谋利这个根本问题上，我们的头脑要特别清醒、立场要特别坚定。To maintain our nature as a Marxist political party under new circumstances, we must be self-driven, know clearly for whom we exercise governance and power and for whose interests we work, and take a firm stance on these fundamental issues.

在这场同严重疫情的殊死较量中，中国人民和中华民族以敢于斗争、敢于胜利的大无畏气概，铸就了生命至上、举国同心、舍生忘死、尊重科学、命运与共的伟大抗疫精神。In the fierce battle against Covid-19, the Chinese people and the Chinese nation have shown extraordinary mettle and fought courageously for victory. While fighting the virus, we have put life above all else, rallied the entire country, braved danger, respected science, and stood together through adversity.

在这里，我代表党和人民庄严宣告，经过全党全国各族人民持续奋斗，我们实现了第一个百年奋斗目标，在中华大地上全面建成了小康社会，历史性地解决了绝对贫困问题，正在意气风发向着全面建成社会主义现代化强国的第二个百年奋斗目标迈进。On this special occasion, it is my honor to declare on behalf of the Party and the people that through the continued efforts of the whole Party and the entire nation, we have realized the First Centenary Goal of building a moderately prosperous society in all respects. This means that we have brought about a historic resolution to the problem of absolute poverty in China, and we are now marching in confident strides towards the Second Centenary Goal of building China into a great modern socialist country in all respects.

在重大风险、强大对手面前，总想过太平日子、不想斗争是不切实际的，得"软骨病"、患"恐惧症"是无济于事的。Confronted by major risks, and powerful opponents, it is unrealistic to think confrontation can be avoided, nor will it help to fear it or evade it.

站立在九百六十多万平方公里的广袤土地上，吸吮着五千多年中华民族漫长奋斗积累的文化养分，拥有十三亿多中国人民聚合的磅礴之力，我们走中国特色社会主义道路，具有无比广阔的时代舞台，具有无比深厚的历史底蕴，具有无比强大的前进定力。Rooted in a land of more than 9.6 million square kilometers, nourished by a culture of more than 5,000 years, and blessed with the strength of more than 1.3 billion people, we have an infinitely vast stage of our era, a heritage of unmatched depth, and incomparable resolve that enable us to forge ahead on the road of socialism with Chinese characteristics.

战略是从全局、长远、大势上作出判断和决策。我们是一个大党，领导的是一个大国，进行的是伟大的事业，要善于进行战略思维，善于从战略上看问题、想问题。Strategic thinking is all about judgment and decision-making. It requires us to take into consideration the overall situation, long-term interests and underlying trends. Ours is a major political party governing a large country and working for a great cause. We must be able to think strategically and plan accordingly.

战胜疫病离不开科技支撑。Novel coronavirus cannot be beaten without science.

这次疫情防控使我们更加深切地认识到，生态文明建设是关系中华民族永续发展的千年大计，必须站在人与自然和谐共生的高度来谋划经济社会发展。Our Covid-19 response has made us more keenly aware that building an eco-civilization is vital to our nation's sustainable development, and our plan of economic and social progress must be based on harmony between humanity and nature.

这是中国共产党和中国人民团结奋斗赢得的历史性胜利，是彪炳中华民族发展史册的历史性胜利，也是对世界具有深远影响的历史性胜利。These were historic feats – feats accomplished by the Communist Party of China and the Chinese people striving in unity, feats that will be forever recorded in the Chinese nation's history, and feats that will profoundly influence the world.

这是中华民族的伟大光荣！这是中国人民的伟大光荣！这是中国共产党的伟大光荣！This is a great and glorious achievement for the Chinese nation, for the Chinese people and for the Communist Party of China.

这50年，中国人民始终发扬自强不息精神，在风云变幻中把握中国前进方向，书写了中国以及人类发展的壮阔史诗。For these 50 years, the Chinese people have demonstrated an untiring spirit and kept to the right direction amid changing circumstances, writing an epic chapter in the story of China and humanity.

这一百年来开辟的伟大道路、创造的伟大事业、取得的伟大成就，必将载入中华民族发展史册、人类文明发展史册！The great path we have pioneered, the great cause we have undertaken, and the great achievements we have made over the past century will go down in the annals of the Chinese nation and of human civilization.

珍惜发展好局面，巩固发展好势头。Make best use of the favorable environment and build momentum for development.

只有更好平衡人与自然的关系，维护生态系统平衡，才能守护人类健康。Only by maintaining a balance between humanity and nature and in our ecosystems can we protect human health.

中国秉持共商共建共享的全球治理观，倡导国际关系民主化，坚持国家不分大小、强弱、贫富一律平等，支持联合国发挥积极作用，支持扩大发展中国家在国际事务中的代表性和发言权。China follows the principle of achieving shared growth through discussion and collaboration in engaging in global governance. China stands for democracy in international relations and the equality of all countries, big or small, strong or weak, rich or poor. China supports the United Nations in playing an active role in international affairs, and supports the efforts of other developing countries to increase their representation and strengthen their voice in international affairs.

中国的昨天已经写在人类的史册上，中国的今天正在亿万人民手中创造，中国的明天必将更加美好。China's past made its mark on human history; China's present is being created by the hands of hundreds of millions of Chinese people; China's future will be even brighter.

中国奉行防御性的国防政策，中国的发展是世界和平力量的增长，无论发展到什么程度，中国永远不称霸、永远不搞扩张。China pursues a defensive national defense policy, and its development strengthens the world's forces for peace. No matter what stage of development it reaches, China will never seek hegemony or engage in expansionism.

中国共产党根基在人民、血脉在人民、力量在人民。In the people, the Party has its roots, its lifeblood and its source of strength.

中国共产党关注人类前途命运，同世界上一切进步力量携手前进，中国始终是世界和平的建设者、全球发展的贡献者、国际秩序的维护者！The Party cares about the future of humanity, and wishes to move forward in parallel with all progressive forces around the world. China has always worked to safeguard world peace, contribute to global development, and preserve international order.

中国共产党和中国人民是在斗争中成长和壮大起来的，斗争精神贯穿于中国革命、建设、改革各个时期。The Communist Party of China and the Chinese people have grown and gained strength in the course of our struggle. Our fighting spirit has been apparent in the whole process of the country's revolution, construction and reform.

中国共产党和中国人民以英勇顽强的奋斗向世界庄严宣告，中华民族迎来了从站起来、富起来到强起来的伟大飞跃，实现中华民族伟大复兴进入了不可逆转的历史进程！Through tenacious struggle, the Party and the Chinese people have shown the world that the Chinese nation has achieved the tremendous transformation from standing up and growing prosperous to becoming strong, and that China's national rejuvenation has become an unstoppable process.

中国共产党建立近百年来，团结带领中国人民所进行的一切奋斗，就是为了把我国建设成为现代化强国，实现中华民族伟大复兴。Over the past hundred years since the founding of the Communist Party of China, all the efforts made by the CPC and by the Chinese people under its leadership have served just one purpose – building China into a strong modern country and realizing national rejuvenation.

中国共产党领导是中国特色社会主义最本质的特征，是中国特色社会主义制度的最大优势，是党和国家的根本所在、命脉所在，是全国各族人民的利益所系、命运所系。The leadership of the Party is the defining feature of socialism with Chinese characteristics and constitutes the greatest strength of this system. It is the foundation and lifeblood of the Party and the country, and the crux upon which the interests and wellbeing of all Chinese people depend.

中国共产党始终把为人类作出新的更大的贡献作为自己的使命。To make new and greater contributions for humanity is our Party's abiding mission.

中国共产党始终代表最广大人民根本利益，与人民休戚与共、生死相依，没有任何自己特殊的利益，从来不代表任何利益集团、任何权势团体、任何特权阶层的利益。The Party has always represented the fundamental interests of all Chinese people; it stands with them in the best and the hardest of times and shares a common destiny with them. The Party has no special interests of its own – it has never represented any individual interest group, power group, or privileged stratum.

中国共产党是为中国人民谋幸福的政党，也是为人类进步事业而奋斗的政党。The Communist Party of China strives for both the wellbeing of the Chinese people and human progress.

中国共产党为什么能，中国特色社会主义为什么好，归根到底是因为马克思主义行。马克思主义之所以行，就在于党不断推进马克思主义中国化时代化并用以指导实践。How does the CPC succeed? Why does Chinese socialism work? Because Marxism works. Because Marxism is adapted by the CPC to the Chinese context, kept up-to-date, and employed to guide our cause.

中国共产党已走过百年奋斗历程。我们党立志于中华民族千秋伟业，致力于人类和平与发展崇高事业，责任无比重大，使命无上光荣。Since its founding a century ago, the Communist Party of China has taken a remarkable journey. Our Party has dedicated itself to achieving lasting greatness for the Chinese nation and committed itself to the noble cause of peace and development for humanity. Our responsibility is unmatched in importance, and our mission is glorious beyond compare.

中国将高举和平、发展、合作、共赢的旗帜，恪守维护世界和平、促进共同发展的外交政策宗旨，坚定不移在和平共处五项原则基础上发展同各国的友好合作，推动建设相互尊重、公平正义、合作共赢的新型国际关系。China will continue to hold high the banner of peace, development, cooperation, and mutual benefit and uphold its fundamental foreign policy goal of preserving world peace and promoting common development. China remains firm in its commitment to strengthening friendship and cooperation with other countries on the basis of the Five Principles of Peaceful Coexistence, and to forging a new form of international relations featuring mutual respect, fairness, justice, and win-win cooperation.

中国将更加注重扩大进口，促进贸易平衡发展。Going forward, China will lay more emphasis on expanding imports, and pursue balanced development of trade.

中国将继续发挥负责任大国作用，积极参与全球治理体系改革和建设，不断贡献中国智慧和力量。China will continue to play its part as a major and responsible country, take an active part in reforming and developing the global governance system, and keep contributing Chinese wisdom and strength to global governance.

中国将推动高质量共建"一带一路"，使更多国家和人民获得发展机遇和实惠。China will promote high-quality Belt and Road cooperation to provide development opportunities and deliver real benefits to more countries and people.

中国将拓展特色服务出口基地，发展服务贸易新业态新模式。China will continue to build bases for exporting particular services and develop new business forms and models in services trade.

中国梦是历史的、现实的，也是未来的；是我们这一代的，更是青年一代的。中华民族伟大复兴的中国梦终将在一代代青年的接力奋斗中变为现实。The Chinese Dream is a dream about the past, the present, and the future. It is a dream of our generation, but even more so, a dream of the younger generations. The Chinese Dream of national rejuvenation will be realized ultimately through the endeavors of young people, generation by generation.

中国人民的前进动力更加强大、奋斗精神更加昂扬、必胜信念更加坚定，焕发出更为强烈的历史自觉和主动精神，中国共产党和中国人民正信心百倍推进中华民族从站起来、富起来到强起来的伟大飞跃。The Chinese people are more inspired than ever to forge ahead, more resolved than ever to work hard, and more confident than ever of securing success. They are filled with a stronger sense of history and initiative. With full confidence, the Communist Party of China and the Chinese people are driving the great transformation of the Chinese nation from standing up and growing prosperous to becoming strong.

中国人民从来没有欺负、压迫、奴役过其他国家人民，过去没有，现在没有，将来也不会有。We have never abused, oppressed or subjugated the people of any other country, and we never will.

中国人民也绝不允许任何外来势力欺负、压迫、奴役我们，谁妄想这样干，必将在14亿多中国人民用血肉筑成的钢铁长城面前碰得头破血流！We will never allow any foreign force to abuse, oppress or subjugate us. Anyone who would attempt to do so will find themselves on a collision course with a great wall of steel forged by over 1.4 billion Chinese people.

中国始终秉持构建人类命运共同体理念，既对本国人民生命安全和身体健康负责，也对全球公共卫生事业尽责。China stands for the vision of building a global community of shared future. China considers it has a responsibility to ensure the lives and health of its own citizens, and also to safeguard global public health.

中国始终坚持维护世界和平、促进共同发展的外交政策宗旨，致力于推动构建人类命运共同体。China has always been committed to its foreign policy goals of upholding world peace and promoting common development, and it is dedicated to promoting a human community with a shared future.

中国式现代化的本质要求是：坚持中国共产党领导，坚持中国特色社会主义，实现高质量发展，发展全过程人民民主，丰富人民精神世界，实现全体人民共同富裕，促进人与自然和谐共生，推动构建人类命运共同体，创造人类文明新形态。The essential requirements of Chinese modernization are as follows: upholding the leadership of the Communist Party of China and socialism with Chinese characteristics, pursuing high-quality development, developing whole-process people's democracy, enriching the people's cultural lives, achieving common prosperity for all, promoting harmony between humanity and nature, building a human community with a shared future, and creating a new form of human advancement.

中国式现代化是全体人民共同富裕的现代化。Chinese modernization is the modernization of common prosperity for all.

中国式现代化是人口规模巨大的现代化。Chinese modernization is the modernization of a huge population.

中国式现代化是人与自然和谐共生的现代化。Chinese modernization is the modernization of harmony between humanity and nature.

中国式现代化是物质文明和精神文明相协调的现代化。Chinese modernization is the modernization of material and cultural-ethical advancement.

中国式现代化是走和平发展道路的现代化。Chinese modernization is the modernization of peaceful development.

中国式现代化,是中国共产党领导的社会主义现代化,既有各国现代化的共同特征,更有基于自己国情的中国特色。Chinese modernization is socialist modernization pursued under the leadership of the Communist Party of China. It contains elements that are common to the modernization processes of all countries, but it is more characterized by features that are unique to the Chinese context.

中国特色社会主义是全面发展、全面进步的伟大事业,没有社会主义文化繁荣发展,就没有社会主义现代化。Building socialism with Chinese characteristics is a great undertaking defined by progress in all areas and endeavors. There can be no socialist modernization without a thriving socialist culture.

中国愿同各国一道,共建开放型世界经济,让开放的春风温暖世界! China

stands ready to work with all countries to build an open world economy, so that the spring breeze of openness will bring warmth to all parts of the world.

中国支持世界贸易组织改革朝着正确方向发展，支持多边贸易体制包容性发展，支持发展中成员合法权益。China supports WTO reform in the right direction. We support the inclusive development of the multilateral trading system, as well as the legitimate rights and interests of the developing members.

中华民族能够经历无数灾厄仍不断发展壮大，从来都不是因为有救世主，而是因为在大灾大难前有千千万万个普通人挺身而出、慷慨前行！ The reason that the Chinese nation has been able to thrive despite countless disasters is never because of a savior, but thanks to hundreds of millions of ordinary people stepping forward to brave the dark for others.

中华民族是历经磨难、不屈不挠的伟大民族，中国人民是勤劳勇敢、自强不息的伟大人民，中国共产党是敢于斗争、敢于胜利的伟大政党。The Chinese nation is a great nation; it has been through hardships and adversity but remains indomitable. The Chinese people are a great people; they are industrious and brave; and they never pause in the pursuit of progress. The Communist Party of China is a great party; it has the courage to fight and the mettle to win.

中华民族拥有在5000多年历史演进中形成的灿烂文明，中国共产党拥有百年奋斗实践和70多年执政兴国经验，我们积极学习借鉴人类文明的一切有益成果，欢迎一切有益的建议和善意的批评，但我们绝不接受"教师爷"般颐指气使的说教！The Chinese nation has fostered a splendid civilization over 5,000 years or more. The Party has also acquired a wealth of experience through its endeavors over the past 100 years and during more than 70 years of governance. At the same time, we are also eager to learn from the fruitful experience of other cultures, and we welcome helpful suggestions and constructive criticisms. We will not, however, accept condescending sermons from those who feel they have the right to lecture us.

中央应对疫情工作领导小组及时研究部署工作，中央指导组积极开展工作，国务院联防联控机制加强统筹协调，各级党委和政府积极作为，同时间赛跑，与病魔较量，形成了抗击病魔的强大合力。With timely planning and action by the Central Leading Group for Coronavirus Response, specific directions and coordination from the central steering group, strong coordination by the State Council joint prevention and control mechanism, and strenuous efforts by Party committees and governments at all levels, a powerful synergy has been formed in the race to fight the virus.

自成立以来，我们党团结带领人民进行革命、建设、改革，根本目的就是为了让人民过上好日子，无论面临多大挑战和压力，无论付出多大牺牲和代价，这一点都始终不渝、毫不动摇。The fundamental goal for the Party since its founding, in uniting the people and leading them in revolution, construction and reform, is to give them a better life. The Party has never wavered in pursuing this goal no matter what challenges and pressure it faces, no matter the sacrifice and the cost.

综合分析国内外形势，当前和今后一个时期，我国发展仍然处于重要战略机遇期，但机遇和挑战都有新的发展变化。With a comprehensive analysis of the domestic and international situation, we are still in an important period of strategic opportunity which will continue, but the challenges and opportunities keep changing.

纵览古今、环顾全球，没有哪一个国家能在这么短的时间内实现几亿人脱贫，这个成绩属于中国，也属于世界，为推动构建人类命运共同体贡献了中国力量！No other country throughout history has been able to lift hundreds of millions out of poverty in such a short period of time. This achievement is China's, but it also belongs to the world, and has contributed Chinese strength to the development of a global community of shared future.

走自己的路，是党的全部理论和实践立足点，更是党百年奋斗得出的历史结论。We must follow our own path – this is the bedrock that underpins all the theories and practices of our Party. More than that, it is the conclusion our Party has drawn from its struggles over the past century.

组织是"形",思想是"魂"。加强党的组织建设,既要"造形",更要"铸魂"。The Party's organization is the body, while its vision is the soul, so to speak. To strengthen the Party's organization, we should build up the body, and more importantly, shape its soul.

最后,我要强调的是,社会主义中国发展到今天,取得的成就不是天上掉下来的,更不是别人恩赐施舍的,而是广大人民群众在党的领导下用勤劳、智慧、勇气干出来的!Finally, I want to emphasize that the achievements of our socialist country have not fallen like manna from Heaven, nor have they been granted by others. They have been achieved by our people through hard work, wisdom and courage under the leadership of the Party.

尊重和保障人权是中国共产党人的不懈追求。Respecting and protecting human rights is an ongoing quest of China's Communists.

做好疫情防控工作,直接关系人民生命安全和身体健康,直接关系经济社会大局稳定,也事关我国对外开放。Our novel coronavirus prevention and control is directly related to people's lives and health, economic development, social stability, and opening up.

附录3 典故解析

A

1. "爱人利物之谓仁"——《庄子·天地》

英译："Compassion means loving and helping others."

解析：汉语原文意思是除了爱人以外，还要施万物以利泽，这种爱就像下雨一般，心无偏执，德泽广被，爱惜万物的生机，就是仁。习近平总书记认为，生命至上，集中体现了中国人民深厚的仁爱传统和中国共产党人以人民为中心的价值追求。"爱人利物之谓仁。"疫情无情人有情。人的生命是最宝贵的，生命只有一次，失去不会再来。在保护人民生命安全面前，我们必须不惜一切代价，我们也能够做到不惜一切代价，因为中国共产党的根本宗旨是全心全意为人民服务，我们的国家是人民当家作主的社会主义国家。

2. "安得广厦千万间，大庇天下寒士俱欢颜！"——杜甫《茅屋为秋风所破歌》

英译："If only I could build a house with thousands upon thousands of rooms, I would bring all the poor people on the earth under its roof and bring smiles to their faces."

解析：汉语原文意思是如何能得到千万间宽敞的大屋，普遍地庇护天底下贫寒的读书人，让他们喜笑颜开。习近平总书记指出，贫困是人类社会的顽疾。反贫困始终是古今中外治国安邦的一件大事。一部中国史，就是一部中华民族同贫困作斗争的历史。杜甫"安得广厦千万间，大庇天下寒士俱欢颜"的憧憬，反映了中华民族对摆脱贫困、丰衣足食的深深渴望。

3. "安而不忘危，存而不忘亡，治而不忘乱"——《周易·系辞下》

英译："One should be mindful of possible danger in times of peace, downfall in times of survival, and chaos in times of stability."

解析：汉语原文意思是在国家安定的时候君子要不忘危险，国家存在的时候要不忘败亡，国家大治的时候要不忘变乱。习近平总书记多次强调要坚持底线思维，告诫全党时刻牢记"安而不忘危，存而不忘亡，治而不忘乱"。新形势下，我国面临复杂多变的发展和安全环境，各种可以预见和难以预见的风险因素明显增多，如果得不到及时有效控制也有可能演变为政治风险。全党同志特别是各级领导干部必须增强风险意识，提高防范政治风险能力。

B

4. "备豫不虞，为国常道。"——吴兢《贞观政要·直谏》

英译："Prepare in advance against the unexpected, which is a basic principle of governing a country."

解析：汉语原文意思是提前做好准备，以防范意料不到的事情发生，这是治理国家的基本原则。习近平总书记指出，"备豫不虞，为国常道"。当前我国正处于一个大有可为的历史机遇期，发展形势总的是好的，但前进道路不可能一帆风顺，越是取得成绩的时候，越是要有如履薄冰的谨慎，越是要有居安思危的忧患，绝不能犯战略性、颠覆性错误。

5. "博学之，审问之，慎思之，明辨之，笃行之。"——《礼记·中庸》

英译："Learn extensively, inquire earnestly, think profoundly, discriminate clearly and practice sincerely."

解析：汉语原文意思是博学，学习要广泛涉猎；审问，有针对性地提问请教；慎思，学会周全地思考；明辨，形成清晰的判断力；笃行，用学习得来的知识和思想指导实践。习近平总书记指出，要笃实，扎扎实实干事，踏踏实实做人。道不可坐论，德不能空谈。于实处用力，从知行合一上下功夫，核心价值观才能内化为人们的精神追求，外化为人们的自觉行动。《礼记》中说："博学之，审问之，慎思之，明辨之，笃行之。"青年有着大好机遇，关键是要迈稳步子、夯实根基、久久为功。心浮气躁，朝三暮四，学一门丢一门，干一行弃一行，无论为学还是创业，都是最忌讳的。

6. "不患寡而患不均，不患贫而患不安。"——《论语·季氏》

英译："He is not concerned lest his people should be poor, but only lest what they have should be ill-apportioned. He is not concerned lest they should be few, but only lest they should be divided against one another."

解析：汉语原文意思是不担忧东西少而担忧分配不均，不担忧贫困而担忧社会不安定。习近平总书记认为，共享理念实质就是坚持以人民为中心的发展思想，体现的是逐步实现共同富裕的要求。共同富裕，是马克思主义的一个基本目标，也是自古以来我国人民的一个基本理想。孔子说："不患寡而患不均，不患贫而患不安。"孟子说："老吾老以及人之老，幼吾幼以及人之幼。"《礼记·礼运》具体而生动地描绘了"小康"社会和"大同"社会的状态。按照马克思、恩格斯的构想，共产主义社会将彻底消除阶级之间、城乡之间、脑力劳动和体力劳动之间的对立和差别，实行各尽所能、按需分配，真正实现社会共享、实现每个人自由而全面的发展。

7. "不困在于早虑，不穷在于早豫。"——刘向《说苑·谈丛》

英译："Prior planning prevents pitfalls and proper preparation preempts perils."

解析：汉语原文意思是要想不陷入困境，就须提前谋划，要想不至绝境，就须事先预防。这体现了居安思危的忧患意识和事预则立的经验智慧。习近平总书记强调从忧患意识把握新发展理念。"不困在于早虑，不穷在于早豫。"随着我国社会主要矛盾变化和国际力量对比深刻调整，我国发展面临的内外部风险空前上升，必须增强忧患意识、坚持底线思维，随时准备应对更加复杂困难的局面。

8. "不谋全局者，不足谋一域。"——陈澹然《寤言·迁都建藩议》

英译："One who fails to plan for the whole situation is incapable of planning for a partial area."

解析：汉语原文意思是不从全局的角度考虑问题，即使治理好一方地区，也是微不足道的。习近平总书记强调坚持从大局出发考虑问题。全面深化改革是关系党和国家事业发展全局的重大战略部署，不是某个领域某个方面的单项改革。"不谋全局者，不足谋一域。"大家来自不同部门和单位，都要从全局看问题，首先要看提出的重大改革举措是否符合全局需要，是否有利于党和国家事业长远发展。

9. "不私，而天下自公。"——马融《忠经·广至理章》

英译："Selflessness in governance creates social equity."

解析：汉语原文意思是（执政者）如果能秉公办事，没有私心，天下自然也就一心为公了。习近平总书记指出，"不私，而天下自公"。我们党没有任何自己特殊的利益，这是我们党敢于自我革命的勇气之源、底气所在。正因为无私，才能本着彻底的唯物主义精神经常检视自身、常思己过，才能摆脱一切利益集团、权势团体、特权阶层的"围猎"腐蚀，并向党内被这些集团、团体、阶层所裹挟的人开刀。

10. "不畏浮云遮望眼" ——王安石《登飞来峰》

英译: "unperturbed by the cloud that obscures our vision"

解析: 汉语原文意思是高瞻远瞩的人,不怕被浮云遮蔽住眼睛。习近平总书记强调,共产党人的斗争是有方向、有立场、有原则的,大方向就是坚持中国共产党领导和我国社会主义制度不动摇。我们的头脑要特别清醒、立场要特别坚定,牢牢把握正确斗争方向,做到在各种重大斗争考验面前"不畏浮云遮望眼"。

11. "不要人夸颜色好,只留清气满乾坤。" ——王冕《墨梅》

英译: "Not bent on praise for its bright colors, but on leaving its fragrance to all."

解析: 汉语原文意思是不需要别人夸它的颜色好看,只需要梅花的清香之气弥漫在天地之间。习近平总书记表示,我们欢迎各位记者朋友在中国多走走、多看看,继续关注中共十九大之后中国的发展变化,更加全面地了解和报道中国。我们不需要更多的溢美之词,我们一贯欢迎客观的介绍和有益的建议,正所谓"不要人夸颜色好,只留清气满乾坤"。

12. "不诱于誉,不恐于诽" ——《荀子·非十二子》

英译: "One should not be seduced by praise, nor should one fear opprobrium."

解析: 汉语原文意思是不为赞誉所诱惑,不为诽谤中伤之言所吓倒。习近平总书记认为,我们党历经百年、成就辉煌,党内党外、国内国外赞扬声很多。越是这样越要发扬自我革命精神,千万不能在一片喝彩声中迷失自我。正所谓"不诱于誉,不恐于诽"。全党同志要永葆自我革命精神,增强全面从严治党永远在路上的政治自觉,决不能滋生已经严到位、严到底的情绪!从最近连续查处的大案要案看,党风廉政建设和反腐败斗争必须一刻也不放松抓、持之以恒抓!

13. "不知耻者,无所不为。" ——欧阳修《集古录跋尾·魏公卿上尊号表》

英译: "A person without shame knows no limits."

解析: 汉语原文意思是一个人如果不知羞耻,就会不问是非、善恶,不顾道德规范,为所欲为,什么伤天害理的事都能做出来。习近平总书记强调,发挥好道德的教化作用,必须以道德滋养法治精神、强化道德对法治文化的支撑作用。再多再好的法律,必须转化为人们内心自觉才能真正为人们所遵行。"不知耻者,无所不为。"没有道德滋养,法治文化就缺乏源头活水,法律实施就缺乏坚实社会基础。

14. "不知人之短，不知人之长，不知人长中之短，不知人短中之长，则不可以用人，不可以教人。"——魏源《默觚·治篇七》

英译："Having no idea of a person's weakness and strength, the weak part of the strength or the strong part of the weakness, we have no ground for appointing or even training that person."

解析：汉语原文意思是不了解一个人的短处，也不了解一个人的长处，不能发现一个人长处中的短处，也不能发现一个人短处里的长处，就无法合理使用人、教导人。习近平总书记认为，用人得当，首先要知人。知人不深、识人不准，往往会出现用人不当、用人失误。"不知人之短，不知人之长，不知人长中之短，不知人短中之长，则不可以用人，不可以教人。"对干部的认识不能停留在感觉和印象上，必须健全考察机制和办法，多渠道、多层次、多侧面深入了解。

C

15. "操其要于上，分其详于下。"——陈亮《论执要之道》

英译："To strengthen planning and design at the top level, and delegate detailed tasks to lower levels with priorities assigned."

解析：汉语原文意思是对于处于上位者而言，做事情最主要的是要抓住事情的关键和掌控做事情的原则；对于处于下位的人而言，要按照上级确定的做事情的原则和事情的发展方向，研究部署这件事情具体该怎么展开，需要从哪些方面入手，决定事情具体该怎么做和落实完成整件事情。习近平总书记指出，构建新发展格局是一个系统工程，既要"操其要于上"，加强战略谋划和顶层设计，也要"分其详于下"，把握工作着力点。

16. "操千曲而后晓声，观千剑而后识器。"——刘勰《文心雕龙·知音》

英译："To understand good music only after singing a thousand songs; to find a fine sword only after appreciating a thousand swords."

解析：汉语原文意思是演奏上千首乐曲才能懂得音乐，观察过上千把宝剑才知道如何识别剑器，强调了实践的重要性。习近平总书记认为，要近距离接触干部，观察干部对重大问题的思考，看其见识见解；观察干部对群众的感情，看其品质情怀；观察干部对待名利的态度，看其境界格局；观察干部处理复杂问题的过程和结果，看其能力水平。考察识别干部，功夫要下在平时，并注意重要关头、关键时刻。"操千曲而后晓声，观千剑而后识器。"干部业绩在实践，干部声名在民间。要多到基层干部群众中、多在乡语口碑中了解干部,既要在"大事"上看德,又要在"小节"中察德。

17."草木植成,国之富也。"——《管子·立政》

英译:"Vegetation is a valuable asset of a country."

解析:汉语原文意思是草木繁殖成长,国家就会富足。习近平总书记指出,要提升生态系统质量和稳定性。这既是增加优质生态产品供给的必然要求,也是减缓和适应气候变化带来不利影响的重要手段。"草木植成,国之富也。"良好生态本身蕴含着经济社会价值。要坚持系统观念,从生态系统整体性出发,推进山水林田湖草沙一体化保护和修复,更加注重综合治理、系统治理、源头治理。

18."长风破浪会有时"——李白《行路难三首(其一)》

英译:"forge ahead like a gigantic ship breaking through strong winds and heavy waves"

解析:汉语原文意思是坚信乘风破浪的时机定会到来。习近平总书记指出,改革开放以来,我们总结历史经验,不断艰辛探索,终于找到了实现中华民族伟大复兴的正确道路,取得了举世瞩目的伟大成就。这条道路就是中国特色社会主义。中华民族的明天,可以说是"长风破浪会有时"。

19."长太息以掩涕兮,哀民生之多艰。"——屈原《离骚》

英译:"Long did I sigh to hold back tears; saddened I am by the grief of my people."

解析:汉语原文意思是长声叹息而泪流满面,为老百姓多灾多难而哀伤。习近平总书记认为,贫困是人类社会的顽疾。反贫困始终是古今中外治国安邦的一件大事。一部中国史,就是一部中华民族同贫困作斗争的历史。屈原"长太息以掩涕兮,哀民生之多艰"的感慨反映了中华民族对摆脱贫困的深深渴望。摆脱贫困,成了中国人民孜孜以求的梦想,也是实现中华民族伟大复兴中国梦的重要内容。

20."常制不可以待变化,一途不可以应无方,刻船不可以索遗剑。"——葛洪《抱朴子·外篇·广譬》

英译:"A fixed system is not able to respond to myriad changes, a single road will not lead to multiple destinations, and a sword lost in a river will not be found by leaving a mark on the boat."

解析：汉语原文意思是固定不变的制度不能应对千变万化的社会，一条道路不可以通达无数的目的地，在行船上刻记号无法找到落入水中的宝剑。习近平总书记指出，共青团要勇于自我革命，始终成为紧跟党走在时代前列的先进组织。对共青团来说，建设什么样的青年组织、怎样建设青年组织是事关根本的重大问题。"常制不可以待变化，一途不可以应无方，刻船不可以索遗剑。"共青团只有勇于自我革命，才能跟上时代前进、青年发展、实践创新的步伐。要把党的全面领导落实到工作的全过程各领域，走好中国特色社会主义群团发展道路，聚焦不断保持和增强政治性、先进性、群众性的目标方向，推动共青团改革向纵深发展。

21. "驰命走驿，不绝于时月"——范晔《后汉书·西域传》

英译："crossed the desert for months on end on post-horses"

解析：汉语原文意思是送信的、传达命令的人奔走不停，生动描绘了古丝绸之路上使者往来不断、商贩不绝于途的繁荣景象。习近平总书记指出，回顾中阿人民交往历史，我们就会想起陆上丝绸之路和海上香料之路。我们的祖先在大漠戈壁上"驰命走驿，不绝于时月"，走在了古代世界各民族友好交往的前列。中阿人民在维护民族尊严、捍卫国家主权的斗争中相互支持，在探索发展道路、实现民族振兴的道路上相互帮助，在深化人文交流、繁荣民族文化的事业中相互借鉴。

22. "迟日江山丽，春风花草香。"——杜甫《绝句二首》

英译："The land bathes in the spring sunshine, and the wind sends the aromas of grass and flowers."

解析：汉语原文意思是江河山川沐浴在春光中多么秀美明丽，阵阵和煦的春风送来花草的香气。"迟日江山丽，春风花草香。"四月的北京，春回大地，万物复苏。习近平总书记用此诗欢迎远道而来的各位宾客。

23. "出入相友，守望相助"——《孟子·滕文公上》

英译："Care for each other and help one another."

解析：汉语原文意思是出入相互做伴，遇到外来的侵害或灾祸时，协同看守瞭望,彼此提供帮助,指人与人之间要互帮互助、和睦共处。习近平总书记指出,中华文明绵延数千年,有其独特的价值体系。中华优秀传统文化已经成为中华民族的基因,植根在中国人内心,潜移默化影响着中国人的思想方式和行为方式。我们提倡和弘扬社会主义核心价值观,必须从中汲取丰富营养,否则就不会有生命力和影响力。

24. "聪者听于无声,明者见于未形"——司马迁《史记·淮南衡山列传》

英译:"A person with sharp ears can hear sounds others cannot, and a person with keen vision can see things others cannot."

解析:汉语原文意思是聪明的人可以于无声处听有声,于无形处见有形,懂得未雨绸缪。习近平总书记指出,"聪者听于无声,明者见于未形"。科技创新永无止境。科技竞争就像短道速滑,我们在加速,人家也在加速,最后要看谁速度更快、谁的速度更能持续。我国广大科技工作者要敢于担当、勇于超越、找准方向、扭住不放,牢固树立敢为天下先的志向和信心,敢于走别人没有走过的路,在攻坚克难中追求卓越,勇于创造引领世界潮流的科技成果。

25. "从善如登,从恶如崩。"——左丘明《国语·周语下》

英译:"Virtue uplifts, while vice debases."

解析:汉语原文意思是做善事就像登山一样艰难,作恶就像崩塌一样迅速,指学好很难,走邪路易。习近平总书记指出,广大青年要把正确的道德认知、自觉的道德养成、积极的道德实践紧密结合起来,自觉树立和践行社会主义核心价值观,带头倡导良好社会风气。要加强思想道德修养,自觉弘扬爱国主义、集体主义、社会主义思想,积极倡导社会公德、职业道德、家庭美德。要牢记"从善如登,从恶如崩"的道理,始终保持积极的人生态度、良好的道德品质、健康的生活情趣。

D

26. "大道之行也,天下为公。"——《礼记·礼运》

英译:"When the Great Way prevailed, a public spirit ruled all under Heaven." / "When the Great Way rules, the land under Heaven belongs to the people."

解析:汉语原文意思是大道(原始共产社会的准则)实行的时代,天下成为公共的,是天下人的天下。习近平总书记强调坚持公平包容,打造平衡普惠的发展模式。"大道之行也,天下为公。"发展的目的是造福人民。要让发展更加平衡,让发展机会更加均等、发展成果人人共享,就要完善发展理念和模式,提升发展公平性、有效性、协同性。

27. "大鹏之动,非一羽之轻也;骐骥之速,非一足之力也。"——王符《潜夫论·释难》

英译: "The roc soars not merely because of the lightness of one of its feathers; the steed gallops not merely because of the strength of one of its legs."

解析:汉语原文意思是大鹏鸟能够冲天飞翔,并不是因为它的某一根羽毛轻盈至极;同样,骏马能够快速奔跑,也并不是因为它的一只脚强大有力。习近平总书记认为,人民是历史的创造者。一切成就都归功于人民,一切荣耀都归属于人民。面向未来,要战胜前进道路上的种种风险挑战,顺利实现中共十九大描绘的宏伟蓝图,必须紧紧依靠人民。正所谓"大鹏之动,非一羽之轻也;骐骥之速,非一足之力也"。中国要飞得高、跑得快,就得汇集和激发近14亿人民的磅礴力量。

28. "大学之道,在明明德,在亲民,在止于至善。"——《礼记·大学》

英译: "The way to great learning is to manifest bright virtue and to treat the people as one's own family, thereby arriving at supreme goodness."

解析:汉语原文意思是大学的宗旨,在于彰显光明的德性,在于亲和民众,在于达到言行的至善。习近平总书记指出,古人说:"大学之道,在明明德,在亲民,在止于至善。"核心价值观,其实就是一种德,既是个人的德,也是一种大德,就是国家的德、社会的德。国无德不兴,人无德不立。如果一个民族、一个国家没有共同的核心价值观,莫衷一是,行无依归,那这个民族、这个国家就无法前进。这样的情形,在我国历史上,在当今世界上,都屡见不鲜。

29. "得众则得国,失众则失国。"——《礼记·大学》

英译: "Win popular support, and you win the country; lose it, and you will lose the country."

解析:汉语原文意思是得到民众的拥戴就能得到整个国家,失去民众的拥护就会失去整个国家。习近平总书记强调,人民立场是中国共产党的根本政治立场,是马克思主义政党区别于其他政党的显著标志。党与人民风雨同舟、生死与共,始终保持血肉联系，是党战胜一切困难和风险的根本保证，正所谓"得众则得国，失众则失国"。

30."德不孤，必有邻。"——《论语·里仁》

英译："A man of high moral quality will never feel lonely."

解析：汉语原文意思是有道德的人是不会孤单的，一定有志同道合的人来和他相伴。习近平总书记指出，像这样的思想和理念，不论过去还是现在，都有其鲜明的民族特色，都有其永不褪色的时代价值。这些思想和理念，既随着时间推移和时代变迁而不断与时俱进，又有其自身的连续性和稳定性。我们生而为中国人，最根本的是我们有中国人的独特精神世界，有百姓日用而不觉的价值观。我们提倡的社会主义核心价值观，就充分体现了对中华优秀传统文化的传承和升华。

31."德不优者，不能怀远；才不大者，不能博见。"——王充《论衡·别通》

英译："A person without virtue has no high aspirations; a person without talent has no keen insights."

解析：汉语原文意思是品德不优秀的人，不会胸怀远大理想；才能不足的人，不会具有渊博的见识。习近平总书记强调，各级党员、干部特别是领导干部都要坚定党性立场，加强党性修养，心怀"国之大者"，遇到问题、做出决策、处理工作首先要从政治上想一想，对照党章、党内政治生活准则、党纪处分条例举一反三，看准能不能干、该不该做，在风浪考验中立得住脚，在诱惑"围猎"面前定得住神，始终做政治上的明白人。正所谓"德不优者，不能怀远；才不大者，不能博见"。

32."德者，本也。"——《礼记·大学》

英译："Virtue is the root."

解析：汉语原文是"德者，本也；财者，末也"，意思是德行才是根本，财富只是小事。习近平总书记指出，要修德，加强道德修养，注重道德实践。"德者，本也。"道德之于个人、之于社会，都具有基础性意义，做人做事第一位的是崇德修身。这就是我们的用人标准为什么是德才兼备、以德为先，因为德是首要、是方向，一个人只有明大德、守公德、严私德，其才方能用得其所。

33. "登高使人心旷，临流使人意远。"——洪应明《菜根谭》

英译："From a mountain top you will enjoy a broader outlook; down by the riverside you will enjoy a pleasant prospect."

解析：汉语原文意思是登上高山会使人心胸开阔，面对清流会使人神清意远。习近平总书记指出，中国特色社会主义新时代是中国人民在新的考验和挑战中创造光明未来的时代，也是中国人民拼搏奋斗创造美好生活的时代。"登高使人心旷，临流使人意远。"广大文艺工作者要紧跟时代步伐，从时代的脉搏中感悟艺术的脉动，把艺术创造向着亿万人民的伟大奋斗敞开，向着丰富多彩的社会生活敞开，从时代之变、中国之进、人民之呼中提炼主题、萃取题材，展现中华历史之美、山河之美、文化之美，抒写中国人民奋斗之志、创造之力、发展之果，全方位全景式展现新时代的精神气象。

34. "蠹众而木折，隙大而墙坏。"——《商君书·修权》

英译："Many worms will disintegrate wood, and a big enough crack will lead to the collapse of a wall."

解析：汉语原文意思是蛀虫多了，木头就要折断，缝隙大了，墙就要倒塌，比喻不利的因素多了，便会招致灾祸。习近平总书记强调，反腐倡廉必须常抓不懈，拒腐防变必须警钟长鸣。要牢记"蠹众而木折，隙大而墙坏"的道理，保持惩治腐败的高压态势，做到有案必查、有腐必惩，坚持"老虎"、"苍蝇"一起打，切实维护人民合法权益，努力做到干部清正、政府清廉、政治清明。

E

35. "恩德相结者，谓之知己；腹心相照者，谓之知心。"——冯梦龙《警世通言·俞伯牙摔琴谢知音》

英译："People drawn to each other by kindness and virtues make good friends; people who hold together with a meeting of minds make bosom friends."

解析：汉语原文意思是施恩于人、德义相交的，可称得上知己；肝胆相照、心心相印的，可称得上知心。习近平总书记指出，古人说："恩德相结者，谓之知己；腹心相照者，谓之知心。"特别值得肯定的是，广大港澳同胞到内地投资兴业，不只是因为看到了商机，而且是希望看到内地摆脱贫困、国家日益富强。大家无偿捐助内地的教科文卫体和扶贫济困等公益事业，不只是为了行善积德，而且是基于与内地人民的同胞之情。每一次内地遇到重大自然灾害时，港澳同胞都是感同身受，最先伸出援手，表现出守望相助、血浓于水的同胞之情。

36."耳闻之不如目见之，目见之不如足践之"——刘向《说苑·政理》

英译："Hearing is not as good as seeing, and seeing is not as good as experiencing."

解析：汉语原文意思是耳朵听到的不如亲眼看到的，亲眼看到的不如自己调查到的。习近平总书记认为，好干部除了要加强学习，还要加强实践。"耳闻之不如目见之，目见之不如足践之。"知识和经验犹如雄鹰之双翼，只有经风雨、见世面，才能飞得更高、飞得更远。越是条件艰苦、困难大、矛盾多的地方，越能锤炼人。干部要深入基层、深入实际、深入群众，在改革发展的主战场、维护稳定的第一线、服务群众的最前沿砥砺品质、提高本领。

F

37."法非从天下，非从地出，发于人间，合乎人心而已。"——《慎子·逸文》

英译："The law does not fall from the sky or grow from the earth; it manifests from among the people and reflects their will."

解析：汉语原文意思是一个国家的法律制度不是从天上掉下来的，也不是从地下长出来的，它产生于人间，符合人们的愿望而已。习近平总书记认为，良法是善治的前提。"法非从天下，非从地出，发于人间，合乎人心而已。"要抓住提高立法质量这个关键，发挥好人大及其常委会在立法工作中的主导作用，坚持尊重和体现客观规律，坚持为了人民、依靠人民，坚持严格依照法定权限和法定程序，深入推进科学立法、民主立法、依法立法。要丰富立法形式，增强立法的针对性、适用性、可操作性。

38."法，国之权衡也，时之准绳也。"——吴兢《贞观政要·论诚信》

英译："Law is the scale of a state and the ethical benchmark for a society."

解析：汉语原文意思是法是国家的秤，是社会的准绳。秤是用来判定轻重的，准绳是用来纠正弯曲的。习近平总书记强调全面贯彻实施宪法，维护宪法权威和尊严。古人说："法者，国之权衡也，时之准绳也。"宪法是国家的根本法，是党和人民意志的集中体现，具有最高的法律地位、法律权威、法律效力。维护宪法权威，就是维护党和人民共同意志的权威；捍卫宪法尊严，就是捍卫党和人民共同意志的尊严；保证宪法实施，就是保证人民根本利益的实现。

39. "法令既行，纪律自正，则无不治之国，无不化之民。"——包拯《上殿札子》

英译："When the law is effective and discipline enforced, the nation is under good governance and people's support is won."

解析：汉语原文意思是只要依法治国法令畅通，纪律和风气自然清正，那样就不会有治不好的国家，也不会有顽固不化的百姓。习近平总书记强调，全面加强纪律建设，用严明的纪律管全党治全党。"法令既行，纪律自正，则无不治之国，无不化之民。"纪律严明是我们党不断从胜利走向胜利的重要保障。党的十九大把纪律建设摆在更加突出位置，纳入党的建设总体布局，表明了用严明的纪律管党治党的坚定决心。

40. "法与时转则治"——《韩非子·心度》

英译："The law must be adaptive to the changing times, so that social order and stability are maintained."

解析：汉语原文意思是法律能随着时代变化而变化，国家就能治理好。习近平总书记指出，"法与时转则治"。随着经济社会不断发展、经济社会生活中各种利益关系不断变化，民法典在实施过程中必然会遇到一些新情况新问题。新技术、新产业、新业态和人们新的工作方式、交往方式、生活方式不断涌现，也给民事立法提出了新课题。要坚持问题导向，适应技术发展进步新需要，在新的实践基础上推动民法典不断完善和发展。

41. "法者，国家所以布大信于天下"——吴兢《贞观政要·论公平》

英译："The law is what the state relies on to gain popular trust."

解析：汉语原文意思是法律是国家用以在全国树立最高威信的。习近平总书记认为，宪法集中体现了党和人民的统一意志和共同愿望，是国家意志的最高表现形式。"法者，国家所以布大信于天下。"可以说，宪法是国家布最大的公信于天下。建章立法需要讲求科学精神，全面认识和自觉运用规律。通过修改宪法使我国宪法更好体现人民意志，更好体现中国特色社会主义制度的优势，更好适应提高中国共产党长期执政能力、推进全面依法治国、推进国家治理体系和治理能力现代化的要求，为新时代坚持和发展中国特色社会主义提供宪法保障。

42. "法者，治之端也" ——《荀子·君道》

英译："The law is the very foundation of governance."

解析：汉语原文意思是法律是国家治理的开端，是国家治理的根本，能够运用明确的制度，是治理好一个国家的开始。习近平总书记认为，我们要坚持以国际法则为基础，不搞唯我独尊。中国古人讲："法者，治之端也。"国际社会应该按照各国共同达成的规则和共识来治理，而不能由一个或几个国家来发号施令。联合国宪章是公认的国与国关系的基本准则。没有这些国际社会共同制定、普遍公认的国际法则，世界最终将滑向弱肉强食的丛林法则，给人类带来灾难性后果。

43. "凡将立国，制度不可不察也" ——《商君书·壹言》

英译："A state system must be established when founding a country."

解析：汉语原文意思是凡是要建立一个国家，对于制度不能不认真考虑。习近平总书记指出，古人说："凡将立国，制度不可不察也。"制度优势是一个国家的最大优势，制度竞争是国家间最根本的竞争。制度稳则国家稳。新中国成立70年来，中华民族之所以能迎来从站起来、富起来到强起来的伟大飞跃，最根本的是因为党领导人民建立和完善了中国特色社会主义制度，形成和发展了党的领导和经济、政治、文化、社会、生态文明、军事、外事等各方面制度，不断加强和完善国家治理。

44. "非尽百家之美，不能成一人之奇" ——刘开《与阮芸台宫保论文书》

英译："Only by learning from hundred schools of thoughts and drawing on their strength can one develop and establish one's own distinct style."

解析：汉语原文意思是不把各家的风格融会贯通，就不能形成自己的特色。习近平总书记认为，世界是丰富多彩的，多样性是人类文明的魅力所在，更是世界发展的活力和动力之源。"非尽百家之美，不能成一人之奇。"文明没有高下、优劣之分，只有特色、地域之别，只有在交流中才能融合，在融合中才能进步。一个国家走的道路行不行，关键要看是否符合本国国情，是否顺应时代发展潮流，能否带来经济发展、社会进步、民生改善、社会稳定，能否得到人民支持和拥护，能否为人类进步事业作出贡献。

45. "非学无以广才,非志无以成学。"——诸葛亮《诫子书》

英译:"One cannot enhance one's ability and wisdom if one does not work hard; neither can one succeed without ambition."

解析:汉语原文意思是不刻苦学习就无从增长见识、提高才干,没有坚定不移的志向就难以完成学业、学有所成。习近平总书记强调广大青年树立和培育社会主义核心价值观,要勤学,下得苦功夫,求得真学问。知识是树立核心价值观的重要基础。我国古人说:"非学无以广才,非志无以成学。"大学的青春时光,人生只有一次,应好好珍惜,为学之要贵在勤奋、贵在钻研、贵在有恒。要勤于学习、敏于求知,注重把所学知识内化于心,形成自己的见解,既要专攻博览,又要关心国家、关心人民、关心世界,学会担当社会责任。

46. "风雨不动安如山"——杜甫《茅屋为秋风所破歌》

英译:"remain as steadfast as a peak in the face of storm"

解析:汉语原文意思是无论处于多大的狂风骤雨,房屋都安稳得像是山一样。习近平总书记认为,中国共产党人的理想信念建立在对马克思主义的深刻理解之上,建立在对历史规律的深刻把握之上。历史和实践反复证明,一个政党有了远大理想和崇高追求,就会坚强有力,无坚不摧,无往不胜,就能经受一次次挫折而又一次次奋起;一名干部有了坚定的理想信念,站位就高了,心胸就开阔了,就能坚持正确政治方向,做到"风雨不动安如山"。信仰认定了就要信上一辈子,否则就会出大问题。

47. "夫孝,德之本也"——《孝经·开宗明义章》

英译:"Filial piety is the root of morality."

解析:汉语原文意思是孝是道德的根本,一切品行的教化都发自孝道。习近平总书记指出,古人讲:"夫孝,德之本也。"自古以来,中国人就提倡孝老爱亲,倡导老吾老以及人之老、幼吾幼以及人之幼。我国已经进入老龄化社会。让老年人老有所养、老有所依、老有所乐、老有所安,关系社会和谐稳定。我们要在全社会大力提倡尊敬老人、关爱老人、赡养老人,大力发展老龄事业,让所有老年人都能有一个幸福美满的晚年。

48. "富贵不能淫,贫贱不能移,威武不能屈"——《孟子·滕文公下》

英译:"Never being corrupted by riches and honors, never departing from principle despite poverty or humble origin, and never submitting to force or threat."

解析：汉语原文意思是真正的大丈夫，富贵不能使他腐化堕落，贫贱不能使他改变志向，武力也不能使他屈服。习近平总书记指出，中国传统文化博大精深，学习和掌握其中的各种思想精华，对树立正确的世界观、人生观、价值观很有益处。古人所说的"富贵不能淫，贫贱不能移，威武不能屈"的浩然正气，体现了中华民族的优秀传统文化和民族精神，我们都应该继承和发扬。

G

49. "盖有非常之功，必待非常之人。"——班固《汉书·武帝纪》

英译："To accomplish extraordinary feats, we must wait for extraordinary persons."

解析：汉语原文意思是要想成就异乎寻常的丰功伟业，必须依靠非同寻常的人才。习近平总书记指出，"盖有非常之功，必待非常之人"。人是科技创新最关键的因素，创新的事业呼唤创新的人才。尊重人才，是中华民族的悠久传统。我国要在科技创新方面走在世界前列，必须在创新实践中发现人才、在创新活动中培育人才、在创新事业中凝聚人才，必须大力培养造就规模宏大、结构合理、素质优良的创新型科技人才。

50. "功崇惟志，业广惟勤"——《尚书·周官》

英译："One must both have great ambition and make tireless efforts to achieve great exploits."

解析：汉语原文意思是取得伟大的功业，是由于有伟大的志向；完成伟大的功业，在于辛勤不懈地工作。习近平总书记指出，"功崇惟志，业广惟勤"。我国仍处于并将长期处于社会主义初级阶段，实现中国梦，创造全体人民更加美好的生活，任重而道远，需要我们每一个人继续付出辛勤劳动和艰苦努力。全国广大工人、农民、知识分子，要发挥聪明才智，勤奋工作，积极在经济社会发展中发挥主力军和生力军作用。一切国家机关工作人员，要克己奉公、勤政廉政，关心人民疾苦，为人民办实事。中国人民解放军全体指战员，中国人民武装警察部队全体官兵，要按照听党指挥、能打胜仗、作风优良的强军目标，提高履行使命能力，坚决捍卫国家主权、安全、发展利益，坚决保卫人民生命财产安全。

51. "功以才成，业由才广。"——《三国志·蜀志·董允传》裴松之注引《襄阳记》

英译："Feats are accomplished by capable people; work develops because of achievers."

解析：汉语原文意思是伟大的功业必须要人才来实现，伟大的事业也因人才方能不断壮大。习近平总书记指出，"功以才成，业由才广"。党和人民事业要不断发展，就要把各方面人才更好使用起来，聚天下英才而用之。我们要以识才的慧眼、爱才的诚意、用才的胆识、容才的雅量、聚才的良方，广开进贤之路，把党内和党外、国内和国外等各方面优秀人才吸引过来、凝聚起来，努力形成人人渴望成才、人人努力成才、人人皆可成才、人人尽展其才的良好局面。

52. "苟利国家生死以，岂因祸福避趋之。"——林则徐《赴戍登程口占示家人》

英译："I am willing to sacrifice my life for my country. How then should I shrink from lesser possible harm?"

解析：汉语原文意思是只要对国家民族有利，即使牺牲自己生命也心甘情愿，绝不会因为自己可能受到灾祸而躲避。习近平总书记指出，做事要有魄力，为官要有担当。凡是有利于党和人民的事，我们就要事不避难、义不逃责，大胆地干、坚决地干，正所谓"苟利国家生死以，岂因祸福避趋之"。

53. "苟利于民，不必法古；苟周于事，不必循旧。"——刘安《淮南子·氾论训》

英译："If it is good for the people, there is no need to follow the practices of antiquity; if it serves the matter at hand, there is no need to observe the conventions of old."

解析：汉语原文意思是只要对人民有好处，就不必一定要效法古人的制度；只要有助于事情的成功，就不必沿袭旧有的规矩。习近平总书记认为，法治领域改革有一个特点，就是很多问题都涉及法律规定。改革要于法有据，但也不能因为现行法律规定就不敢越雷池一步，那是无法推进改革的，正所谓"苟利于民不必法古，苟周于事不必循旧"。需要推进的改革，将来可以先修改法律规定再推进。对涉及改革的事项，中央全面深化改革领导小组要认真研究和督办。

54. "苟日新，日日新，又日新。"——《礼记·大学》

英译："If you can in one day renovate yourself, do so from day to day. Yea, let there be daily renovation."

解析：汉语原文意思是如果能每天除旧更新，就要天天除旧更新，不间断地更新又更新。习近平总书记指出，广大青年一定要勇于创新创造。创新是民族进步的灵魂，是一个国家兴旺发达的不竭源泉，也是中华民族最深沉的民族禀赋，正所谓"苟日新，日日新，又日新"。生活从不眷顾因循守旧、满足现状者，从不等待不思进取、坐享其成者，而是将更多机遇留给善于和勇于创新的人们。青年是社会上最富活力、最具创造性的群体，理应走在创新创造前列。

55. "孤举者难起，众行者易趋"——魏源《默觚·治篇八》

英译："The going may be tough when one walks alone, but it gets easier when people walk together."

解析：汉语原文意思是一个人独自举起重物可能会很困难，但许多人一块儿抬着，则容易行走得快。习近平总书记指出，"孤举者难起，众行者易趋"。新冠肺炎疫情阴霾未散，世界经济复苏前路坎坷，各国人民更需要同舟共济、共克时艰。中国愿同各国一道，共建开放型世界经济，让开放的春风温暖世界！

56. "观时而制法，因事而制礼"——《战国策·赵策二》

英译："Laws should be made based on the developments of the times, and rituals should be instituted to meet specific needs."

解析：汉语原文意思是根据时代的发展制定法律，根据事情的变化制定制度。习近平总书记指出，"观时而制法，因事而制礼"。党中央考虑启动这次宪法修改的一个重要因素，就是深化国家监察体制改革的需要。深化国家监察体制改革是党中央决策和推进的重大政治体制改革，需要在国家机构顶层设计上作出重要调整和完善，涉及宪法修改问题。从推进国家监察体制改革的过程看，比较好地处理了深化改革和推进法治的关系，贯彻了凡属重大改革都要于法有据的要求，彰显了党坚持在宪法法律范围内活动的执政原则。

57. "国虽大，好战必亡"——《司马法·仁本》

英译："A warlike state, however big it may be, will eventually perish."

解析：汉语原文意思是国家即便再强大，如果喜欢战争也必然会灭亡。习近平总书记强调，中华民族是爱好和平的民族。一个民族最深沉的精神追求，一定要在其薪火相传的民族精神中来进行基因测序。有着5000多年历史的中华文明，始终崇尚和平，和平、和睦、和谐的追求深深植根于中华民族的精神世界之中，深深溶化在中国人民的血脉之中。中国自古就提出了"国虽大，好战必亡"的箴言。中国历史上曾经长期是世界上最强大的国家之一，但没有留下殖民和侵略他国的记录。我们坚持走和平发展道路，是对几千年来中华民族热爱和平的文化传统的继承和发扬。

58. "国以民为本，社稷亦为民而立"——朱熹《四书章句集注·孟子集注·尽心章句下》

英译："The people are the foundation of a country, and are also what the rule of a country is for."

解析：汉语原文意思是国家以人民为根本，也是为人民而设立。习近平总书记指出，"国以民为本，社稷亦为民而立"。加强党的政治建设，要紧扣民心这个最大的政治，把赢得民心民意、汇集民智民力作为重要着力点。要站稳人民立场，贯彻党的群众路线，同人民想在一起、干在一起，坚决反对"四风"特别是形式主义、官僚主义，始终保持党同人民群众的血肉联系。

59. "国之称富者，在乎丰民"——钟会《刍荛论》

英译："A country is truly prosperous only when its people are prosperous."

解析：汉语原文意思是国家真正的富强，在于让百姓都能富裕起来。习近平总书记强调正确认识和把握实现共同富裕的战略目标和实践途径。"国之称富者，在乎丰民。"财富的创造和分配是各国都面对的重大问题。在我国社会主义制度下，既要不断解放和发展社会生产力，不断创造和积累社会财富，又要防止两极分化，切实推动人的全面发展、全体人民共同富裕取得更为明显的实质性进展。

H

60. "海不辞水，故能成其大"——《管子·形势解》

英译："The ocean is vast because it rejects no rivers."

解析：汉语原文意思是大海不拒绝点滴的水，才能浩瀚无边。习近平总书记指出，"海不辞水，故能成其大"。中国是世界上最大的发展中国家，非洲是发展中国家最集中的大陆，中非早已结成休戚与共的命运共同体。我们愿同非洲人民心往一处想、劲往一处使，共筑更加紧密的中非命运共同体，为推动构建人类命运共同体树立典范。

61. "浩渺行无极,扬帆但信风。"——尚颜《送朴山人归新罗》

英译:"Boundless is the ocean where we sail with the wind."

解析:汉语原文意思是广阔无垠的大海没有尽头,扬起风帆向着目的地御风而行。习近平总书记指出,"浩渺行无极,扬帆但信风"。亚太是我们共同发展的空间,我们都是亚太这片大海中前行的风帆。亚太未来发展攸关亚太经合组织每个成员的利益。

62. "合天下之众者财,理天下之财者法"——王安石《度支副使厅壁题名记》

英译:"It is wealth that binds the people of a country together, and it is the law that governs the wealth of a country."

解析:汉语原文意思是能聚合天下之民众的是财富,治理天下经济的是法令。法令不当,则经济形势虽好也无从管理。国家必须掌握全国之财力、物力,才能使全国民众齐心合力而效力于国家。习近平总书记指出,搞社会主义市场经济是我们党的一个伟大创造。既然是社会主义市场经济,就必然会产生各种形态的资本。"合天下之众者财,理天下之财者法。"我们要探索如何在社会主义市场经济条件下发挥资本的积极作用,同时有效控制资本的消极作用。

63. "和而不同"——《论语·子路》

英译:"harmony without uniformity"

解析:汉语原文意思是君子能够与他人和谐相处,却不盲从附和。总书记认为,中华优秀传统文化已经成为中华民族的基因,植根在中国人内心,潜移默化影响着中国人的思想方式和行为方式,这样的思想和理念,不论过去还是现在都有其鲜明的民族特点,具有永不褪色的时代价值。

64. "河海不择细流,故能就其深"——司马迁《史记·李斯列传》

英译:"The ceaseless inflow of rivers makes the ocean deep."

解析:汉语原文意思是江河湖海不拒绝细小溪流的汇入,所以能成就它的深广。习近平总书记认为,商品、资金、技术、人员流通,可以为经济增长提供强劲动力和广阔空间。"河海不择细流,故能就其深。"如果人为阻断江河的流入,再大的海,迟早都有干涸的一天。我们要促进贸易和投资自由化便利化,旗帜鲜明反对保护主义,推动经济全球化朝着更加开放、包容、普惠、平衡、共赢的方向发展。

65. "横眉冷对千夫指，俯首甘为孺子牛。"——鲁迅《自嘲》

英译："Holding my head high in defiance of the enemy's attacks, bowing my head low in obedience to the people."

解析：汉语原文意思是横眉怒对那些各路来的敌人的指责，俯下身子甘愿为老百姓做孺子牛。习近平总书记指出，要有"横眉冷对千夫指，俯首甘为孺子牛"的精神，歌颂真善美、针砭假恶丑。对正能量要敢写敢歌，理直气壮，正大光明。对丑恶事要敢怒敢批，大义凛然，威武不屈。要弘扬行风艺德，树立文艺界良好社会形象，营造自尊自爱、互学互鉴、天朗气清的行业风气。

66. "红日初升，其道大光。"——梁启超《少年中国说》

英译："The red rising sun will light up the road ahead."

解析：汉语原文意思是红日刚刚升起，道路充满霞光。习近平总书记指出，"红日初升，其道大光"。只要中非友好的接力棒能够在青年一代手中不断相传，中非命运共同体就一定会更具生机活力，中华民族伟大复兴的中国梦和非洲人民团结振兴的非洲梦就一定能够早日实现！

67. "惟江上之清风，与山间之明月，耳得之而为声，目遇之而成色，取之无禁，用之不竭"——苏轼《赤壁赋》

英译："Only the gentle breeze caressing the river and the bright moonlight pouring down on the mountains are a bounty and ceaseless feast for the eye and the ear that nature offers."

解析：汉语原文意思是只有江上的清风以及山间的明月，听到便成了声音，进入眼帘便绘出形色，取得这些不会有人禁止，感受这些也不会有竭尽的忧虑。习近平总书记认为，党的领导干部更要对组织和人民常怀感恩敬畏之心，对功名利禄要知足，对物质享受和个人待遇要知止。"惟江上之清风，与山间之明月，耳得之而为声，目遇之而成色，取之无禁，用之不竭。"苏轼的这份情怀，正是今人所欠缺的，也是最为珍贵的。生不带来、死不带去。想通这个道理，就一定能够以身作则、以上率下，以清廉养浩然正气。

68. "祸患常积于忽微，而智勇多困于所溺"——欧阳修《新五代史·伶官传》

英译："Disasters often result from neglecting the smallest things; the wise and brave are often trapped by their minor indulgences."

解析：汉语原文意思是祸患常常是由一些微小的失误累积而成的，而人的智慧和勇气常常被他们所沉迷的事物困扰。习近平总书记指出，正衣冠，主要是在照镜子的基础上，按照为民务实清廉的要求，勇于正视缺点和不足，严明党的纪律特别是政治纪律，敢于触及思想、正视矛盾和问题，从自己做起，从现在改起，端正行为，自觉把党性修养正一正、把党员义务理一理、把党纪国法紧一紧，保持共产党人良好形象。正视和解决自身存在的问题需要勇气，但这样做最主动。"祸患常积于忽微，而智勇多困于所溺。"养成勤正衣冠的习惯，能收到防微杜渐之效。

69."祸几始作，当杜其萌；疾证方形，当绝其根。"——何坦《西畴老人常言·原治》

英译："We must nip troubles in the bud and eliminate illnesses at their earliest stage."

解析：汉语原文意思是在祸患刚出现时，就迅速解决于萌芽状态；当身体显示出病症时，就立刻医治以免留下病根。习近平总书记强调正确认识和把握防范化解重大风险。20世纪90年代以来，我国有效应对了亚洲金融危机、国际金融危机、新冠肺炎疫情等重大考验。现在，我国经济金融领域风险隐患很多，但总体可控。要坚持底线思维。古人说："祸几始作，当杜其萌；疾证方形，当绝其根。"我们要发挥好党的领导和我国社会主义制度优势，见微知著，抓早抓小，着力避免发生重大风险或危机。

J

70."机者如神，难遇易失"——魏收《魏书·傅永传》

英译："Opportunities are rare and hard to grasp, and easy to lose."

解析：汉语原文意思是机遇很难把握，它难以遇到，却又容易失去。习近平总书记指出，我国是经济全球化的积极参与者和坚定支持者，也是重要建设者和主要受益者。我国经济发展进入新常态，妥善应对我国经济社会发展中面临的困难和挑战，更加需要扩大对外开放。"机者如神，难遇易失。"我们必须审时度势，努力在经济全球化中抢占先机、赢得主动。

71."己所不欲，勿施于人。"——《论语·颜渊》

英译："Don't do unto others what you don't want others to do unto you." / "not doing to others what we would not have done to ourselves"

解析：汉语原文意思是自己不想做的事情，不要强加给别人。习近平总书记强调相互尊重，坚守国际关系基本准则。东方文化讲究"己所不欲，勿施于人"，平等相待、和合与共是我们的共同诉求。我们率先倡导和平共处五项原则和"万隆精神"，中国在东盟对话伙伴中最先加入《东南亚友好合作条约》。我们照顾彼此重大关切，尊重各自发展路径，以真诚沟通增进理解和信任，以求同存异妥处分歧和问题，共同维护和弘扬亚洲价值观。

72. "家给人足，四海之内无一夫不获其所。"——孙中山《同盟会宣言》

英译："every family living in plenty, with not a single person left behind"

解析：汉语原文意思是主持家业就要使每一个人富足，四海之内没有一个成年男子不在他应在的位置上。习近平总书记认为，贫困是人类社会的顽疾。反贫困始终是古今中外治国安邦的一件大事。一部中国史，就是一部中华民族同贫困作斗争的历史。近代以后，由于封建统治的腐朽和西方列强的入侵，中国政局动荡、战乱不已、民不聊生，贫困的梦魇更为严重地困扰着中国人民。摆脱贫困，成了中国人民孜孜以求的梦想，也是实现中华民族伟大复兴中国梦的重要内容。

73. "见不贤而内自省"——《论语·里仁》

英译："When we see a bad example we should turn to check our own conduct."

解析：汉语原文意思是看见没有德行的人，自己就要反省是否有和他一样的错误。习近平总书记指出，正风反腐，人人有责，要当参与者，不当旁观者。每名党员干部都应坚决摒弃"看戏"心态，真正从别人身上吸取教训，把未病当作有病防，坚守底线、追求高标准，不断提高自身免疫力。要加强纪律教育，不搞不教而诛，用身边人身边事开展警示教育，用典型案例当头棒喝，使更多的干部红脸出汗、知错知止，"见不贤而内自省"，使铁的纪律转化为党员、干部的日常习惯和自觉遵循。

74. "见出以知入，观往以知来"——《列子·说符》

英译："One can tell the inside of a thing by observing its outside and see future developments by reviewing the past."

解析：汉语原文意思是看见外表就可以知道内里，观察过往就可以预知未来。这句话可以引申解释为，由表及里，透过现象可以看到事物的本质；以史为鉴，学习历史可以掌握未来的发展规律。习近平总书记指出，"见出以知入，观往以知来"。一个国家、一个民族要振兴，就必须在历史前进的逻辑中前进、在时代发展的潮流中发展。中国扩大高水平开放的决心不会变，同世界分享发展机遇的决心不会变，推动经济全球化朝着更加开放、包容、普惠、平衡、共赢方向发展的决心不会变。

75. "见善如不及，见不善如探汤。"——《论语·季氏》

英译："Contemplating good and pursuing it, as if you could not reach it; contemplating evil, and shrinking from it, as you would from thrusting a hand into boiling water."

解析：汉语原文意思是看到善的行为，就唯恐自己达不到；看到不善的行为，就好像把手伸到开水中一样赶快避开。习近平总书记指出，坚决反对腐败，防止党在长期执政条件下腐化变质，是我们必须抓好的重大政治任务。反腐败高压态势必须继续保持，坚持以零容忍态度惩治腐败。对腐败分子，发现一个就要坚决查处一个。要抓早抓小，有病就马上治，发现问题就及时处理，不能养痈遗患。"见善如不及，见不善如探汤。"领导干部要心存敬畏，不要心存侥幸。

76. "见善则迁，有过则改。"——《周易·益》

英译："Learning from fine things that may appear and correcting any mistakes that may occur."

解析：汉语原文意思是君子见到善人善事善行，就要追随、效仿；发现自己有过错时，也要毫不犹豫地改正。习近平总书记认为，道德之于个人、之于社会，都具有基础性意义，做人做事第一位的是崇德修身。这就是我们的用人标准为什么是德才兼备、以德为先，因为德是首要、是方向，一个人只有明大德、守公德、严私德，其才方能用得其所。修德，既要立意高远，又要立足平实。要立志报效祖国、服务人民，这是大德，养大德者方可成大业。同时，还得从做好小事、管好小节开始起步，"见善则迁，有过则改"，踏踏实实修好公德、私德，学会劳动、学会勤俭、学会感恩、学会助人、学会谦让、学会宽容、学会自省、学会自律。

77. "禁微则易，救末者难。"——范晔《后汉书·桓荣丁鸿列传》

英译："Curing an illness is easy at the start, but saving a terminal patient is hard."

解析：汉语原文意思是抑制不良之事于萌芽阶段很容易，到酿成大祸时再来挽救就很困难了。习近平总书记认为，人的身体有了毛病，就要看医生，就要打针吃药，重了还要动手术。人的思想和作风有了毛病，也必须抓紧治。如果讳疾忌医，就可能小病拖成大病，由病在表皮发展到病入膏肓，最终无药可治，正所谓"禁微则易，救末者难"。各级党组织要采取有力措施，帮助有问题的党员、干部找准"病症"，对症下药，该吃中药的吃中药，该吃西药的吃西药，或者中西医结合，该动手术的动手术，切实体现全面从严治党的要求。

78."鞠躬尽瘁，死而后已。"——诸葛亮《后出师表》
英译："giving all, till the heart beats its last"
解析：汉语原文意思是勤勤恳恳，竭尽心力，到死为止。习近平总书记指出，各种文史知识，中国优秀传统文化，领导干部也要学习，以学益智，以学修身。中国传统文化博大精深，学习和掌握其中的各种思想精华，对树立正确的世界观、人生观、价值观很有益处。中华民族的优秀传统文化和民族精神，我们都应该继承和发扬。我们不仅要了解中国的历史文化，还要睁眼看世界，了解世界上不同民族的历史文化，去其糟粕，取其精华，从中获得启发，为我所用。

79."举直错诸枉，则民服；举枉错诸直，则民不服。"——《论语·为政》
英译："People will obey you if you promote righteous men and suppress evil men. And they will disobey you if you do the contrary."
解析：汉语原文意思是推选任用贤明正直的人，将其置于品行作风不正的人之上，就会使民众信服，还会产生良好的导向作用；推选任用品行作风不正的人，置于贤明正直的人之上，民众就不会信服。习近平总书记指出，推进公正司法，要以优化司法职权配置为重点，健全司法权力分工负责、相互配合、相互制约的制度安排。各级党组织和领导干部都要旗帜鲜明支持司法机关依法独立行使职权，绝不容许利用职权干预司法。"举直错诸枉，则民服；举枉错诸直，则民不服。"司法人员要刚正不阿，勇于担当，敢于依法排除来自司法机关内部和外部的干扰，坚守公正司法的底线。要坚持以公开促公正、树公信，构建开放、动态、透明、便民的阳光司法机制，杜绝暗箱操作，坚决遏制司法腐败。

80."君子检身，常若有过"——《亢仓子·训道篇》
英译："A man of virtue often examines himself as a fallible person."

解析：汉语原文意思是君子要时时反省检查自己，就像自己经常会有缺点过失那样。习近平总书记认为，不忘初心、牢记使命，说到底是要解决党内存在的违背初心和使命的各种问题。关键是要有正视问题的自觉和刀刃向内的勇气。无论什么时候，问题总是客观存在的，我们要以"君子检身，常若有过"的态度来检视发现自身不足，做到知耻而后勇。要坚持问题导向，真刀真枪解决问题。讳疾忌医、有病不治，本来可以医好的病症就会拖成不治之症。从实际情况看，党内存在的各种突出问题表现多样，我们要全面查找、全面发力。

81. "君子坦荡荡"——《论语·述而》

英译："A gentleman is broad-minded."

解析：汉语原文意思是君子心胸开阔，能够包容别人。习近平总书记认为，中华文明绵延数千年，有其独特的价值体系。中华优秀传统文化已经成为中华民族的基因，植根在中国人内心，潜移默化影响着中国人的思想方式和行为方式。今天，我们提倡和弘扬社会主义核心价值观，必须从中汲取丰富营养，否则就不会有生命力和影响力。

82. "君子义以为质"——《论语·卫灵公》

英译："A gentleman takes morality as his bedrock."

解析：汉语原文意思是君子以义作为立身之本。习近平总书记指出，我们生而为中国人，最根本的是我们有中国人的独特精神世界，有百姓日用而不觉的价值观。我们提倡的社会主义核心价值观，就充分体现了对中华优秀传统文化的传承和升华。

83. "君子喻于义"——《论语·里仁》

英译："A gentleman has a good knowledge of righteousness."

解析：汉语原文意思是君子明白大义，以道义为标准辨别是非曲直。习近平总书记指出，县委书记作为县里的权力人物和公众人物，要注意道德操守，道德上失足有时比某些工作失误杀伤力还要大。我国古代就要求县令"导扬风化"。要自觉弘扬和践行社会主义核心价值观，加强道德修养，追求健康情趣，慎重对待朋友交往，时刻检点自己生活的方方面面，引导全县形成健康向上的社会风尚。要不断体会和弘扬先人传承下来的传统美德，如"大道之行也，天下为公"、"不义而富且贵，于我如浮云"、"君子喻于义"、"言必信，行必果"、"德不孤,必有邻"、"人而无信,不知其可也",等等,为为人处世、安身立命提供重要启示。

K

84. "砍头不要紧,只要主义真。"——夏明翰《就义诗》

英译:"I shall hold to my beliefs even at the cost of my life."

解析:汉语原文意思是砍下"我"的头颅并不可怕,只要"我"的理想和信仰共产主义是真理。习近平总书记指出,加强党的政治建设,必须把维护党中央权威和集中统一领导作为首要任务。党内所有的政治问题,归根到底就是对党是否忠诚。忠诚是共产党人必须具备的优秀品格。任何时候任何情况下,党的领导干部在政治上都要站得稳、靠得住,对党忠诚老实、与党中央同心同德,严守政治纪律和政治规矩,不断增强政治定力、纪律定力、道德定力、抵腐定力,把"四个意识"转化成听党指挥、为党尽责的实际行动。

85. "孔子登东山而小鲁,登泰山而小天下。"——《孟子·尽心上》

英译:"When Confucius looks down from the peak of the Dongshan Mountain, the local Kingdom of Lu comes into view; when he looks down from the peak of Mount Tai, the whole land comes into view."

解析:汉语原文意思是孔子登上家乡的东山,整个鲁国尽收眼底,觉得鲁国变小了;登上泰山,天下就会一览无余,感觉天下也变小了。习近平总书记指出,"孔子登东山而小鲁,登泰山而小天下"。面对世界大发展大变革大调整的新形势,为更好推进人类文明进步事业,我们必须登高望远,正确认识和把握世界大势和时代潮流。

L

86. "老吾老,以及人之老;幼吾幼,以及人之幼。"——《孟子·梁惠王上》

英译:"Respect others' elders as one respects one's own, and care for others' children as one cares for one's own." / "Do reverence to the elders in your own family and extend it to those in other families; show loving care to the young in your own family and extend it to those in other families."

解析:汉语原文意思是在赡养孝敬自己的长辈时不应忘记其他与自己没有亲缘关系的老人,在抚养教育自己的小辈时不应忘记其他与自己没有血缘关系的小孩。习近平总书记认为，共享理念实质就是坚持以人民为中心的发展思想，体现的是逐步实现共同富裕的要求。共同富裕，是马克思主义的一个基本目标，也是自古以来我国人民的一个基本理想。孟子说："老吾老以及人之老，幼吾幼以及人之幼。"按照马克思、恩格斯的构想，共产主义社会将彻底消除阶级之间、城乡之间、脑力劳动和体力劳动之间的对立和差别，实行各尽所能、按需分配，真正实现社会共享、实现每个人自由而全面的发展。

87."理辩则气直，气直则辞盛，辞盛则文工。"——李翱《答朱载言书》

英译："A good and well-constructed argument makes one feel upright and righteous; only by feeling upright and righteous can one be eloquent and articulate; only with articulate eloquence can one create well-structured and meaningful writing."

解析：汉语原文意思是（文章）道理明辨才能气势刚正，气势刚正才能辞藻华美，辞藻华美才显出文章技巧。习近平总书记认为，古往今来，优秀文艺作品必然是思想内容和艺术表达有机统一的结果。正所谓"理辩则气直，气直则辞盛，辞盛则文工"。只有把美的价值注入美的艺术之中，作品才有灵魂，思想和艺术才能相得益彰，作品才能传之久远。要把提高质量作为文艺作品的生命线，内容选材要严、思想开掘要深、艺术创造要精，不断提升作品的精神能量、文化内涵、艺术价值。

88."力，形之所以奋也。"——《墨经》

英译："Force is the reason that an object moves."

解析：汉语原文意思是动力是使物体运动的原因。习近平总书记指出，充分认识创新是第一动力，提供高质量科技供给，着力支撑现代化经济体系建设。《墨经》中写道，"力，形之所以奋也"，就是说动力是使物体运动的原因。要以提高发展质量和效益为中心，以支撑供给侧结构性改革为主线，把提高供给体系质量作为主攻方向，推动经济发展质量变革、效率变革、动力变革，显著增强我国经济质量优势。要通过补短板、挖潜力、增优势，促进资源要素高效流动和资源优化配置，推动产业链再造和价值链提升，满足有效需求和潜在需求，实现供需匹配和动态均衡发展，改善市场发展预测，提振实体经济发展信心。

89."立善法于天下，则天下治；立善法于一国，则一国治。"——王安石《周公》

英译："If good laws are established under Heaven, then there will be order under

Heaven; if good laws are established in a state, then there will be order in that state."

解析：汉语原文意思是在天下制定完善的法律，天下就会太平；在一国制定完善的法律，一国就能安定。习近平总书记指出，加快完善中国特色社会主义法律体系，以良法促进发展、保障善治。"立善法于天下，则天下治；立善法于一国，则一国治。"改革开放以来，在党的领导下，经过各方面努力，我国用 30 多年时间形成了中国特色社会主义法律体系，这是人类法治史上一项了不起的成就。同时，也要看到，时代在进步，实践在发展，不断对法律体系建设提出新需求，法律体系必须与时俱进加以完善。

90."立文之道，惟字与义。"——刘勰《文心雕龙·指瑕》
英译："Writing is about expressing ideas through the optimal use of words."
解析：汉语原文意思是文章写作的基本途径，不外用字和立义两个方面。习近平总书记指出，"立文之道，惟字与义"。文艺只有向上向善才能成为时代的号角。止于至善，方能臻于至美。广大文艺工作者要发扬中国文艺追求向上向善的优良传统，把社会主义核心价值观生动活泼体现在文艺创作之中，把有筋骨、有道德、有温度的东西表现出来，倡导健康文化风尚，摒弃畸形审美倾向，用思想深刻、清新质朴、刚健有力的优秀作品滋养人民的审美观价值观，使人民在精神生活上更加充盈起来。

91."立志而圣，则圣矣；立志而贤，则贤矣。"——王守仁《教条示龙场诸生》
英译："A person who aspires to be a saint will become a saint; and a person who aspires to be a sage will become a sage."
解析：汉语原文意思是一个人如果立志成为圣人，就会成为圣人；如果立志成为贤人，就会成为贤人。习近平总书记指出，新时代中国青年要树立远大理想。青年的理想信念关乎国家未来。青年理想远大、信念坚定，是一个国家、一个民族无坚不摧的前进动力。青年志存高远，就能激发奋进潜力，青春岁月就不会像无舵之舟漂泊不定。正所谓"立志而圣则圣矣，立志而贤则贤矣"。青年的人生目标会有不同，职业选择也有差异，但只有把自己的小我融入祖国的大我、人民的大我之中，与时代同步伐、与人民共命运，才能更好实现人生价值、升华人生境界。离开了祖国需要、人民利益，任何孤芳自赏都会陷入越走越窄的狭小天地。

92. "路遥知马力，日久见人心。"——《争报恩》

英译："Just as distance tests a horse's strength, time will show a person's sincerity."

解析：汉语原文意思是路途遥远，才可以知道马的力气的大小；经历的事情多了，时间长了，才可识别人心的善恶好歹。习近平总书记指出，中国有句谚语，叫作"路遥知马力，日久见人心"。中拉关系的发展历程已经并将继续证明，双方关系发展是开放的发展、包容的发展、合作的发展、共赢的发展。我们坚信，一个更高水平的中拉全面合作伙伴关系，必将更有力地促进双方共同发展，也有利于地区和世界的和平、稳定、繁荣。

93. "履不必同，期于适足；治不必同，期于利民。"——魏源《默觚·治篇五》

英译："People don't need to wear the same shoes; they should find what suit their feet. Governments don't have to adopt the same model of governance; they should find what benefits their people."

解析：汉语原文意思是每一个人的鞋子大小不必相同，关键是要适合自己的脚；每个国家的治理方法不必雷同，关键是要有利于人民。习近平总书记指出，弘扬丝路精神，就是要尊重道路选择。"履不必同，期于适足；治不必同，期于利民。"一个国家发展道路合不合适，只有这个国家的人民才最有发言权。正像我们不能要求所有花朵都变成紫罗兰这一种花，我们也不能要求有着不同文化传统、历史遭遇、现实国情的国家都采用同一种发展模式。否则，这个世界就太单调了。阿拉伯国家正在自主探索发展道路。我们愿意同阿拉伯朋友分享治国理政经验，从各自古老文明和发展实践中汲取智慧。

M

94. "民非谷不食，谷非地不生"——《管子·八观》

英译："Without farming, no food can be produced. And without arable land, no crops can grow."

解析：汉语原文意思是人民没有谷物就没有吃的东西，谷物没有土地就无处生长。习近平总书记指出，"民非谷不食，谷非地不生"。耕地是粮食生产的命根子。早在 2013 年，我就讲过要像保护大熊猫那样保护耕地，严防死守 18 亿亩耕地红线。这些年，我先后对清理整治大棚房、违建别墅、乱占耕地建房和遏制耕地"非农化"、防止"非粮化"等提出要求，有关部门打了一套组合拳。但是，耕地乱象仍屡禁不止。我们土地是不少，但同 14 亿人口的需求一比，又是稀缺资源！要采取"长牙齿"的硬措施，落实最严格的耕地保护制度。

95. "民惟邦本"——《尚书·五子之歌》

英译："The people are the foundation of a state."

解析：汉语原文意思是百姓应该是国家的根本。习近平总书记认为，民生是人民幸福之基、社会和谐之本。民生连着民心、民心凝聚民力，做好保障和改善民生工作，事关群众福祉和社会和谐稳定。

96. "明镜所以照形，古事所以知今。"——陈寿《三国志·吴志·孙奋传》

英译："One needs to clean the mirror before taking a look at oneself, and should learn the lessons of the past before making the decisions of today." / "Looking at the mirror we know about ourselves; reflecting on the past we know what to do now."

解析：汉语原文意思是对照明镜是为了看清自己的面容，研究历史是为了了解今天的时势。习近平总书记强调，"明镜所以照形，古事所以知今"。今天，我们回顾历史，不是为了从成功中寻求慰藉，更不是为了躺在功劳簿上、为回避今天面临的困难和问题寻找借口，而是为了总结历史经验、把握历史规律，增强开拓前进的勇气和力量。

97. "明者因时而变，知者随事而制。"——桓宽《盐铁论·忧边》

英译："A wise man changes his way as circumstances change; a knowledgeable person alters his means as times evolve." / "A smart man changes his approach as circumstances change; a wise person alters his means as times evolve."

解析：汉语原文意思是聪明的人会根据时代变迁来调整应对策略，智慧的人会随着世事变化来制定治理规则。习近平总书记指出，在长期实践中，我们党的宣传思想工作积累了十分丰富的经验。这些经验来之不易、弥足珍贵，是做好今后工作的重要遵循，一定要认真总结、长期坚持，并在实践中不断丰富和发展。"明者因时而变，知者随事而制。"宣传思想工作创新，重点要抓好理念创新、手段创新、基层工作创新，努力以思想认识新飞跃打开工作新局面，积极探索有利于破解工作难题的新举措新办法，把创新的重心放在基层一线。

98. "谋度于义者必得，事因于民者必成。"——《晏子春秋·内篇问上》

英译："Designs for justice prevail, and actions to benefit the people succeed."

解析：汉语原文意思是谋划时考虑符合道义的就一定能够实现，做事时注重顺从民意的就一定能够成功。习近平总书记指出，中国古人说："谋度于义者必得，事因于民者必成。"让我们把人民对美好生活的向往放在心头，把维护和平、促进发展的时代使命扛在肩上，携手前行，接续奋斗，构建更为紧密的中国—东盟命运共同体，共创更加繁荣美好的地区和世界！

N

99."内无妄思，外无妄动。"——《朱子语类·学六·持守》

英译："We will not act recklessly if we think right."

解析：汉语原文意思是心中没有胡思乱想，行为上就不会轻举妄动。习近平总书记指出，要弘扬忠诚老实、公道正派、实事求是、清正廉洁等价值观，使党员、干部在严肃认真的党内政治生活中加强党性锻炼，锤炼政治能力，提高思想境界和政治觉悟。古人说："内无妄思，外无妄动。"党的领导干部更要对组织和人民常怀感恩敬畏之心，对功名利禄要知足，对物质享受和个人待遇要知止。

100."能用众力，则无敌于天下矣；能用众智，则无畏于圣人矣。"——陈寿《三国志·吴志·吴主传》

英译："If you can employ the strength of the people, you will be invincible under Heaven; if you can employ the wisdom of the people, no sage will be cleverer than you."

解析：汉语原文意思是如果能够充分发挥和凝聚众人的力量与智慧，就可以所向无敌、无所畏惧。习近平总书记指出，要紧紧依靠人民。人民是我们党执政的最大底气。古人说："能用众力，则无敌于天下矣；能用众智，则无畏于圣人矣。"我国社会主义民主是维护人民根本利益的最广泛、最真实、最管用的民主。我们要坚持人民民主，更好把人民的智慧和力量凝聚到党和人民事业中来。

101."农，天下之本，务莫大焉。"——司马迁《史记·孝文本纪》

英译："Agriculture is the foundation of a country and the top priority in governance."

解析：汉语原文意思是农业是国家的根本，是最重要的事情。习近平总书记指出，"农，天下之本，务莫大焉"。历史和现实都告诉我们，农为邦本，本固邦宁。我们要坚持用大历史观来看待农业、农村、农民问题，只有深刻理解了"三农"问题，才能更好理解我们这个党、这个国家、这个民族。必须看到，全面建设社会主义现代化国家，实现中华民族伟大复兴，最艰巨最繁重的任务依然在农村，最广泛最深厚的基础依然在农村。

Q

102．"其作始也简，其将毕也必巨。"——《庄子·人间世》

英译："A promising cause may seem simple at the beginning, yet proves great on completion."

解析：汉语原文意思是做任何事，开头的时候总是相对比较简单和细微，但快要到结尾的时候，却往往变得纷繁巨大，使得原来要完成的计划和达成的预期目标，成为一项复杂而艰巨的任务。习近平总书记指出，"其作始也简，其将毕也必巨"。我们党团结带领人民取得了举世瞩目的伟大成就，这值得我们骄傲和自豪。同时，事业发展永无止境，共产党人的初心永远不能改变。唯有不忘初心，方可告慰历史、告慰先辈，方可赢得民心、赢得时代，方可善作善成、一往无前。

103．"骐骥一跃，不能十步；驽马十驾，功在不舍。锲而舍之，朽木不折；锲而不舍，金石可镂。"——《荀子·劝学》

英译："If a gallant steed leaps only once, it can cover a distance of no more than ten steps; if an inferior horse travels for ten days, it can go a long way because of perseverance. If a sculptor stops chipping halfway, he cannot even cut dead wood, but if he keeps chipping, he can engrave metal and stone."

解析：汉语原文意思是骏马一跃，也不会达到十步；劣马跑十天，也能跑得很远；雕刻东西，如果刻了一下就放下，朽木也不会刻断；如果不停刻下去，金属和石头都可以雕空。习近平总书记认为，科技创新永无止境。科技竞争就像短道速滑，我们在加速，人家也在加速，最后要看谁速度更快、谁的速度更能持续。荀子说："骐骥一跃，不能十步；驽马十驾，功在不舍。锲而舍之，朽木不折；锲而不舍，金石可镂。"我国广大科技工作者要敢于担当、勇于超越、找准方向、扭住不放，牢固树立敢为天下先的志向和信心，敢于走别人没有走过的路，在攻坚克难中追求卓越，勇于创造引领世界潮流的科技成果。

104. "恰同学少年，风华正茂"——毛泽东《沁园春·长沙》

英译："Young we were, schoolmates, at life's full flowering."

解析：汉语原文意思是同学们正值青春年少，神采飞扬，才华横溢。习近平总书记指出，要勤学，下得苦功夫，求得真学问。知识是树立核心价值观的重要基础。大学阶段"恰同学少年，风华正茂"，有老师指点，有同学切磋，有浩瀚的书籍引路，可以心无旁骛求知问学。此时不努力，更待何时？要勤于学习、敏于求知，注重把所学知识内化于心，形成自己的见解，既要专攻博览，又要关心国家、关心人民、关心世界，学会担当社会责任。

105. "千军易得，一将难求！"——马致远《汉宫秋》

英译："It is easy to muster a 1,000-man army, but hard to find a capable general."

解析：汉语原文意思是征集众多的兵士很容易，寻求一个好的主帅却很困难。习近平总书记指出，建设网络强国，要把人才资源汇聚起来，建设一支政治强、业务精、作风好的强大队伍。"千军易得，一将难求"，要培养造就世界水平的科学家、网络科技领军人才、卓越工程师、高水平创新团队。

106. "千里之行，始于足下。"——《老子》

英译："A journey of one thousand miles begins with the first step."

解析：汉语原文意思是千里的远行，是从脚下第一步开始走出来的。习近平总书记指出，从小做起，就是要从自己做起、从身边做起、从小事做起，一点一滴积累，养成好思想、好品德。"千里之行，始于足下。"每个人的生活都是由一件件小事组成的，养小德才能成大德。

107. "千磨万击还坚劲，任尔东西南北风。"——郑燮《竹石》

英译："In the face of all blows, not bending low, it still stands fast. Whether from east, west, south or north the wind doth blast."

解析：汉语原文意思是历尽磨难，依旧坚韧挺拔；傲然挺立，任凭你四面来风。习近平总书记指出，中国特色社会主义是社会主义而不是其他什么主义，科学社会主义基本原则不能丢，丢了就不是社会主义。一个国家实行什么样的主义，关键要看这个主义能否解决这个国家面临的历史性课题。历史和现实都告诉我们，只有社会主义才能救中国，只有中国特色社会主义才能发展中国，这是历史的结论、人民的选择。随着中国特色社会主义不断发展，我们的制度必将越来越成熟，我国社会主义制度的优越性必将进一步显现，我们的道路必将越走越宽广。我们就是要有这样的道路自信、理论自信、制度自信，真正做到"千磨万击还坚劲，任尔东西南北风"。

108."千淘万漉虽辛苦，吹尽狂沙始到金。"——刘禹锡《浪淘沙九首（其八）》
英译："Gold glitters only after countless washings and sievings."
解析：汉语原文意思是淘金的工作虽然十分艰辛，需要千遍万遍地过滤，但只有把泥沙淘尽，才能得到闪闪发光的黄金。习近平总书记指出，要明辨，善于明辨是非，善于决断选择。关键是要学会思考、善于分析、正确抉择，做到稳重自持、从容自信、坚定自励。要树立正确的世界观、人生观、价值观，掌握了这把总钥匙，再来看看社会万象、人生历程，一切是非、正误、主次，一切真假、善恶、美丑，自然就洞若观火、清澈明了，自然就能作出正确判断、作出正确选择。正所谓"千淘万漉虽辛苦，吹尽狂沙始到金"。

109."亲仁善邻"——《左传·隐公六年》
英译："The Chinese nation always values amity and friendship with neighbors."
解析：汉语原文意思是与邻者亲近、与邻邦友好。这是我们坚持的原则。习近平总书记指出，铭记伟大胜利，推进伟大事业，必须维护世界和平和正义，推动构建人类命运共同体。中华民族历来秉持"亲仁善邻"的理念。作为负责任大国，中国坚守和平、发展、公平、正义、民主、自由的全人类共同价值，坚持共商共建共享的全球治理观，坚定不移走和平发展、开放发展、合作发展、共同发展道路。只要坚持走和平发展道路，同各国人民一道推动构建人类命运共同体，就一定能够迎来人类和平与发展的美好未来！

110."青春虚度无所成，白首衔悲亦何及。"——权德舆《放歌行》
英译："If you idle away your youth and achieve nothing, it's no good lamenting in old age."
解析：汉语原文意思是如果在年轻的时候虚度光阴、一无所成，等到年老的时候，恐怕也就只有空自悲叹、追悔莫及了。习近平总书记认为，新时代中国青年要练就过硬本领。青年是苦练本领、增长才干的黄金时期。"青春虚度无所成，白首衔悲亦何及。"当今时代，知识更新不断加快，社会分工日益细化，新技术新模式新业态层出不穷。这既为青年施展才华、竞展风采提供了广阔舞台，也对青年能力素质提出了新的更高要求。不论是成就自己的人生理想，还是担当时代的神圣使命，青年都要珍惜韶华、不负青春，努力学习掌握科学知识，提高内在素质，锤炼过硬本领，使自己的思维视野、思想观念、认识水平跟上越来越快的时代发展。

111. "青年者，国家之魂"——李大钊《〈晨钟〉之使命——青春中华之创造》

英译："Young people are the soul of a country."

解析：汉语原文意思是青年人是国家的灵魂，是国家的希望。习近平总书记指出，李大钊说过："青年者，国家之魂。"过去、现在、将来青年工作都是党的工作中一项战略性工作。各级党委（党组）要倾注极大热忱研究青年成长规律和时代特点，拿出极大精力抓青年工作，做青年朋友的知心人、青年工作的热心人、青年群众的引路人。各级党组织要落实党建带团建制度机制，经常研究解决共青团工作中的重大问题，热情关心、严格要求团干部，支持共青团按照群团工作特点和规律创造性地开展工作。

112. "青山一道同云雨，明月何曾是两乡。"——王昌龄《送柴侍御》

英译："Green hills bathe in the same cloud and rain. The same moon lights up towns however far away."

解析：汉语原文意思是虽然我们相隔两地，但共沐同一青山的云雨，共享一轮明月的清辉，又何尝分离过呢？习近平总书记指出，"青山一道同云雨，明月何曾是两乡"。让我们携起手来，站在历史正确的一边，站在人类进步的一边，为实现世界永续和平发展，为推动构建人类命运共同体而不懈奋斗！

113. "穷则变，变则通，通则久。"——《周易·系辞下》

英译："Limits lead to changes; changes lead to solutions; solutions lead to development."

解析：汉语原文意思是事物发展到了极点则变化，变化则通达，能通达，则能恒久。习近平总书记指出，新时代全面深化改革决心不能动摇、勇气不能减弱。科技体制改革要敢于啃硬骨头，敢于涉险滩、闯难关，破除一切制约科技创新的思想障碍和制度藩篱，正所谓"穷则变，变则通，通则久"。

114. "求木之长者，必固其根本；欲流之远者，必浚其泉源"——魏徵《谏太宗十思疏》

英译："For a tree to grow tall, a strong and solid root is essential; for a river to reach far, an unimpeded source is necessary."

解析：汉语原文意思是想要树木成长，必须固定根基；想要泉水长流，必须疏通源头。习近平总书记指出，可持续，就是要发展和安全并重以实现持久安全。"求木之长者，必固其根本；欲流之远者，必浚其泉源。"发展是安全的基础，安全是发展的条件。贫瘠的土地上长不成和平的大树，连天的烽火中结不出发展的硕果。对亚洲大多数国家来说，发展就是最大安全，也是解决地区安全问题的"总钥匙"。

115. "取之有制，用之有节，则裕；取之无制，用之不节，则乏。"——张居正《论时政疏》

英译："Utilized with restraint, resources will be abundant; otherwise, they will be scarce."

解析：汉语原文意思是取财有限度、用财有节制，国家就会越来越富裕；取财无限度、用财无节制，国家就会越来越困乏。习近平总书记指出，要坚持节约优先。"取之有制、用之有节则裕，取之无制、用之不节则乏。"要实施全面节约战略，推进各领域节约行动。在生产领域，要推进资源全面节约、集约、循环利用，降低单位产品能耗物耗，加快制造业技术改造，提高投入产出效率，深入开展"光盘"等粮食节约行动，广泛开展创建绿色机关、绿色家庭、绿色社区、绿色出行等行动。

R

116. "人而无信，不知其可也。"——《论语·为政》

英译："If a man does not keep his word, what is he good for?"

解析：汉语原文意思是人要是失去了信用或不讲信用，不知道他还可以做什么。习近平总书记指出，我们要增强两国互信。中国人历来讲究"信"。2000多年前，孔子就说："人而无信，不知其可也。"信任是人与人关系的基础、国与国交往的前提。我们要防止浮云遮眼，避免战略误判，就要通过经常性沟通，积累战略互信。这个问题解决好了，中美合作基础就会更加坚实，动力就会更加强劲。

117. "人患不知其过。既知之，不能改，是无勇也。"——韩愈《五箴（并序）》

英译："It is most pitiful that one does not know one's mistakes, and those who know but do not change have no courage."

解析：汉语原文意思是人最大的忧患就是不知道自己的过失，既然知道了，不能改正，就是没有勇气。习近平总书记指出，"人患不知其过，既知之，不能改，是无勇也"。要把"改"字贯穿始终，立查立改、即知即改，能够当下改的，明确时限和要求，按期整改到位；一时解决不了的，要盯住不放，通过不断深化认识、增强自觉，明确阶段目标，持续整改。整改落实要防止虎头蛇尾、久拖不决，防止搞纸上整改、虚假整改，防止以简单问责基层干部代替整改责任落实，防止以整改为名，层层填表报数，增加基层负担。

118. "人间正道是沧桑"——毛泽东《七律·人民解放军占领南京》

英译："seas becoming mulberry fields"

解析：汉语原文意思是人生的正道和真理是在经历了沧桑和变迁之后才能够领悟和实现的。习近平总书记指出，近代以后，中华民族遭受的苦难之重、付出的牺牲之大，在世界历史上都是罕见的。但是，中国人民从不屈服，不断奋起抗争，终于掌握了自己的命运，开始了建设自己国家的伟大进程，充分展示了以爱国主义为核心的伟大民族精神。中华民族的今天，正可谓"人间正道是沧桑"。改革开放以来，我们总结历史经验，不断艰辛探索，终于找到了实现中华民族伟大复兴的正确道路，取得了举世瞩目的伟大成就。

119. "人生天地间，长路有险夷。"——元好问《临汾李氏任运堂二首》

英译："As you move on, the road ahead is bound to be strewn with difficulties and obstacles."

解析：汉语原文意思是人生在天地之间，所经历的道路必然有艰难险阻。习近平总书记指出，进一步发扬革命精神，始终保持艰苦奋斗的昂扬精神。"人生天地间，长路有险夷。"世界上没有哪个党像我们这样，遭遇过如此多的艰难险阻，经历过如此多的生死考验，付出过如此多的惨烈牺牲。一百年来，在应对各种困难挑战中，我们党锤炼了不畏强敌、不惧风险、敢于斗争、勇于胜利的风骨和品质。这是我们党最鲜明的特质和特点。

120. "人生万事须自为，跬步江山即寥廓。"——范柠《王氏能远楼》

英译："One must experience everything in life for oneself; every step counts on the path to a wider world."

解析：汉语原文意思是人生的许多事情都要靠自己去做，只要迈步向前，日积月累，就可以进入一个无比广阔的世界。习近平总书记指出，"人生万事须自为，跬步江山即寥廓"。追求进步，是青年最宝贵的特质，也是党和人民最殷切的希望。新时代的广大共青团员，要做理想远大、信念坚定的模范，带头学习马克思主义理论，树立共产主义远大理想和中国特色社会主义共同理想，自觉践行社会主义核心价值观，大力弘扬爱国主义精神；要做刻苦学习、锐意创新的模范，带头立足岗位、苦练本领、创先争优，努力成为行业骨干、青年先锋；要做敢于斗争、善于斗争的模范，带头迎难而上、攻坚克难，做到不信邪、不怕鬼、骨头硬；要做艰苦奋斗、无私奉献的模范，带头站稳人民立场，脚踏实地、求真务实，吃苦在前、享受在后。

121. "人生自古谁无死？留取丹心照汗青。"——文天祥《过零丁洋》

英译："dying with a loyal heart shining in the pages of history"

解析：汉语原文意思是自古以来，人都不免一死，但怀有一颗爱国之心，能够为国尽忠，死后仍可光照千秋，青史留名。习近平总书记认为，各种文史知识，中国优秀传统文化，领导干部也要学习，以学益智，以学修身。中国传统文化博大精深，学习和掌握其中的各种思想精华，对树立正确的世界观、人生观、价值观很有益处。"人生自古谁无死，留取丹心照汗青"的献身精神体现了中华民族的优秀传统文化和民族精神，我们都应该继承和发扬。

122. "仁者爱人"——《孟子·离娄下》

英译："The benevolent man loves others."

解析：汉语原文意思是仁者对他人充满仁爱之心。习近平总书记指出，世间万物，人是最宝贵的，人的生命更是唯一的。无论何时何地都要时刻把人民放在心中，保护人民生命安全和身体健康可以不惜一切代价。这不仅是中华文化精神中的重要概念、实现中华民族伟大复兴的梦想的文化力量，在全球抗疫的态势下，也应该成为一些过度诠释个人主义、自由主义的国家的镜鉴。

123. "任重而道远者，不择地而息"——韩婴《韩诗外传》卷一

英译："People on a long and arduous journey will not stop and opt for an easy one before reaching the destination."

解析：汉语原文意思是身负重担而路途遥远的人，不会刻意挑选某地而安身憩息。习近平总书记指出，"任重而道远者，不择地而息"。中共十八大以来，我们高举改革开放的旗帜，以前所未有的力度推进全面深化改革，作出顶层设计，在经济、政治、文化、社会、生态文明建设等领域一共推出 1600 多项改革方案，其中许多是事关全局、前所未有的重大改革，如市场体制改革、宏观调控体制改革、财税体制改革、金融体制改革、国有企业改革、司法体制改革、教育体制改革、生态文明建设体制改革、党和国家机构改革、监察体制改革、国防和军队改革等。每逢重要场合，我都要谈改革、谈开放，强调要敢于啃硬骨头、敢于涉险滩，拿出壮士断腕的勇气，把改革进行到底。

124. "如临深渊，如履薄冰"——《诗经·小雅·小旻》

英译："as if we were standing on the edge of an abyss, and treading on thin ice"

解析：汉语原文意思是（君子修身讲究谨慎）犹如站在悬崖边上，或脚踩在薄薄的冰面上一样，时时唯恐失坠。习近平总书记指出，老百姓的衣食住行，社会的日常运行，国家机器的正常运转，执政党的建设管理，都有大量工作要做。要始终把人民放在心中最高的位置，牢记人民重托，牢记责任重于泰山。这样一个大国，这样多的人民，这么复杂的国情，领导者要深入了解国情，了解人民所思所盼，要有"如履薄冰，如临深渊"的自觉，要有"治大国如烹小鲜"的态度，丝毫不敢懈怠，丝毫不敢马虎，必须夙夜在公、勤勉工作。

125. "如身使臂，如臂使指，叱咤变化，无有留难，则天下之势一矣。"——吕中《类编皇朝大事记讲义·太祖皇帝》

英译："The body employs the arms and the arms employ the fingers without any difficulty, then the country runs as a whole."

解析：汉语原文意思是治理国家要做到像身体支配手臂、手臂支配手指那样，指挥自如，没有困阻，这样一来全国上下便步调一致、行动统一。习近平总书记指出，我们党是按照马克思主义建党原则建立起来的政党，我们党建立了包括党的中央组织、地方组织、基层组织在内的严密组织体系。这是世界上任何其他政党都不具有的强大优势。党中央是大脑和中枢，党中央必须有定于一尊、

一锤定音的权威，这样才能"如身使臂，如臂使指，叱咤变化，无有留难，则天下之势一矣"。党的地方组织的根本任务是确保党中央决策部署贯彻落实，有令即行、有禁即止。党组在党的组织体系中具有特殊地位，要贯彻落实党中央和上级党组织决策部署，发挥好把方向、管大局、保落实的重要作用。每个党员特别是领导干部都要强化党的意识和组织观念，自觉做到思想上认同组织、政治上依靠组织、工作上服从组织、感情上信赖组织。

126. "若无德，则虽体魄智力发达，适足助其为恶"——蔡元培《在爱国女学校之演说》

英译："He who is strong physically and talented but has no virtue will end up on the side of vice."

解析：汉语原文意思是如果没有道德，即使身体强壮、智力发达，也是助纣为虐，正好帮助其为非作歹。习近平总书记指出，要修德，加强道德修养，注重道德实践。蔡元培先生说过："若无德，则虽体魄智力发达，适足助其为恶。"道德之于个人、之于社会，都具有基础性意义，做人做事第一位的是崇德修身。这就是我们的用人标准为什么是德才兼备、以德为先，因为德是首要、是方向，一个人只有明大德、守公德、严私德，其才方能用得其所。

S

127. "山重水复疑无路，柳暗花明又一村。"——陆游《游山西村》

英译："When one doubts whether there is a way out from the endless mountains and rivers, one suddenly finds a village shaded by soft willows and bright flowers."

解析：汉语原文意思是山峦重叠、水流曲折，正担心无路可走，突然出现了一个柳绿花红的小山村。习近平总书记指出，亚太一直是世界经济增长的重要引擎，在世界经济复苏缺乏动力的背景下，亚太经济体应该拿出敢为天下先的勇气，推动建立发展创新、增长联动、利益融合的开放型经济发展方式。只有这样，才能做到"山重水复疑无路，柳暗花明又一村"，使亚太经济在世界经济复苏中发挥引领作用。

128. "山积而高，泽积而长。"——刘禹锡《唐故监察御史赠尚书右仆射王公神道碑铭》

英译："Readiness to converge with others makes a mountain high and a river mighty."

解析：汉语原文意思是山是由土石日积月累而高耸起来的，江河湖泽是由点滴之水长期积聚而成的。习近平总书记指出，"山积而高，泽积而长"。中国是亚洲安全观的积极倡导者，也是坚定实践者，中方将一步一个脚印加强同各方的安全对话和合作，共同探讨制定地区安全行为准则和亚洲安全伙伴计划，使亚洲国家成为相互信任、平等合作的好伙伴。

129. "善禁者，先禁其身而后人"——荀悦《申鉴·政体》

英译："He who is good at governing through restriction should first restrict himself then others."

解析：汉语原文意思是善于用禁令治理社会的人，必然先按照禁令要求自身，而后才去要求别人。习近平总书记指出，工作作风上的问题绝对不是小事，如果不坚决纠正不良风气，任其发展下去，就会像一座无形的墙把我们党和人民群众隔开，我们党就会失去根基、失去血脉、失去力量。抓改进工作作风，各项工作都很重要，但最根本的是要坚持和发扬艰苦奋斗精神。改进工作作风的任务非常繁重，中央八项规定是一个切入口和动员令。中央八项规定既不是最高标准，更不是最终目的，只是我们改进作风的第一步，是我们作为共产党人应该做到的基本要求。"善禁者，先禁其身而后人。"各级领导干部要以身作则、率先垂范，说到的就要做到，承诺的就要兑现。

130. "善为政者，弊则补之，决则塞之"——桓宽《盐铁论·申韩》

英译："Those with a sound grasp of governance will leave no problems unresolved and no defects unrepaired."

解析：汉语原文意思是善于治国理政的人，一旦发现弊端便会马上补救，看到有漏洞存在就会立即填补，不会任由问题发展扩大。习近平总书记指出，坚持与时俱进，进一步提升特别行政区治理水平。古人说："善为政者，弊则补之，决则塞之。"要适应现代社会治理发展变化及其新要求，推进公共行政等制度改革，提高政府管治效能，促进治理体系和治理能力现代化。要把依法办事作为特别行政区治理的基本准则，不断健全完善依法治澳的制度体系。要善用科技，加快建设智慧城市，以大数据等信息化技术推进政府管理和社会治理模式创新，不断促进政府决策科学化、社会治理精准化、公共服务高效化。

131. "善战者，立于不败之地，而不失敌之败也。"——《孙子兵法·军形篇》

英译："Those skilled in warfare make sure they are invincible and miss no chance of overwhelming their enemies."

解析：汉语原文意思是善战者总是做好充分准备，先确保自己不失败，然后在战斗中寻找一切战胜敌人的机会，战则必胜。习近平总书记指出，"善战者，立于不败之地，而不失敌之败也"。唯有主动迎战、坚决斗争才有生路出路，才能赢得尊严、求得发展，逃避退缩、妥协退让只会招致失败和屈辱，只能是死路一条。我们必须把握新的伟大斗争的历史特点，发扬斗争精神，把握斗争方向，把握斗争主动权，坚定斗争意志，掌握斗争规律，增强斗争本领，有效应对重大挑战、抵御重大风险、克服重大阻力、解决重大矛盾，战胜前进道路上的一切艰难险阻，不断夺取新时代伟大斗争的新胜利。

132. "尚贤者，政之本也。"——《墨子·尚贤上》

英译："Exaltation of the virtuous is fundamental to governance."

解析：汉语原文意思是尊重推崇贤才，任用品行高尚、能力突出的人，是治理好国家的根本。习近平总书记指出，"尚贤者，政之本也"。各级党委和政府要认真贯彻党和国家关于留学人员工作的方针政策，更大规模、更有成效地培养我国改革开放和社会主义现代化建设急需的各级各类人才。环境好，则人才聚、事业兴；环境不好，则人才散、事业衰。要健全工作机制，增强服务意识，加强教育引导，搭建创新平台，善于发现人才、团结人才、使用人才，为留学人员回国工作、为国服务创造良好环境，促使优秀人才脱颖而出。

133. "少年辛苦终身事，莫向光阴惰寸功。"——杜荀鹤《题弟侄书堂》

英译："Work hard when young, and you will have a future; time flies, and you should not slacken your efforts."

解析：汉语原文意思是年轻时候的努力是有益终身的大事，对着匆匆逝去的光阴，不要丝毫放松自己的努力。习近平总书记指出，听说有的同学喜欢比吃穿，比有没有车接车送，比爸爸妈妈是干什么工作的，这样就比偏了。一定不能比这些。"自古雄才多磨难，从来纨绔少伟男"、"少年辛苦终身事，莫向光阴惰寸功"。要比就比谁更有志气、谁更勤奋学习、谁更热爱劳动、谁更爱锻炼身体、谁更有爱心。

134. "少壮不努力,老大徒伤悲。"——《乐府诗集·长歌行》

英译:"A young idler, an old beggar."

解析:汉语原文意思是年轻力壮的时候不奋发图强,到了老年再悲伤也没用了。习近平总书记指出,少年儿童培育和践行社会主义核心价值观,要适应年龄和特点,主要是要做到记住要求、心有榜样、从小做起、接受帮助。从小做起,就是要从自己做起、从身边做起、从小事做起,一点一滴积累,养成好思想、好品德。"少壮不努力,老大徒伤悲。"每个人的生活都是由一件件小事组成的,养小德才能成大德。

135. "奢靡之始,危亡之渐"——《新唐书·褚遂良传》

英译:"Self-indulgence and extravagance lead to decline and demise."

解析:汉语原文意思是奢靡行为开始之时也是危亡渐渐来临之际。习近平总书记指出,我们一定要牢记"奢靡之始,危亡之渐"的古训,对作风之弊、行为之垢来一次大排查、大检修、大扫除,切实解决人民群众反映强烈的突出问题。

136. "慎易以避难,敬细以远大"——《韩非子·喻老》

英译:"We should manage the small and simple things with care so as to avoid difficulties and disasters."

解析:汉语原文意思是谨慎地对待容易的事,就可以避免危难;认真地处理细小环节,就可以远离大灾。习近平总书记指出,我们必须清醒看到,当前和今后一个时期,虽然我国发展仍然处于重要战略机遇期,但机遇和挑战都有新的发展变化,机遇和挑战之大都前所未有,总体上机遇大于挑战。古人说:"慎易以避难,敬细以远大。"全党必须继续谦虚谨慎、艰苦奋斗,调动一切可以调动的积极因素,团结一切可以团结的力量,全力办好自己的事,锲而不舍实现我们的既定目标。

137. "生年不满百,常怀千岁忧。"——《古诗十九首》

英译:"We worry about the next one thousand years when we are only to last less than a hundred."

解析:汉语原文意思是人活在世上通常不满百岁,又何苦心里老是记挂着千万年后的忧愁。习近平总书记指出,理想信念不可能凭空产生,也不可能轻而易举坚守。我们要经受住"四大考验"、抵御住"四种危险",必须立足当前、着眼长远,深刻认识共产主义远大理想和中国特色社会主义共同理想的辩证关系,既不能离开发展中国特色社会主义事业、实现民族复兴的现实工作而空谈远大理想,也不能因为实现共产主义是一个漫长的历史过程就讳言甚至丢掉远大理想。正所谓"生年不满百,常怀千岁忧"。

138. "生于忧患,死于安乐。"——《孟子·告子下》

英译:"One prospers in worries and hardships, and perishes in ease and comfort."

解析:汉语原文意思是忧愁祸患使人生存发展,安逸享乐使人萎靡死亡。习近平总书记指出,今年是新中国成立70周年,我们党在全国执政也70年了。古人说:"生于忧患,死于安乐。"我们党作为世界第一大党,没有什么外力能够打倒我们,能够打倒我们的只有我们自己。应该看到,在长期执政条件下,各种弱化党的先进性、损害党的纯洁性的因素无时不有,各种违背初心和使命、动摇党的根基的危险无处不在,如果不严加防范、及时整治,久而久之,必将积重难返,小问题就会变成大问题、小管涌就会沦为大塌方,甚至可能酿成全局性、颠覆性的灾难。

139. "胜非其难也,持之者其难也。"——刘安《淮南子·道应训》

英译:"The most difficult part of victory is not the winning, but the sustaining."

解析:汉语原文意思是取得胜利并不是最难的事情,保持住胜利、巩固胜利成果才是最难的。习近平总书记指出,"胜非其难也,持之者其难也"。我们要切实做好巩固拓展脱贫攻坚成果同乡村振兴有效衔接各项工作,让脱贫基础更加稳固、成效更可持续。对易返贫致贫人口要加强监测,做到早发现、早干预、早帮扶。对脱贫地区产业要长期培育和支持,促进内生可持续发展。对易地扶贫搬迁群众要搞好后续扶持,多渠道促进就业,强化社会管理,促进社会融入。

140. "石可破也,而不可夺坚;丹可磨也,而不可夺赤。"——《吕氏春秋·诚廉》

英译:"A rock can be smashed, but its pieces will still be hard; cinnabar can be ground, but its powder will still be red."

解析:汉语原文意思石头可以被击破打碎,但不可以改变它坚硬的质地;朱砂可以被研磨耗损,但不可以改变它赤红的色彩。习近平总书记指出,"石可破也,而不可夺坚;丹可磨也,而不可夺赤"。理想信念的坚定,来自思想理论的坚定。

认识真理，掌握真理，信仰真理，捍卫真理，是坚定理想信念的精神前提。

141. "适己而忘人者，人之所弃；克己而立人者，众之所戴。" ——方孝孺《杂铭》

英译："Those who seek comfort only for themselves will ultimately be denounced, while those who sacrifice their own interests for the success of others will be hailed."

解析：汉语原文意思是只为自己着想而不顾及他人的人，人们会离他而去；克制自己的私欲以利他人的人，人们会拥戴他。习近平总书记指出，"适己而忘人者，人之所弃；克己而立人者，众之所戴"。发展是世界各国的权利，而不是少数国家的专利。我们要推动各国加强发展合作、各国人民共享发展成果，提升全球发展的公平性、有效性、协同性，共同反对任何人搞技术封锁、科技鸿沟、发展脱钩。我相信，任何以阻挠他国发展、损害他国人民生活为要挟的政治操弄都是不得人心的，也终将是徒劳的！

142. "收百世之阙文，采千载之遗韵。" ——陆机《文赋》

英译："collecting even incomplete articles and essays from previous generations, and gathering even heritage that may have been neglected or ignored by our forebears"

解析：汉语原文意思是吸收百代的文章精华，广泛采纳千年文章的风华，收采百世千载遗留下来的文章，并要努力别出心裁。习近平总书记指出，博大精深的中华文明是中华民族独特的精神标识，是当代中国文化的根基，也是文艺创新的宝藏。中国文化历来推崇"收百世之阙文，采千载之遗韵"。要深入挖掘中华优秀传统文化蕴含的思想观念、人文精神、道德规范，把艺术创造力和中华文化价值融合起来，把中华美学精神和当代审美追求结合起来，激活中华文化生命力。故步自封、陈陈相因谈不上传承，割断血脉、凭空虚造不能算创新。要把握传承和创新的关系，学古不泥古、破法不悖法，让中华优秀传统文化成为文艺创新的重要源泉。

143. "水能载舟，亦能覆舟。" ——吴兢《贞观政要·政体》

英译："The same water that keeps a ship afloat can also sink it."

解析：汉语原文意思是统治者如船，老百姓如水，水既能让船安稳地航行，也能将船推翻吞没，沉于水中。习近平总书记指出，"红船精神"昭示我们，党和人民的关系就好比舟和水的关系，"水可载舟，亦可覆舟"。革命战争年代，正是在"红船精神"引领下,我们党从民族大义和人民群众的根本利益出发,充分发动并紧紧依靠人民群众夺取了政权,从此成为在全国掌握政权并长期执政的执政党。

144. "顺木之天,以致其性"——柳宗元《种树郭橐驼传》

英译:"We should respect a tree's nature, and let it grow freely."

解析:汉语原文意思是顺应树木生长的自然规律,使其按照自身的习性成长,才能高大茂盛。习近平总书记指出,要按照人才成长规律改进人才培养机制,"顺木之天,以致其性",避免急功近利、拔苗助长。要坚持竞争激励和崇尚合作相结合,促进人才资源合理有序流动。要广泛吸引海外优秀专家学者为我国科技创新事业服务。要在全社会积极营造鼓励大胆创新、勇于创新、包容创新的良好氛围,既要重视成功,更要宽容失败,完善好人才评价指挥棒作用,为人才发挥作用、施展才华提供更加广阔的天地。

145. "四维不张,国乃灭亡"——《管子·牧民》

英译:"propriety, righteousness, honesty and a sense of shame – the four anchors of our moral foundation, and a question of life and death for the country"

解析:汉语原文中的"四维",指礼、义、廉、耻四种纲纪,如果不能厉行礼、义、廉、耻这治国的四大纲纪,国家就有灭亡的危险。习近平总书记指出,每个时代都有每个时代的精神,每个时代都有每个时代的价值观念。国有四维,礼义廉耻,"四维不张,国乃灭亡"。这是中国先人对当时核心价值观的认识。

146. "虽有智慧,不如乘势。"——《孟子·公孙丑上》

英译:"It is wiser to avail oneself of a favorable situation than to reply on one's mere wisdom."

解析:汉语原文意思是即使有智慧,也不如很好地运用形势。习近平总书记指出,"虽有智慧,不如乘势"。了解历史才能看得远,理解历史才能走得远。要教育引导全党胸怀中华民族伟大复兴战略全局和世界百年未有之大变局,树立大历史观,从历史长河、时代大潮、全球风云中分析演变机理、探究历史规律,提出因应的战略策略,增强工作的系统性、预见性、创造性。

147. "所谓大学者,非谓有大楼之谓也,有大师之谓也。"——梅贻琦

英译:"The key to the success of a university lies in having a lot of highly accomplished gurus rather than imposing buildings."

解析:汉语原文意思是一所大学之所以成为大学,并不在于它有多少幢大楼,而在于它有多少名大师。习近平总书记指出,教师承担着最庄严、最神圣的使命。梅贻琦先生说:"所谓大学者,非谓有大楼之谓也,有大师之谓也。"我体会,这样的大师,既是学问之师,又是品行之师。教师要时刻铭记教书育人的使命,甘当人梯,甘当铺路石,以人格魅力引导学生心灵,以学术造诣开启学生的智慧之门。

T

148. "太上有立德,其次有立功,其次有立言"——《左传·襄公二十四年》

英译:"The highest attainment is to exemplify virtue; the second highest is to perform great deeds; the third highest is to put forth noble ideas."

解析:汉语原文意思是人生最高的境界是树立德行,其次是建功立业,然后是著书立说。习近平总书记指出,希望大家坚持用明德引领风尚。《左传》讲"太上有立德,其次有立功,其次有立言",立德是最高的境界。文化文艺工作者、哲学社会科学工作者都肩负着启迪思想、陶冶情操、温润心灵的重要职责,承担着以文化人、以文育人、以文培元的使命。大家社会影响力大,理应以高远志向、良好品德、高尚情操为社会作出表率。

149. "天不言而四时行,地不语而百物生。"——李白《上安州裴长史书》

英译:"Heaven and earth do not speak, yet the seasons change and all things grow."

解析:汉语原文意思是天地不会说话,但不影响四季运行,也不影响百物生长。习近平总书记指出,坚持人与自然和谐共生。人与自然是生命共同体。生态环境没有替代品,用之不觉,失之难存。"天不言而四时行,地不语而百物生。"当人类合理利用、友好保护自然时,自然的回报常常是慷慨的;当人类无序开发、粗暴掠夺自然时,自然的惩罚必然是无情的。人类对大自然的伤害最终会伤及人类自身,这是无法抗拒的规律。

150. "天地与我并生,而万物与我为一。"——《庄子·齐物论》

英译:"Heaven and earth coexist with me; all things and I are one."

解析：汉语原文意思是天地与"我"同生，万物与"我"是一体的，喻指人与自然是生命共同体，应和谐相处。习近平总书记指出，人与自然是生命共同体。生态环境没有替代品，用之不觉，失之难存。"天地与我并生，而万物与我为一。"当人类合理利用、友好保护自然时，自然的回报常常是慷慨的；当人类无序开发、粗暴掠夺自然时，自然的惩罚必然是无情的。人类对大自然的伤害最终会伤及人类自身，这是无法抗拒的规律。

151. "天地之大，黎元为本。"——房玄龄等《晋书·宣帝纪》

英译："In a country, the people are the most important."

解析：汉语原文意思是天地虽然广袤无垠，但是黎民百姓才是国家的根本。习近平总书记指出，从根本宗旨把握新发展理念。古人说："天地之大，黎元为本。"人民是我们党执政的最深厚基础和最大底气。为人民谋幸福、为民族谋复兴，这既是我们党领导现代化建设的出发点和落脚点，也是新发展理念的"根"和"魂"。只有坚持以人民为中心的发展思想，坚持发展为了人民、发展依靠人民、发展成果由人民共享，才会有正确的发展观、现代化观。

152. "天人合一"

英译："the harmony of Nature and man"

解析：汉语原文意思是人与自然万物相生相依。习近平总书记指出，中华文明有其独特的价值体系，都具有鲜明的民族特色，具有永不褪色的时代价值，这些思想和理念，既随着时间推移和时代变迁而不断与时俱进，又有其自身的连续性和稳定性。

153. "天下不能常治，有弊所当革也；犹人身不能常安，有疾所当治也。"——何坦《西畴常言》

英译："To ensure lasting peace, problems must be addressed when they arise; to enjoy eternal health, people must go to the doctor when they get ill."

解析：汉语原文意思是天下没有永远的安定太平，出现问题及时修正革弊，才能使国家长治久安，这就像人难免会生病，生了病就要及时对症下药进行治疗一样。习近平总书记指出，要在自我净化上下功夫，通过过滤杂质、清除毒素、割除毒瘤，不断纯洁党的队伍，保证党的肌体健康。古人说："天下不能常治，有弊所当革也；犹人身不能常安，有疾所当治也。"治病救人，哪能不吃药，对那些顽症须下点猛药才行，对有病毒扩散风险的肿瘤还得动刀子。

154. "天下难事，必作于易；天下大事，必作于细。"——《老子》

英译："Difficult things are done starting from easy ones; a great undertaking begins with minor work."

解析：汉语原文意思是处理难事的时候一定要从简易简单的方面入手，处理大的事情一定要从细微的地方做起。习近平总书记指出，"天下难事，必作于易；天下大事，必作于细"。成功的背后，永远是艰辛努力。青年要把艰苦环境作为磨炼自己的机遇，把小事当作大事干，一步一个脚印往前走。滴水可以穿石。只要坚韧不拔、百折不挠，成功就一定在前方等你。

155. "天下兴亡，匹夫有责"——顾炎武《日知录·正始》

英译："Everyone is responsible for his country's rise or fall."

解析：汉语原文意思是国家兴盛或衰亡，每个普通的人都有责任。习近平总书记指出，在中国人民抗日战争的壮阔进程中，形成了伟大的抗战精神，中国人民向世界展示了天下兴亡、匹夫有责的爱国情怀，视死如归、宁死不屈的民族气节，不畏强暴、血战到底的英雄气概，百折不挠、坚忍不拔的必胜信念。

156. "天下之势不盛则衰，天下之治不进则退。"——吕祖谦《东莱博议·葵丘之会》

英译："The momentum of the world either flourishes or declines; the governance of the world either progresses or regresses." / "If a dynasty cannot continue to rise, it will fall; if a country cannot improve its governance, the state of order will deteriorate."

解析：汉语原文意思是天下各种力量此消彼长，不强盛就会走向衰落；治理国家若不寻求发展进步，社会则将面临倒退。习近平总书记指出，"天下之势不盛则衰，天下之治不进则退"。世界总是在矛盾运动中发展的，没有矛盾就没有世界。纵观历史，人类正是在战胜一次次考验中成长、在克服一场场危机中发展。我们要在历史前进的逻辑中前进、在时代发展的潮流中发展。

157. "天下之事，不难于立法，而难于法之必行。"——张居正《请稽查章奏随事考成以修实政疏》

英译："The most difficult thing about law is not legislation but law enforcement."

解析：汉语原文意思是天下的事情，制定法令并不困难，难的是认真切实地贯彻执行。习近平总书记指出，"天下之事，不难于立法，而难于法之必行"。推进法治体系建设，重点和难点在于通过严格执法、公正司法、全民守法，推进法律正确实施，把"纸上的法律"变成"行动中的法律"。要健全法律面前人人平等保障机制，维护国家法制统一、尊严、权威，一切违反宪法法律的行为都必须予以追究。各级党组织和领导干部都要旗帜鲜明支持司法机关依法独立行使职权，绝不容许利用职权干预司法、插手案件。

158. "天行健，君子以自强不息。"——《周易·乾》

英译："Just as Heaven maintains vigor through movement, a gentleman makes unremitting efforts to perfect himself."

解析：汉语原文意思是天的运动刚强劲健，相应于此，君子处世，应像天一样，自我力求进步，刚毅坚卓，发奋图强，永不停息。习近平总书记指出，"天行健，君子以自强不息"。一个民族之所以伟大，根本就在于在任何困难和风险面前都从来不放弃、不退缩、不止步，百折不挠为自己的前途命运而奋斗。从5000多年文明发展的苦难辉煌中走来的中国人民和中华民族，必将在新时代的伟大征程上一路向前，任何人任何势力都不能阻挡中国人民实现更加美好生活的前进步伐！

159. "听言不如观事，观事不如观行。"——傅玄《傅子·通志》

英译："Approach tells more than words, and conduct reveals more than approach."

解析：汉语原文意思是要想甄别一个人，与其听他说话，不如看他做事；与其看他做事，不如观察他的行为。习近平总书记指出，中国特色社会主义制度和国家治理体系具有丰富的实践成果。"听言不如观事，观事不如观行。"我国国家制度和国家治理体系管不管用、有没有效，实践是最好的试金石。

160. "同乎流俗，合乎污世。"——《孟子·尽心下》

英译："just following the herd and being in concord with the filthy world"

解析：汉语原文意思是思想、言行低俗，就会与恶劣的风气、污浊的世道相合。

习近平总书记指出，奉行好人主义，出发点就有问题，因为好的是自己，坏的是风气、是事业。大量事实表明，一些地方和单位正气不彰、邪气蔓延，工作局面长期打不开，矛盾问题积累一大堆，同好人主义的盛行有密不可分的关系。

161. "图之于未萌，虑之于未有。"——刘昫等《旧唐书·柳亨传附柳泽传》

英译："Nip the problem in the bud when it is in the making; prepare yourself for risks yet to emerge."

解析：汉语原文意思是在祸患尚未萌发时就预先提防，在灾祸没有到来时未雨绸缪。习近平总书记指出，有效防范生态环境风险。生态环境安全是国家安全的重要组成部分，是经济社会持续健康发展的重要保障。"图之于未萌，虑之于未有。"要始终保持高度警觉，防止各类生态环境风险积聚扩散，做好应对任何形式生态环境风险挑战的准备。

W

162. "万物并育而不相害，道并行而不相悖。"——《礼记·中庸》

英译："All living things grow side by side without harming one another; the sun, moon and seasons rotate according to their own laws without hindering each other."

解析：汉语原文意思是万物竞相生长，但是彼此之间并不妨害；日月运行、四时更替各有各的规律，相互不冲突。习近平总书记指出，我们要努力建立一个远离封闭、开放包容的世界。中国有句古话："万物并育而不相害，道并行而不相悖。"文明的繁盛、人类的进步，离不开求同存异、开放包容，离不开文明交流、互学互鉴。历史呼唤着人类文明同放异彩，不同文明应该和谐共生、相得益彰，共同为人类发展提供精神力量。

163. "万物得其本者生，百事得其道者成"——刘向《说苑·谈丛》

英译："Plants with strong roots grow well, and efforts with the right focus ensure success."

解析：汉语原文意思是世间万物，只有保住根本才能生长；一切事情，只有符合道义才能成功。习近平总书记强调与时俱进完善和发展中国特色社会主义制度和国家治理体系。"万物得其本者生，百事得其道者成。"随着中国特色社会主义进入新时代，我国发展处于新的历史方位，我国社会主要矛盾已经转化为人民日益增长的美好生活需要和不平衡不充分的发展之间的矛盾，我国国家治理面临许多新任务新要求，必然要求中国特色社会主义制度和国家治理体系更加完善、不断发展。

164."万物各得其和以生，各得其养以成"——《荀子·天论》

英译："All beings flourish when they live in harmony and receive nourishment from nature." / "All things must be in harmony with nature to grow, and obtain from nature to thrive."

解析：汉语原文意思是自然万物各自得到阴阳形成的和气而产生，各自得到相应的滋养而成长。习近平总书记指出，"万物各得其和以生，各得其养以成"。生物多样性使地球充满生机，也是人类生存和发展的基础。保护生物多样性有助于维护地球家园，促进人类可持续发展。

165."为国也，观俗立法则治，察国事本则宜。不观时俗，不察国本，则其法立而民乱，事剧而功寡。"——《商君书·算地》

英译："In governing a country, a wise ruler establishes laws through observing popular customs, thus bringing order. He understands the fundamentals of the land he rules, thus implementing appropriate policies. Where the customs of the times are ignored and the fundamentals of the land neglected, the people will fall into disorder even when laws are made. And the ruler may be kept busy but will achieve little."

解析：汉语原文意思是治理国家，只有在充分考察风俗的基础上，才能制定合适的法规；只有在弄清国情的基础上，才能抓住国家的根本任务。如果不观察当时的风俗，不抓住国家的根本任务，那么法令制定后民众就会混乱，政务再繁忙也没有什么效果。习近平总书记指出，必须坚持从中国实际出发。走什么样的法治道路、建设什么样的法治体系，是由一个国家的基本国情决定的。"为国也，观俗立法则治，察国事本则宜。不观时俗，不察国本，则其法立而民乱，事剧而功寡。"全面推进依法治国，必须从我国实际出发，同推进国家治理体系和治理能力现代化相适应，既不能罔顾国情、超越阶段，也不能因循守旧、墨守成规。

166."为世用者，百篇无害；不为用者，一章无补。"——王充《论衡·自纪》

英译："Writings, if useful to society, are never enough even if there are more than a hundred of them; while if useless, one single page is far too many."

解析：汉语原文意思是对社会有用的文章，写一百篇也没有害处；对社会没用的文章，哪怕就是写一章也没有益处。这体现了好作品对社会的重要价值和积极作用。习近平总书记指出，立德树人的人，必先立己；铸魂培根的人，必先铸己。那些在历史长河中经久不衰的经典，都体现了文学家、艺术家襟怀和学识的贯通、道德和才情的交融、人品和艺品的统一。正所谓"为世用者，百篇无害；不为用者，一章无补"。

167. "为有牺牲多壮志，敢教日月换新天。"——毛泽东《七律·到韶山》

英译："Our minds grow stronger for the martyrs' sacrifice, daring to make the sun and the moon shine in the new sky."

解析：汉语原文意思是因为有这么多敢为自己伟大理想而去牺牲的人，敢去改变旧的日月换新的天地。习近平总书记指出，一百年来，中国共产党团结带领中国人民，以"为有牺牲多壮志，敢教日月换新天"的大无畏气概，书写了中华民族几千年历史上最恢宏的史诗。这一百年来开辟的伟大道路、创造的伟大事业、取得的伟大成就，必将载入中华民族发展史册、人类文明发展史册。

168. "为政之道，以顺民心为本"——程颐《代吕晦叔应诏疏》

英译："Conforming to the will of the people is the key to governance."

解析：汉语原文意思是为官执政的道理，在于以顺应民心为根本。习近平总书记强调充分发挥人大代表作用，做到民有所呼、我有所应。"为政之要，以顺民心为本。"人民代表大会制度之所以具有强大生命力和显著优越性，关键在于深深植根于人民之中。一切国家机关和国家工作人员必须牢固树立人民公仆意识，把人民放在心中最高位置，保持同人民的密切联系，倾听人民意见和建议，接受人民监督，努力为人民服务。

169. "为治之本，务在于安民。安民之本，在于足用。"——刘安《淮南子·诠言训》

英译："The essence of governance is livelihood, and the essence of livelihood is sufficiency."

解析：汉语原文意思是治理国家的根本，就在于使老百姓生活安定；使老百姓生活安定的根本，在于财物用度充足。习近平总书记指出，我们应该坚持互利共赢，共同推动经济社会发展更好造福人民。中国古人说："为治之本，务在于安民；安民之本，在于足用。"推动发展、安居乐业是各国人民共同愿望。为了人民而发展，发展才有意义；依靠人民而发展，发展才有动力。世界各国应该坚持以人民为中心，努力实现更高质量、更有效率、更加公平、更可持续、更为安全的发展。要破解发展不平衡不充分问题，提高发展的平衡性、协调性、包容性。要增强人民发展能力，形成人人参与、人人享有的发展环境，创造发展成果更多更公平惠及每一个国家每一个人的发展局面。

170. "为治之要，莫先于用人"——司马光《资治通鉴·魏纪五》

英译："Employing capable officials represents the top priority of governance."

解析：汉语原文意思是治理国家的关键在于如何选用人才。习近平总书记指出，我们党历来高度重视选贤任能，始终把选人用人作为关系党和人民事业的关键性、根本性问题来抓。治国之要，首在用人，也就是古人说的："尚贤者，政之本也。""为政之要，莫先于用人。"

171. "惟以改过为能，不以无过为贵。"——司马光《资治通鉴·唐纪四十五》

英译："It is admirable to correct one's mistakes, and it's not commendable not to make any mistakes."

解析：汉语原文意思是有了错误能够改正才最为重要，不要把不犯错误当成可贵的事情。习近平总书记指出，我们党作为世界第一大党，没有什么外力能够打倒我们，能够打倒我们的只有我们自己。古人说："惟以改过为能，不以无过为贵。"应该看到，在长期执政条件下，各种弱化党的先进性、损害党的纯洁性的因素无时不有，各种违背初心和使命、动摇党的根基的危险无处不在，如果不严加防范、及时整治，久而久之，必将积重难返，小问题就会变成大问题、小管涌就会沦为大塌方，甚至可能酿成全局性、颠覆性的灾难。

172. "畏则不敢肆而德以成，无畏则从其所欲而及于祸。"——吕坤《呻吟语·修身》

英译："With awe in mind, one will be prudent in word and deed, and therefore cultivate virtue; without awe in mind, one will act rashly, and therefore bring disaster to oneself."

解析：汉语原文意思是心中有所敬畏，言行不敢放纵，才能养成美好的德行操守；反之，心中无戒惧，就会肆意妄为，招致祸端。习近平总书记指出，讲规矩、守底线，首先要有敬畏心。心有所畏，方能言有所戒、行有所止。但仍有一些干部我行我素，顶风违纪。他们不是不知道纪律规矩，而是根本没有敬畏之心。他们所犯的哪一项不是党纪国法所明令禁止的？所作所为的哪一件没有前车之鉴？古人讲："畏则不敢肆而德以成，无畏则从其所欲而及于祸。"没有敬畏之心，就什么乱七八糟的事都干得出来。

173."文章合为时而著，歌诗合为事而作。"——白居易《与元九书》

英译："Prose and poetry are composed to reflect the times and reality."

解析：汉语原文意思是诗文创作要贴近实际，把握时代脉搏，反映社会现实。习近平总书记指出，希望大家坚持与时代同步伐。古人讲："文章合为时而著，歌诗合为事而作。"所谓"为时"、"为事"，就是要发时代之先声，在时代发展中有所作为。

174."文者，贯道之器也"——李汉《昌黎先生集序》

英译："Literature is the channel by which ideas are disseminated."

解析：汉语原文意思是文章是贯通道理的工具。习近平总书记认为，文化是民族的精神命脉，文艺是时代的号角。古人说："文者，贯道之器也。"新时代新征程是当代中国文艺的历史方位。广大文艺工作者要深刻把握民族复兴的时代主题，把人生追求、艺术生命同国家前途、民族命运、人民愿望紧密结合起来，以文弘业、以文培元、以文立心、以文铸魂，把文艺创造写到民族复兴的历史上、写在人民奋斗的征程中。

175."我劝天公重抖擞，不拘一格降人才。"——龚自珍《己亥杂诗》

英译："I beg Old Man Heaven to bestir himself, and send down talented people of more kinds than one."

解析：汉语原文意思是"我"奉劝上天要重新振作精神，不要拘泥一定规格以降下更多的人才。习近平总书记指出，未来总是属于年青人的。拥有一大批创新型青年人才，是国家创新活力之所在，也是科技发展希望之所在。"我劝天公重抖擞，不拘一格降人才。"广大院士不仅要做科技创新的开拓者，更要做提携后学的领路人。希望广大院士肩负起培养青年科技人才的责任，甘为人梯，言传身教，慧眼识才，不断发现、培养、举荐人才，为拔尖创新人才脱颖而出铺路搭桥。广大青年科技人才要树立科学精神、培养创新思维、挖掘创新潜能、提高创新能力，在继承前人的基础上不断超越。

176. "无实事求是之意，有哗众取宠之心。"——毛泽东《改造我们的学习》

英译："no intention of seeking truth from facts, but only a desire to curry favor by claptrap"

解析：汉语原文意思是在做研究工作和实际工作时，不是采取老老实实地从实际出发的态度，而是脱离实际，用夸夸其谈的方法博得大家的称赞和好评，这实际上是党性不纯的一种表现。习近平总书记指出，既要"身入"基层，更要"心到"基层，听真话、察真情，真研究问题、研究真问题，不能搞作秀式调研、盆景式调研、蜻蜓点水式调研，"无实事求是之意，有哗众取宠之心"是不行的！这就是严重的形式主义、官僚主义！要在深入分析思考上下功夫，去粗取精、去伪存真，由此及彼、由表及里，找到事物的本质和规律，找到解决问题的办法。

177. "吾心信其可行，则移山填海之难，终有成功之日；吾心信其不可行，则反掌折枝之易，亦无收效之期也。"——孙中山《建国方略》

英译："If I believe I can do it, then I am able to complete any difficult task – even moving a mountain or filling up a sea; if I don't think I can do it, then I may not succeed in even the easiest tasks like flipping over my hands or breaking off a twig."

解析：汉语原文意思是如果有信心把事做成，就算像移山填海一样困难，终有一天也会成功；如果没有信心，即便像翻手掌、折树枝那样容易，想要实现也只会遥遥无期。习近平总书记指出，要矢志不移自主创新，坚定创新信心，着力增强自主创新能力。只有自信的国家和民族，才能在通往未来的道路上行稳致远。自力更生是中华民族自立于世界民族之林的奋斗基点，自主创新是我们攀登世界科技高峰的必由之路。"吾心信其可行，则移山填海之难，终有成功之日；吾心信其不可行，则反掌折枝之易，亦无收效之期也。"

178. "五谷者，万民之命，国之重宝也。"——范蠡《范子计然》

英译："Grain sustains life and is vital to the nation."

解析：汉语原文意思是粮食是天下百姓生命之所系，是国家之至宝。习近平总书记指出，"五谷者，万民之命，国之重宝"。我反复强调，粮食多一点少一点是战术问题，粮食安全是战略问题。今年应对新冠肺炎疫情，粮食和重要农副产品供给充裕功不可没，充分印证了这一点。

179. "五色交辉，相得益彰；八音合奏，终和且平。"——冯友兰《三松堂全集》

英译："The matching of different colors leads to greater beauty, and the combination of different musical instruments creates harmony and peace."

解析：汉语原文意思是多种颜色交相辉映，在互相映衬下更加彰显；各种声音一起合奏，在彼此交响中达到平衡与和谐。习近平总书记指出，弘扬丝路精神，就是要促进文明互鉴。人类文明没有高低优劣之分，因为平等交流而变得丰富多彩，正所谓"五色交辉，相得益彰；八音合奏，终和且平"。中阿双方坚持以开放包容心态看待对方，用对话交流代替冲突对抗，创造了不同社会制度、不同信仰、不同文化传统的国家和谐相处的典范。

180. "务农重本，国之大纲。"——房玄龄等《晋书·文六王传》

英译："Attaching importance to agricultural development is the fundamental plan of the country."

解析：汉语原文意思是重视发展农业，是国家的根本大计。习近平总书记指出，"务农重本，国之大纲"。历史和现实都告诉我们，农为邦本，本固邦宁。我们要坚持用大历史观来看待农业、农村、农民问题，只有深刻理解了"三农"问题，才能更好理解我们这个党、这个国家、这个民族。必须看到，全面建设社会主义现代化国家，实现中华民族伟大复兴，最艰巨最繁重的任务依然在农村，最广泛最深厚的基础依然在农村。

181. "物必先腐也，而后虫生之。"——苏轼《范增论》

英译："Worms can only grow in something rotten."

解析：汉语原文意思是东西必定自身先腐烂了，然后才生蛆虫，比喻内部先有弱点或腐败，坏事或奸邪就容易发生滋长。习近平总书记指出，反对腐败、建设廉洁政治，保持党的肌体健康，始终是我们党一贯坚持的鲜明政治立场。党风廉政建设，是广大干部群众始终关注的重大政治问题。"物必先腐也，而后虫生之。"近年来，一些国家因长期积累的矛盾导致民怨载道、社会动荡、政权垮台，其中贪污腐败就是一个很重要的原因。大量事实告诉我们，腐败问题越演越烈，最终必然会亡党亡国！我们要警醒啊！

182. "物有甘苦，尝之者识；道有夷险，履之者知。"——刘基《拟连珠》

英译："To know the flavor of a thing, one must taste it; to know what lies ahead on a path, one must walk it."

解析：汉语原文意思是任何事物都有甘苦之分，只有尝试过才会知道；天下道路都有平坦坎坷之分，只有自己走过才会明白。习近平总书记指出，"物有甘苦，尝之者识；道有夷险，履之者知"。在这场波澜壮阔的抗疫斗争中，我们积累了重要经验，收获了深刻启示。

183. "物之不齐，物之情也。"——《孟子·滕文公上》

英译："It is natural for things to be different."

解析：汉语原文意思是物品千差万别，这是客观情形、自然规律。习近平总书记认为，文明交流互鉴不应该以独尊某一种文明或者贬损某一种文明为前提。中国人在2000多年前就认识到了"物之不齐，物之情也"的道理。推动文明交流互鉴，可以丰富人类文明的色彩，让各国人民享受更富内涵的精神生活、开创更有选择的未来。

X

184. "先天下之忧而忧，后天下之乐而乐"——范仲淹《岳阳楼记》

英译："being the first to worry about the affairs of the state and the last to enjoy oneself"

解析：汉语原文意思是在天下人忧之前先忧，在天下人乐之后才乐。习近平总书记指出，希望广大留学人员继承和发扬留学报国的光荣传统，做爱国主义的坚守者和传播者，秉持"先天下之忧而忧，后天下之乐而乐"的人生理想，始终把国家富强、民族振兴、人民幸福作为努力志向，自觉使个人成功的果实结在爱国主义这棵常青树上。大家都要牢记，无论身在何处，祖国和人民始终惦记着你们，祖国永远是你们温暖的精神家园。

185. "贤良之士众，则国家之治厚；贤良之士寡，则国家之治薄。"——《墨子·尚贤上》

英译："If a country has a huge pool of talent, good governance is ensured; otherwise, poor governance is unavoidable."

解析：汉语原文意思是国家拥有的贤能良德之才越多，那么国家治理的根基就越深厚；拥有的贤能良才越少，那么国家治理的根基就越浅薄。习近平总书记强调抓好执政骨干队伍和人才队伍建设。古人说："贤良之士众，则国家之治厚；贤良之士寡，则国家之治薄。"干部工作也好，人才工作也好，本质上都是用人问题。我们要应变局、育新机、开新局、谋复兴，关键是要把党的各级领导班子和干部队伍建设好、建设强。

186."乡愿，德之贼也。"——《论语·阳货》

英译："The 'honest villager' spoils true virtue."

解析：汉语原文意思是没有道德修养的伪君子，就是破坏道德的人。习近平总书记指出，对共产党人来说，"好好先生"并不是真正的好人。奉行好人主义的人，没有公心、只有私心，没有正气、只有俗气，以为"坚持原则是非多、碰到硬茬麻烦多、平平稳稳好处多、拉拉扯扯朋友多"。自古以来，人们就对这种人嗤之以鼻。孔子说："乡愿，德之贼也。"就是说那些不分是非、不得罪乡里的"好好先生"，其实是破坏道德的人。

187."消未起之患，治未病之疾，医之于无事之前"——葛洪《抱朴子·内篇·地真》

英译："Remove health risks before they emerge and treat ailments before they are serious, thus preventing illnesses before they arise."

解析：汉语原文意思是在祸患还尚未兴起时就消除它，在疾病还没有发展成重症之前就治愈它，在无疾患之前就进行预防保健。习近平总书记指出，古人说："消未起之患、治未病之疾，医之于无事之前。"法治建设既要抓末端、治已病，更要抓前端、治未病。我国国情决定了我们不能成为"诉讼大国"。我国有14亿人口，大大小小的事都要打官司，那必然不堪重负！要推动更多法治力量向引导和疏导端用力，完善预防性法律制度，坚持和发展新时代"枫桥经验"，完善社会矛盾纠纷多元预防调处化解综合机制，更加重视基层基础工作，充分发挥共建共治共享在基层的作用，推进市域社会治理现代化，促进社会和谐稳定。

188."行百里者半于九十。"——《战国策·秦策五》

英译："The last one tenth of the journey demands half the effort." / "A thing is yet to be done until it is done."

解析：汉语原文意思是一百里的路程，尽管已走了九十里，也只能算是走了一半。习近平总书记指出，我们比历史上任何时期都更接近实现中华民族伟大复兴的目标，比历史上任何时期都更有信心、更有能力实现这个目标。行百里者半九十。距离实现中华民族伟大复兴的目标越近，我们越不能懈怠，越要加倍努力，越要动员广大青年为之奋斗。

189. "行之力则知愈进，知之深则行愈达"——张栻《论语解·序》

英译："Practice improves understanding and a deeper understanding guides further practice."

解析：汉语原文意思是越是深入实践，知识越能不断增长，认识越能不断精进；有了更深刻的认识，实践才更有方向感。习近平总书记认为，只有顺应历史潮流，积极应变，主动求变，才能与时代同行。"行之力则知愈进，知之深则行愈达。"改革开放40年积累的宝贵经验是党和人民弥足珍贵的精神财富，对新时代坚持和发展中国特色社会主义有着极为重要的指导意义，必须倍加珍惜、长期坚持，在实践中不断丰富和发展。

190. "雄关漫道真如铁"——毛泽东《忆秦娥·娄山关》

英译："storming an iron-wall pass"

解析：汉语原文意思是雄壮的关隘坚硬如铁难以逾越。习近平总书记指出，中华民族的昨天，可以说是"雄关漫道真如铁"。近代以后，中华民族遭受的苦难之重、付出的牺牲之大，在世界历史上都是罕见的。但是，中国人民从不屈服，不断奋起抗争，终于掌握了自己的命运，开始了建设自己国家的伟大进程，充分展示了以爱国主义为核心的伟大民族精神。

191. "学而不思则罔，思而不学则殆。"——《论语·为政》

英译："Reading without thinking makes one muddled; thinking without reading makes one flighty."

解析：汉语原文意思是只是学习却不思考就会感到迷茫而无所适从，只是思考却不学习就会心中充满疑惑而无定见。习近平总书记指出，要明辨，善于明辨是非，善于决断选择。"学而不思则罔，思而不学则殆。"是非明，方向清，路子正，人们付出的辛劳才能结出果实。面对世界的深刻复杂变化，面对信息时代各种思潮的相互激荡，面对纷繁多变、鱼龙混杂、泥沙俱下的社会现象，面对学业、情感、职业选择等多方面的考量，一时有些疑惑、彷徨、失落，是正常的人生经历。关键是要学会思考、善于分析、正确抉择，做到稳重自持、从容自信、坚定自励。

192. "学如弓弩，才如箭镞"——袁枚《续诗品·尚识》

英译："Learning is the bow, while competence is the arrow."

解析：汉语原文意思是学问的根基好比弓弩，才能好比箭头，只要依靠厚实的见识来引导，就可以让才能很好发挥作用。习近平总书记指出，广大青年一定要练就过硬本领。学习是成长进步的阶梯，实践是提高本领的途径。青年的素质和本领直接影响着实现中国梦的进程。古人说："学如弓弩，才如箭镞。"青年人正处于学习的黄金时期，应该把学习作为首要任务，作为一种责任、一种精神追求、一种生活方式，树立梦想从学习开始、事业靠本领成就的观念，让勤奋学习成为青春远航的动力，让增长本领成为青春搏击的能量。

193. "学所以益才也，砺所以致刃也。"——刘向《说苑·建本》

英译："Through learning we improve ability, as through the whetstone knives are honed."

解析：汉语原文意思是要想增长才干，就要努力学习；要使刀刃锋利，就得勤加磨砺。习近平总书记指出，新中国成立之初组建海军，党中央决定肖劲光同志担任海军司令员。肖劲光同志从没接触过海军，自己还是个"旱鸭子"，但他边干边学，使我国海军从无到有、迅速壮大，出色完成了党中央交给的任务。许多从战争年代走来的老一辈革命家也都是在实践中成长为经济、科技、外交等领域的行家里手的。"学所以益才也，砺所以致刃也。"

194. "学者非必为仕，而仕者必如学。"——《荀子·大略》

英译："One may or may not study for the purpose of becoming an official, but officials must be learned to fulfill their duties."

解析：汉语原文意思是读书人不一定都要做官，但为官者必须坚持学习以不负平生所学。习近平总书记指出，从这个角度讲，领导干部学习不学习不仅仅是自己的事情，本领大小也不仅仅是自己的事情，而是关乎党和国家事业发展的大事情。这也就是古人所说的"学者非必为仕，而仕者必为学"。只有加强学习，才能增强工作的科学性、预见性、主动性，才能使领导和决策体现时代性、把握规律性、富于创造性，避免陷入少知而迷、不知而盲、无知而乱的困境，才能克服本领不足、本领恐慌、本领落后的问题。

Y

195. "衙斋卧听萧萧竹,疑是民间疾苦声。些小吾曹州县吏,一枝一叶总关情。"——郑板桥《潍县署中画竹呈年伯包大中丞括》

英译:"When I hear the rustles of bamboo leaves outside my study,

I feel it is the wails of hungry people;

For petty county officials like us,

Every concern of the people weighs in our heart."

解析:汉语原文意思是在一个凄风冷雨的夜晚,"我"在县衙书斋躺着休息,听见风吹竹叶发出萧萧之声,立即联想是百姓啼饥号寒的怨声,"我们"这些小小的州县官,老百姓的一举一动都牵动着"我们"的感情。习近平总书记指出,历朝历代都高度重视县级官员选拔任用。许多名人志士为官从政是从县一级起步的。北宋政治家王安石,二十七岁担任浙江鄞县(今宁波市鄞州区)知县,任职三年,"治绩大举,民称其德",为以后革新变法打下了基础。清代郑板桥长期在河南范县、山东潍县担任知县,其诗句"衙斋卧听萧萧竹,疑是民间疾苦声。些小吾曹州县吏,一枝一叶总关情"千古流传。陶渊明、狄仁杰、包拯、海瑞等很多人都当过县令、知县。

196. "言必信,行必果"——《论语·子路》

英译:"Be true in word and resolute in deed."

解析:汉语原文意思是说话一定讲诚信,做事一定果断。习近平总书记指出,"言必信,行必果"。农村贫困人口如期脱贫、贫困县全部摘帽、解决区域性整体贫困,是全面建成小康社会的底线任务,是我们做出的庄严承诺。

197. "尧有欲谏之鼓,舜有诽谤之木"——《吕氏春秋·自知》

英译:"Emperor Yao set up a drum for people to beat and offer their advice, and Emperor Shun set up wooden boards for people to write down their criticisms."

解析:汉语原文意思是尧有供想进谏的人敲击的鼓,舜有供书写批评意见的木柱。习近平总书记指出,大家读历史都知道,《吕氏春秋》里讲:"尧有欲谏之鼓,舜有诽谤之木。""谏鼓"、"谤木"就是为了收集舆论。这说明古人就很懂得发挥舆论的作用。

198. "一命而偻，再命而伛，三命而俯。循墙而走，亦莫余敢侮。饘于是，鬻于是，以糊余口。"——《左传·昭公七年》

英译："Head down when I was promoted the first time, back hunched when promoted the second time, and waist bent when promoted the third time. No one insults me if I keep close to the wall when walking along the street. What I need only is this vessel to cook porridge in."

解析：汉语原文意思是每逢有任命提拔时都越来越谨慎，一次提拔要低着头，再次提拔要曲背，三次提拔要弯腰，连走路都靠墙走，生活中只要有这只鼎煮粥糊口就可以了。习近平总书记指出，敢于担当，是为了党和人民事业，而不是个人风头主义，飞扬跋扈、唯我独尊并不是敢于担当。春秋时期宋国大夫正考父是几朝元老，但他对自己要求很严，他在家庙的鼎上铸下铭训："一命而偻，再命而伛，三命而俯。循墙而走，亦莫余敢侮。饘于是，鬻于是，以糊余口。"我们的干部都是党的干部，权力都是党和人民赋予的，更应该在工作中敢作敢为、锐意进取，在做人上谦虚谨慎、戒骄戒躁。

199. "一年之计，莫如树谷；十年之计，莫如树木；终身之计，莫如树人。"——《管子·权修》

英译："If you want one year of prosperity, then grow grain; if you want ten years of prosperity, then grow trees; if you want one hundred years of prosperity, then you cultivate people."

解析：汉语原文意思是若是为一年谋算，没有比种植庄稼更合适的；若是为十年谋划，没有比栽种树木更合适的；而若是要为一生制定规划，就没有比培养人才更合适的。习近平总书记指出，我国科技队伍规模是世界上最大的，这是我们必须引以为豪的。但是我们在科技队伍上也面对着严峻挑战，就是创新型科技人才结构性不足矛盾突出，世界级科技大师缺乏，领军人才、尖子人才不足，工程技术人才培养同生产和创新实践脱节。"一年之计，莫如树谷；十年之计，莫如树木；终身之计，莫如树人。"我们要把人才资源开发放在科技创新最优先的位置，改革人才培养、引进、使用等机制，努力造就一批世界水平的科学家、科技领军人才、工程师和高水平创新团队，注重培养一线创新人才和青年科技人才。

200. "一时之强弱在力,千古之胜负在理。"——《东周列国志》

英译:"The powerful may get the upper hand for the time being, but justice will ultimately prevail."

解析:汉语原文意思是一时的强大可能取决于平常谁更强势,但长期的胜利还是要看谁顺应潮流、谁更在理。习近平总书记强调走公平正义之路。"一时强弱在于力,千秋胜负在于理。"解决国际上的事情,不能从所谓"实力地位"出发,推行霸权、霸道、霸凌,应该以联合国宪章宗旨和原则为遵循,坚持共商共建共享。要践行真正的多边主义,反对打着所谓"规则"旗号破坏国际秩序、制造对抗和分裂的行径。要恪守互利共赢的合作观,拆除割裂贸易、投资、技术的高墙壁垒,营造包容普惠的发展前景。

201. "一语不能践,万卷徒空虚。"——林鸿《饮酒》

英译:"There is no use in reading 10,000 books if we cannot even put one of their words into practice."

解析:汉语原文意思是假如一句话都不能付诸实践,纵然读万卷诗书也是枉然。习近平总书记指出,"一语不能践,万卷徒空虚"。要教育引导广大党员干部了解民情、掌握实情,搞清楚问题是什么、症结在哪里,拿出破解难题的实招、硬招。调查研究要注重实效,使调研的过程成为加深对党的创新理论领悟的过程,成为保持同人民群众血肉联系的过程,成为推动事业发展的过程。要防止为调研而调研,防止搞"出发一车子、开会一屋子、发言念稿子"式的调研,防止扎堆调研、"作秀式"调研。

202. "壹引其纲,万目皆张。"——《吕氏春秋·用民》

英译:"As long as the fundamental principles are upheld, all work will fall in place."

解析:汉语原文意思是一提起网上的大绳,所有的网眼就都张开了。习近平总书记指出,"壹引其纲,万目皆张"。党的十八大以来,我们全力推进党的政治建设,健全维护党中央权威和集中统一领导的各项制度,党的团结统一更加巩固。

203. "以其昏昏使人昭昭。"——《孟子·尽心下》

英译:"Those in the dark are in no position to light the way for others."

解析:汉语原文意思是自己都没有搞清楚,却想让别人明白。习近平总书记指出,中央要转变工作作风,能不能多一点学习、多一点思考,少一点无谓的应酬、少一点形式主义的东西,这也是转变工作作风的重要内容。群众说,现在,有的干部学风不浓、玩风太盛。这样"以其昏昏,使人昭昭"是不行的!是要贻误工作、贻误大事的!不注意学习,忙于事务,思想就容易僵化、庸俗化。

204. "以至公无私之心,行正大光明之事"——吕坤《呻吟语·应务》

英译:"do honest and upright things justly, selflessly, and conscientiously"

解析:汉语原文意思是要怀着一颗至公无私的心,做正大光明的事情。习近平总书记指出,要紧紧牵住司法责任制这个牛鼻子,凡是进入法官、检察官员额的,要在司法一线办案,对案件质量终身负责。法官、检察官要有审案判案的权力,也要加强对他们的监督制约,把对司法权的法律监督、社会监督、舆论监督等落实到位,保证法官、检察官做到"以至公无私之心,行正大光明之事",把司法权关进制度的笼子,让公平正义的阳光照进人民心田,让老百姓看到实实在在的改革成效。

205. "亦余心之所善兮,虽九死其犹未悔。"——屈原《离骚》

英译:"For the ideal that I hold dear to my heart, I will not regret a thousand deaths to die."

解析:汉语原文意思是"我"心中追求的真善美,纵使为此要九死一生"我"也不会懊悔。习近平总书记认为,创新从来都是九死一生,但我们必须有"亦余心之所善兮,虽九死其犹未悔"的豪情。我国广大科技工作者要有强烈的创新信心和决心,既不妄自菲薄,也不妄自尊大,勇于攻坚克难、追求卓越、赢得胜利,积极抢占科技竞争和未来发展制高点。

206. "有朋自远方来,不亦乐乎?"——《论语·学而》

英译:"What a joy to have friends coming from afar!"

解析:汉语原文意思是朋友远道而来与"我"相识相交,这是何等欣慰快乐的事呀。习近平总书记指出,六月的青岛,风景如画。在这美好的时节,欢迎大家来到这里,出席上海合作组织成员国元首理事会第十八次会议。早在 2500 多年前,中国古代伟大的思想家孔子就说:"有朋自远方来,不亦乐乎?"今天,孔子的故乡山东喜迎远道而来的各方贵宾,我们在这里共商上海合作组织发展大计,具有特殊意义。

207. "于安思危,于治忧乱。"——魏源《默觚·学篇七》

英译:"Be alert to danger in times of peace, and be wary of unrest in times of stability."

解析:汉语原文意思是即使居于安乐的环境里,也要想到可能出现的危险;即使处在稳定的境况中,也要忧虑可能发生的动乱。习近平总书记强调防范政治风险。"于安思危,于治忧乱。"我们党在内忧外患中诞生,在磨难挫折中成长,在战胜风险挑战中壮大,始终有着强烈的忧患意识、风险意识。

208. "与人不求备,检身若不及"——《尚书·伊训》

英译:"being strict with oneself and lenient with others"

解析:汉语原文意思是要宽以待人,不要苛责他人;要严于律己,向着更高的目标不断自加压力。习近平总书记指出,干部的党性修养、思想觉悟、道德水平不会随着党龄的增加而自然提高,也不会随着职务的升迁而自然提高,而需要终身努力。要时刻用党章、用共产党员标准要求自己,要有"与人不求备,检身若不及"的精神,时刻自重自省自警自励,努力做到老老实实做人,踏踏实实干事,清清白白为官。

209. "与人为善"——《孟子·公孙丑上》

英译:"Do things for the good of others."

解析:汉语原文意思是同别人一道行善做好事,后多指善意助人。习近平总书记指出,在5000多年的文明发展中,中华民族一直追求和传承着和平、和睦、和谐的坚定理念。以和为贵,与人为善,己所不欲、勿施于人等观念和传统在中国代代相传,深深植根于中国人的精神中,深深体现在中国人的行为上。

210. "与天下同利者,天下持之;擅天下之利者,天下谋之。"——《管子·版法解》

英译:"A sovereign who shares the interests of the people will have their support; a sovereign who denies the interests of the people will provoke their opposition."

解析:汉语原文意思是与天下人同利的,天下人就拥护他;独占天下人利益的,天下人就图谋对付他。习近平总书记指出,始终坚持人民至上。古人讲:"与天下同利者,天下持之;擅天下之利者,天下谋之。"党章明确规定,我们党没有自己特殊的利益,党在任何时候都把群众利益放在第一位。这是我们党作为马克思主义政党区别于其他政党的显著标志。在重大疫情面前，我们一开始就鲜明提出把人民生命安全和身体健康放在第一位。我们在全国范围调集最优秀的医生、最先进的设备、最急需的资源，全力以赴投入疫病救治，救治费用全部由国家承担。人民至上、生命至上，保护人民生命安全和身体健康可以不惜一切代价！

211. "玉不琢，不成器；人不学，不知义。"——《三字经》

英译："A jade uncut will not be a useful vessel; a man without learning will not know the way."

解析：汉语原文意思是玉不经过雕琢，不会成为器物；人不经过刻苦学习，就不会懂得处世的道理。习近平总书记指出，接受帮助，就是要听得进意见，受得了批评，在知错就改、越改越好的氛围中健康成长。一个人不可能十全十美，总是在克服缺点、纠正错误的过程中进步的，正所谓"玉不琢，不成器；人不学，不知义"。少年儿童正在形成世界观、人生观、价值观的过程中，需要得到帮助。

212. "云帆高张，昼夜星驰"——《天妃灵应之记》

英译："sailing the oceans day and night"

解析：汉语原文意思是高高张挂起船帆，昼夜兼程，一路疾驰。习近平总书记指出，回顾中阿人民交往历史，我们就会想起陆上丝绸之路和海上香料之路。我们的祖先在大漠戈壁上"驰命走驿，不绝于时月"，在汪洋大海中"云帆高张，昼夜星驰"，走在了古代世界各民族友好交往的前列。

Z

213. "宰相必起于州部，猛将必发于卒伍。"——《韩非子·显学》

英译："Prime ministers must have served as local officials, and great generals must have risen from the ranks."

解析：汉语原文意思是宰相都是从基层州部中锻炼上来的，猛将都是从军队卒伍中摔打出来的。习近平总书记指出，中国有句古话，"宰相必起于州部，猛将必发于卒伍"。我们现在的干部遴选机制也是一级一级的。干部有了丰富的基层经历，就能更好树立群众观点，知道国情，知道人民需要什么，在实践中不断积累各方面经验和专业知识，增强工作能力和才干。这是做好工作的基本条件。

附录3 典故解析

214. "凿井者，起于三寸之坎，以就万仞之深。" ——刘昼《刘子·崇学》

英译："A deep well is dug starting with a shallow pit."

解析：汉语原文意思是凿井的人从挖很浅的土坑开始，最后才挖成万丈深井。习近平总书记指出，青年的价值取向决定了未来整个社会的价值取向，而青年又处在价值观形成和确立的时期，抓好这一时期的价值观养成十分重要。这就像穿衣服扣扣子一样，如果第一粒扣子扣错了，剩余的扣子都会扣错。人生的扣子从一开始就要扣好。"凿井者，起于三寸之坎，以就万仞之深。"青年要从现在做起、从自己做起，使社会主义核心价值观成为自己的基本遵循，并身体力行大力将其推广到全社会去。

215. "政之所兴，在顺民心。政之所废，在逆民心。" ——《管子·牧民》

英译："Decrees may be followed if they are in accordance with the aspirations of the people; they may be ineffective if they are against the aspirations of the people."

解析：汉语原文意思是政权之所以能兴盛，在于顺应民心；政权之所以废弛，则因为违逆民心。习近平总书记指出，坚持群众路线，就要坚持全心全意为人民服务的根本宗旨。"政之所兴在顺民心，政之所废在逆民心。"全心全意为人民服务，是我们党一切行动的根本出发点和落脚点，是我们党区别于其他一切政党的根本标志。党的一切工作，必须以最广大人民根本利益为最高标准。检验我们一切工作的成效，最终都要看人民是否真正得到了实惠，人民生活是否真正得到了改善，人民权益是否真正得到了保障。面对人民过上更好生活的新期待，我们不能有丝毫自满和懈怠，必须再接再厉，使发展成果更多更公平惠及全体人民，朝着共同富裕方向稳步前进。

216. "知其事而不度其时则败" ——陆贽《论缘边守备事宜状》

英译："You are bound to fail if you only know what to do but without knowing the situation."

解析：汉语原文意思是仅仅知道事情本身却不懂得审时度势就会失败。习近平总书记指出，"知其事而不度其时则败"。尽管国际国内环境发生了深刻复杂变化，但我国发展重要战略机遇期的重大判断没有改变。从国际看，世界政治经济形势总体上有利于维护世界和平与发展大局，世界经济在深度调整中曲折复苏，全球治理体系深刻变革，国际力量对比趋向平衡，我国发展具有相对稳定的外部环境。从国内看，我国物质基础雄厚、人力资本丰富、市场空间广阔、发展潜力巨大，经济长期向好基本面没有改变。经济发展进入新常态，在增长速度不可避免换挡的同时，经济发展方式加快转变，经济结构不断优化，发展动力持续转换，改革开放释放出新的发展活力，良好发展态势可以保持。

217. "知政失者在草野"——王充《论衡·书解》

英译："It is the people who know whether a decree is good or not."

解析：汉语原文意思是知道政治有过失的人在民间。习近平总书记指出，坚持群众路线，就要真正让人民来评判我们的工作。"知政失者在草野。"任何政党的前途和命运最终都取决于人心向背。"人心就是力量。"我们党的党员人数，放在人民中间还是少数。我们党的宏伟奋斗目标，离开了人民支持就绝对无法实现。我们党的执政水平和执政成效都不是由自己说了算，必须而且只能由人民来评判。

218. "知之者不如好之者，好之者不如乐之者。"——《论语·雍也》

英译："Regarding knowledge, those who are devoted to it learn better than those who are aware of it, and those who enjoy it the most are the best students."

解析：汉语原文意思是对于学习，了解怎么学习的人，不如喜爱学习的人；喜爱学习的人，又不如以学习为乐的人。习近平总书记认为，兴趣是激励学习的最好老师。"知之者不如好之者，好之者不如乐之者。"讲的就是这个道理。领导干部应该把学习作为一种追求、一种爱好、一种健康的生活方式，做到好学乐学。

219. "志不立，天下无可成之事。"——王守仁《教条示龙场诸生》

英译："Without resolve, one can accomplish nothing."

解析：汉语原文意思是志向不确立，天下就没有可以办成的事情。习近平总书记指出，"志不立，天下无可成之事"。理想信念动摇是最危险的动摇，理想信念滑坡是最危险的滑坡。一个政党的衰落，往往从理想信念的丧失或缺失开始。我们党是否坚强有力，既要看全党在理想信念上是否坚定不移，更要看每一位党员在理想信念上是否坚定不移。

220. "志不强者智不达，言不信者行不果。"——《墨子·修身》

英译："The weak-minded cannot be wise; the dishonest cannot succeed."

解析：汉语原文意思是意志不坚强的，智慧一定不高；说话不讲信用的，行动一定不果敢。习近平总书记强调坚定担当责任，不断增强进行伟大斗争的意志和本领。"志不强者智不达，言不信者行不果。"我们党在内忧外患中诞生、在历经磨难中成长、在攻坚克难中壮大，锤炼了不畏强敌、不惧风险、敢于斗争、敢于胜利的风骨和品质。为了肩负历史重任，为了党和人民事业，无论敌人如何强大、道路如何艰险、挑战如何严峻，党总是绝不畏惧、决不退缩，不怕牺牲、百折不挠。

221."志高则其言洁，志大则其辞弘，志远则其旨永。"——叶燮《原诗·外篇上》
英译："A cultivated person of noble and lofty aspirations can produce succinct and vigorous expressions of profound thoughts."
解析：汉语原文意思是志趣高雅的人，其作品的语言就会纯净；志气宏大的人，其作品的文辞就会雄健；志向远大的人，其作品的思想就会深邃。习近平总书记指出，希望广大文艺工作者坚持弘扬正道，在追求德艺双馨中成就人生价值。"志高则其言洁，志大则其辞弘，志远则其旨永。"文艺承担着成风化人的职责。广大文艺工作者要把个人的道德修养、社会形象与作品的社会效果统一起来，坚守艺术理想，追求德艺双馨，努力以高尚的操守和文质兼美的作品，为历史存正气、为世人弘美德、为自身留清名。

222."志合者，不以山海为远"——葛洪《抱朴子·外篇》
英译："Nothing, not even mountains and seas, can separate people with common goals and ideals."
解析：汉语原文意思是志同道合者，即便相隔山海万里，也不觉遥远。习近平总书记指出，中国有句古话，志合者，不以山海为远。我们来自世界四大洲的5个国家，为了构筑伙伴关系、实现共同发展的宏伟目标走到了一起，为了推动国际关系民主化、推进人类和平与发展的崇高事业走到了一起。求和平、谋发展、促合作、图共赢，是我们共同的愿望和责任。

223."志之难也，不在胜人，在自胜也。"——《韩非子·喻老》
英译："The key to achieving your aspirations lies not in overcoming others but in overcoming your own weaknesses."

解析：汉语原文意思是立志困难，不在于胜过别人，而在于战胜自己，克服懦夫懒汉思想。习近平总书记指出，坚持调动广大贫困群众积极性、主动性、创造性，激发脱贫内生动力。"志之难也，不在胜人，在自胜。"脱贫必须摆脱思想意识上的贫困。我们注重把人民群众对美好生活的向往转化成脱贫攻坚的强大动能，实行扶贫和扶志扶智相结合，既富口袋也富脑袋，引导贫困群众依靠勤劳双手和顽强意志摆脱贫困、改变命运。

224."志之所趋，无远弗届；穷山距海，不能限也。志之所向，无坚不入；锐兵精甲，不能御也。"——金缨《格言联璧·学问》

英译："Aspirations can reach any place however far it is, even over mountains and seas; and it can break through any defense however tough it is, even as strong as the best armor and shield."

解析：汉语原文意思是一个人要有远大的志向，就算再遥远的距离也能到达，即使是高山大海，也无法阻挡；一个人要有坚定的志向，必会无坚不摧，即使是精兵坚甲，也不能抵挡。这句话告诉我们一个重要的道理，人要有远大的志向。习近平总书记指出，理想信念就是人的志向。古人说："志之所趋，无远勿届，穷山距海，不能限也。志之所向，无坚不入，锐兵精甲，不能御也。"志存高远的人，再遥远的地方也能达到，再坚固的东西也能突破。在革命、建设、改革各个历史时期，有无数共产党员为了党和人民事业英勇牺牲了，支撑他们的就是"革命理想高于天"的精神力量。

225."治大国，若烹小鲜"——《老子》

英译："Governing a big country is as delicate as frying a small fish."

解析：汉语原文意思是"烹小鲜"不能随意翻动，调料要恰到好处，火候要掌握得当，治理国家也是如此，要有审慎负责的态度。习近平总书记指出，这样一个大国，这样多的人民，这么复杂的国情，领导者要深入了解国情，了解人民所思所盼，要有"治大国如烹小鲜"的态度，丝毫不敢懈怠，丝毫不敢马虎，必须夙夜在公、勤勉工作。

226."治国常富，而乱国常贫。"——《管子·治国》

英译："Stability brings a country prosperity while instability may well plunge it into poverty."

解析：汉语原文意思是局势安定的国家，常常是富足的；局势动乱的国家，常常是贫穷的。习近平总书记指出，"治国常富，而乱国常贫"。安全是发展的前提，人类是不可分割的安全共同体。事实再次证明，冷战思维只会破坏全球和平框架，霸权主义和强权政治只会危害世界和平，集团对抗只会加剧21世纪安全挑战。

227. "治国无其法则乱，守法而不变则衰。"——欧阳询等《艺文类聚》

英译："A country that is not ruled by law will descend into chaos; a country that sticks to outdated laws will fall into decline."

解析：汉语原文意思是治理国家，没有法度就会混乱，固守法度而不知变革就会衰落。习近平总书记指出，"治国无其法则乱，守法而不变则衰"。要加快完善中国特色社会主义法律体系，使之更加科学完备、统一权威。要研究丰富立法形式，可以搞一些"大块头"，也要搞一些"小快灵"，增强立法的针对性、适用性、可操作性。

228. "治国犹如栽树，本根不摇则枝叶茂荣。"——吴兢《贞观政要·政体》

英译："Governing a country is like planting a tree. If the roots are firm, the branches and leaves flourish."

解析：汉语原文意思是治理国家就像种树一样，只要树根稳固不动摇，就能枝繁叶茂。习近平总书记指出，"治国犹如栽树，本根不摇则枝叶茂荣"。我们治国理政的本根，就是中国共产党的领导和我国社会主义制度。在这一点上，必须理直气壮、旗帜鲜明。党的领导必须是全面的、系统的、整体的，必须体现到经济建设、政治建设、文化建设、社会建设、生态文明建设和国防军队、祖国统一、外交工作、党的建设等各方面。哪个领域、哪个方面、哪个环节缺失了弱化了，都会削弱党的力量，损害党和国家事业。

229. "治国之道，富民为始"——司马迁《史记·平津侯主父列传》

英译："The key to running a country is to first enrich the people."

解析：汉语原文意思是治理国家之道，首先要使百姓富裕起来。习近平总书记指出，坚持以人民为中心的发展思想，坚定不移走共同富裕道路。"治国之道，富民为始。"我们始终坚定人民立场，强调消除贫困、改善民生、实现共同富裕是社会主义的本质要求，是我们党坚持全心全意为人民服务根本宗旨的重要体现，是党和政府的重大责任。

230."治其本，朝令而夕从；救其末，百世不改也。"——苏轼《关陇游民私铸钱与江淮漕卒为盗之由》

英译："If the root cause of a problem is addressed, there will be immediate change for the better; if only trivial matters are addressed, the problem will stay forever."

解析：汉语原文意思是从根本上进行治理，政令将会很迅速得到执行；只从细枝末叶进行治理，经过一百代也不能有所改变。习近平总书记指出，党的十八大以来，在全面从严治党实践中，我们深刻认识到，党内存在的很多问题都同政治问题相关联，都是因为党的政治建设没有抓紧、没有抓实。"治其本，朝令而夕从；救其末，百世不改也。"不从政治上认识问题、解决问题，就会陷入头痛医头、脚痛医脚的被动局面，就无法从根本上解决问题。我们把党的政治建设摆上突出位置，在坚定政治信仰、增强"四个意识"、维护党中央权威和集中统一领导、严明党的政治纪律和政治规矩、加强和规范新形势下党内政治生活、净化党内政治生态、正风肃纪、反腐惩恶等方面取得明显成效。

231."忠诚印寸心，浩然充两间。"——蔡和森《少年行——北上过洞庭有感》

英译："My loyalty comes from the bottom of my heart, and it stretches all the way from the Earth to the Heavens."

解析：汉语原文意思是用生命铸就忠诚，浩然之气充盈于天地之间。习近平总书记指出，加强党的政治建设，必须把维护党中央权威和集中统一领导作为首要任务。党内所有的政治问题，归根到底就是对党是否忠诚。忠诚是共产党人必须具备的优秀品格。"忠诚印寸心，浩然充两间"的坚毅，"砍头不要紧，只要主义真"的无畏，腹中满是草根而宁死不屈的气节，十指钉入竹签而永不叛党的坚贞，无数先烈用鲜血诠释了对党的忠诚。对党忠诚必须是纯粹的、无条件的，是政治标准、更是实践标准，鲜明体现在坚决贯彻党中央决策部署上。

232."褚小者不可以怀大，绠短者不可以汲深。"——《庄子·至乐》

英译："A small bag cannot hold large things; a short rope cannot reach a deep well."

解析：汉语原文意思是口袋小了装不下大的东西，井绳短了打不到深处的水，后世常用来比喻能力薄弱者难以胜任重大任务，因而人们要不断提高自己的才干。习近平总书记强调勤学苦练、增强本领。"褚小者不可以怀大，绠短者不可以汲深。"我们处在前所未有的变革时代,干着前无古人的伟大事业,如果知识不够、眼界不宽、能力不强,就会耽误事。年轻干部精力充沛、思维活跃、接受能力强,正处在长本事、长才干的大好时期,一定要珍惜光阴、不负韶华,如饥似渴学习,一刻不停提高。

233."自古雄才多磨难,从来纨绔少伟男。"——王宝池《七律·劝学》

英译:"A hard life breeds great talents, whereas an easy life is not the way to cultivate great men."

解析:汉语原文意思是古往今来凡是有所建树的英雄豪杰都经历过很多磨难,而娇生惯养之辈很少有人能成就一番大业。习近平总书记认为,从小做起,就是要从自己做起、从身边做起、从小事做起,一点一滴积累,养成好思想、好品德。千里之行,始于足下。每个人的生活都是由一件件小事组成的,养小德才能成大德。听说有的同学喜欢比吃穿,比有没有车接车送,比爸爸妈妈是干什么工作的,这样就比偏了。一定不能比这些。"自古雄才多磨难,从来纨绔少伟男。"要比就比谁更有志气、谁更勤奋学习、谁更热爱劳动、谁更爱锻炼身体、谁更有爱心。

234."自信人生二百年,会当水击三千里。"——毛泽东《七古·残句》

英译:"I'm sure to live for 200 years, and will swim for 3,000 *li*."

解析:汉语原文意思是"我"相信人生会有二百年,那自然要游泳击水三千里,抒发了不畏艰难、奋发图强的豪情壮志。习近平总书记指出,全党要坚定道路自信、理论自信、制度自信、文化自信。当今世界,要说哪个政党、哪个国家、哪个民族能够自信的话,那中国共产党、中华人民共和国、中华民族是最有理由自信的。有了"自信人生二百年,会当水击三千里"的勇气,我们就能毫无畏惧面对一切困难和挑战,就能坚定不移开辟新天地、创造新奇迹。

235."自知者英,自胜者雄。"——王通《中说·周公篇》

英译:"Heroes are those who know themselves and can surpass themselves."

解析:汉语原文意思是能正确评估自己的人是俊伟之人,能战胜自己的私心杂念的人是杰出之人,说明人贵在能够自知自胜。习近平总书记指出,"自知者英,自胜者雄"。民族复兴梦想越接近,改革开放任务越繁重,越要加强党的建设。安不忘危,才是生存发展之道。我们党面临的"四大考验"、"四种危险"是长期的、复杂的、严峻的。要坚持党中央集中统一领导，在各级党组织和广大党员、干部中强化政治意识、大局意识、核心意识、看齐意识，确保在思想上政治上行动上始终同党中央保持高度一致。

主要参考书目

英文参考书目

Hacker, Diana. *A Writer's Reference* [M]. 2nd ed. New York: Bedford Books of St. Martin's Press, 1992.

Xi Jinping. *Understanding Xi Jinping's Educational Philosophy* [M]. Beijing: Foreign Language Teaching and Research Press, Higher Education Press, 2022.

Xi Jinping. *XI JINPING: SPEECHES ON DIPLOMACY I* [M]. Beijing: Central Compilation & Translation Press, 2022.

Xi Jinping. *XI JINPING: SPEECHES ON DIPLOMACY II* [M]. Beijing: Central Compilation & Translation Press, 2022.

Xi Jinping. *XI JINPING: THE GOVERNANCE OF CHINA I* [M]. Beijing: Foreign Languages Press, 2014.

Xi Jinping. *XI JINPING: THE GOVERNANCE OF CHINA II* [M]. Beijing: Foreign Languages Press, 2017.

Xi Jinping. *XI JINPING: THE GOVERNANCE OF CHINA III* [M]. Beijing: Foreign Languages Press, 2020.

Xi Jinping. *XI JINPING: THE GOVERNANCE OF CHINA IV* [M]. Beijing: Foreign Languages Press, 2022.

中文参考书目

陈望道. 修辞学发凡[M]. 上海：复旦大学出版社，2008.

辞海编辑委员会. 辞海[M]. 上海：上海辞书出版社，2012.

丁往道、吴冰. 英语写作基础教程[M]. 第三版. 北京：高等教育出版社，2014.

李梓铭等. 汉译英基础教程[M]. 北京：北京理工大学出版社，2018.

任文、李长栓. 高级汉英笔译教程[M]. 北京：外语教学与研究出版社，2022.

司显柱等. 汉译英教程[M]. 上海：东华大学出版社，2016.

王雪明、杨子. 典籍英译中深度翻译的类型与功能——以《中国翻译话语英译选集》（上）为例[J]. 中国翻译，2012（3）：103-108.

王振平. 科普翻译中的注释[J]. 科技英语学习，2006（6）：58.

温秀颖等. 英语翻译教程[M]. 天津：南开大学出版社，2001.

习近平. 习近平谈治国理政（第二卷）[M]. 北京：外文出版社，2017.

习近平. 习近平谈治国理政（第三卷）[M]. 北京：外文出版社，2020.

习近平. 习近平谈治国理政（第四卷）[M]. 北京：外文出版社，2022.

习近平. 习近平谈治国理政（第一卷）[M]. 北京：外文出版社，2014.

习近平. 习近平外交演讲集（第二卷）[M]. 北京：中央文献出版社，2022.

习近平. 习近平外交演讲集（第一卷）[M]. 北京：中央文献出版社，2022.

习近平. 习近平总书记教育重要论述讲义[M]. 北京：外语教学与研究出版社、高等教育出版社，2022.

印晓红. 汉英语篇翻译教程[M]. 北京：清华大学出版社，2017.

曾剑平、胡莹. 《习近平谈治国理政》的翻译融通策略[J]. 新余学院学报，2017（5）：67-72.

张弓. 现代汉语修辞学[M]. 石家庄：河北教育出版社，1993.

张威. 汉英翻译教程[M]. 北京：外语教学与研究出版社，2022.

章振邦. 新编英语语法[M]. 第三版. 上海：上海外语教育出版社，2000.